DROPPING BRITAIN'S FIRST H-BOMB

The publication of this edition is dedicated to Ken Hubbard.

Britain's first
thermonuclear
bomb (H-Bomb),
code named 'Short
Granite', exploded
off Malden Island
on 15 May 1957.
This photograph
was taken from the
cameras installed
in Valiant XD818,
captained by Wg
Cdr KG Hubbard,
OC 49 Squadron
RAF.

DROPPING BRITAIN'S FIRST H-BOMB

The Story of Operation *Grapple* 1957/58

Group Captain Kenneth Hubbard OBE, DFC, AFC
and
Michael Simmons

Pen & Sword
AVIATION

This edition published in Great Britain in 2008 by
Pen & Sword Aviation
An imprint of
Pen & Sword Books Ltd
47 Church Street
Barnsley
South Yorkshire
S70 2AS

Copyright © K. G. Hubbard and M. J. Simmons 2008

ISBN 978 1 84415 747 1

First published in 1985 as Operation 'Grapple' by Ian Allan Ltd, London.

Typeset in Palatino by
Phoenix Typesetting, Auldgirth, Dumfries.

Printed and bound in England
By CPI UK

Pen & Sword Books Ltd incorporates the Imprints of Pen & Sword Aviation,
Pen & Sword Family History, Pen & Sword Maritime, Pen & Sword Military,
Wharncliffe Local History, Pen & Sword Select, Pen & Sword Military Classics,
Leo Cooper, Remember When, Seaforth Publishing and Frontline Publishing

For a complete list of Pen & Sword titles please contact
PEN & SWORD BOOKS LIMITED
47 Church Street, Barnsley, South Yorkshire, S70 2AS, England
E-mail: enquiries@pen-and-sword.co.uk
Website: www.pen-and-sword.co.uk

Contents

Glossary

ADC	Aide-de-camp
ACM	Air Chief Marshal
Air Cdre	Air Commodore
AM	Air Marshal
AOC	Air Officer Commanding
AVM	Air Vice-Marshal
BCBS	Bomber Command Bombing School
CFS	Central Flying School
C-in-C	Commander-in-Chief
DCAS	Deputy Chief Air Staff
EAAS	Empire Air Armament School
EAFS	Empire Air Flying School
EANS	Empire Air Navigation School
EMI	Electro Magnetic Indicator
Flg Off	Flying Officer
Flt Lt	Flight Lieutenant
Flt Sgt	Flight Sergeant
Form 700	RAF Aircraft Technical Log
FTS	Flying Training School
GCA	Ground Control Approach
Gp Capt	Group Captain
HF	High Frequency
ILS	Instrument Landing System
JOC	Joint Operation Control
MRAF	Marshal Royal Air Force
NCO	Non-Commissioned Officer
nm	nautical miles
OC	Officer Commanding

OCU	Operational Conversion Unit
PSO	Personal Staff Officer
QFE	Airfield Barometric Pressure Setting
QNH	Regional Barometric Pressure Setting
RV	Rendezvous Point on Bombing Circuit
Sgt	Sergeant
SNCO	Senior Non-Commissioned Officer
Sqn Ldr	Squadron Leader
TFC	Task Force Commander
VHF	Very High Frequency
Wg Cdr	Wing Commander

The Authors

Group Captain Kenneth Hubbard

Group Captain Hubbard joined the Royal Air Force in August 1940, commissioned as a pilot in May 1941 and was posted to CFS RAF Cranwell for training as a flying instructor. As instructor he served with No. 12 FTS RAF Grantham 1941-43. In 1943, Hubbard was posted to No. 205 Group in Italy. He completed an operational tour with No. 70 Squadron, flying Wellingtons. During the period he was promoted to Squadron Leader and awarded the DFC. After a spell as Flight Commander at No. 77 OTU at Quastina in Palestine he returned to No. 70 Squadron, now with Liberators, and was later Group Training Officer.

From August 1946 Hubbard commanded No. 104 Squadron based in Egypt with Lancasters. Posted to the Empire Armament School at RAF Manby he flew Lancaster *Thor 1* and Lincoln *Thor 2 to* South Africa and Canada in 1948. He joined the Directing Staff of the Flying College on its formation at RAF Manby.

As a Squadron Leader Hubbard was Station Commander of RAF Shaibah 1951-53 when this station was involved in the evacuation of British personnel from Abadan. He received the OBE in 1953.

Following an appointment as PSO to the Air Member for Personnel, and attendance at the RAF Staff College, he was promoted and posted to the V bomber force in January 1955. On completion of Valiant conversion at No. 232 OCU RAF Gaydon, Wg Cdr Hubbard took command of No. 49 Squadron at RAF Wittering in September 1956.

No. 49 Squadron was specifically tasked with the live drops element of Operation Grapple. The operation culminated on 15 May 1957 with the first live drop of a British megaton yield weapon, the dropping aircraft being captained by Wg Cdr Hubbard. He and his crew received immediate awards of the AFC.

At the conclusion of the Grapple test series he served at HQ Bomber Command and, as Group Captain, commanded the RAF stations of El Adem and Scampton; the latter station was at that time the base for the Blue Steel-equipped Vulcan B2s of Nos 27, 83 and 617 Squadrons. His final RAF appointment was Group Captain Training at HQ Transport Command. Gp Capt Hubbard left the RAF in 1966 and tried farming in the West Country. This was not to his liking and he joined his cousin's Geoffrey Hubbard's refrigeration engineering group in 1974 as Sales and Marketing Director of the Vehicle Air-Conditioning Division. Gp Capt Hubbard retired in 1987 and lived quietly with his wife Margaret at Blythburgh in Suffolk. Gp Capt Ken Hubbard was President of the Megaton Club formed from members of No. 49 Squadron who participated in Operation Grapple. The members met annually at the RAF Club Piccadilly.

Group Captain Kenneth Gilbert Hubbard OBE, DFC, AFC died on the 22nd January 2004 aged 83 years.

Michael Simmons

Michael Simmons was born in Suffolk on 25 May 1947. On leaving school he served a Marine Engineering apprenticeship and continued in this profession until joining Hubbard Engineering Co as a Development Engineer specialising in vehicle air-conditioning systems.

In 1974, K. G. Hubbard, a cousin of G. A. Hubbard, Chairman of the Hubbard-Reader Group, had joined the company to be responsible for the marketing and sales of vehicle air-conditioning systems. From this moment Michael Simmons and Ken Hubbard commenced working together within the company, with Michael Simmons being responsible for the technical aspect, directly under Ken Hubbard.

In 1976 Michael Simmons took up a new appointment managing a Vehicle Installation Centre, which was based at Greenwich, London, and was subsequently made a Director of Hubbard Engineering Co.

Some four years later he returned to Head Office and when Ken Hubbard retired as Marketing Director in June 1982 to concentrate on other activities within the Group, he took over his responsibilities within sales.

'Grapple' was first thought of in 1976 and the project was started in 1983 with the first publication under the title of *Operation Grapple* in 1985.

Today Michael Simmons works for an International refrigeration manufacturing company in the UK in a sales and marketing capacity.

KG Hubbard and MJ Simmons at the RAF Museum, Hendon.

Preface

In assembling the contents of this book, it was difficult to decide at what point in my service career the '49' story should commence. However, since my appointment had been decided by the Air Secretary's department during the latter phase of the Royal Air Force Staff College course, I felt it was appropriate to commence at this time when the course postings were announced in December 1955.

From here, the book unfolds my experiences as the officer destined to command No. 49 Squadron, equipped with the new four-jet Vickers Valiant V bombers, during the years 1956 to 1958 when the squadron was detailed to carry out special live thermonuclear megaton weapon trials in the South Pacific as part of Operation Grapple.

Due attention has been given to all aspects of matters classified as sensitive to security and, for this reason, the story does not provide a detailed insight to any operational procedure effective in the Royal Air Force today.

This book is intended as a tribute to all members of No. 49 Squadron who served under my command during this unique period in our history. Our task was highly specialised and called for exceptionally high professional standards by both air and ground crews. I could not have wished for a more dedicated team of people who, at all times, responded to the very exacting requirements made of them, often under the most trying environmental conditions.

K. G. Hubbard

Acknowledgements

The authors wish to record their appreciation for the assistance and co-operation received from the following friends, colleagues and professional people who have contributed in various ways towards the compilation of this book: Daphne Godbold for typing all letters and correspondence and the original manuscript; Lance Cooper (photographer) for his expertise in reproducing photographs and diagrams included in this book; Air Cdre Henry Probert for allowing us access to the records of 49 Squadron (MoD, RAF Air Historical Branch); Humphrey Wynne for his guidance in all aspects of this book; Wg Cdr William Wood (RAF Museum); Gp Capt Peter Dodsworth (Station Commander) and Flt Lt Andrew de Labat (RAF Wittering); Brian Trubshaw and Norman Barfield (British Aerospace); Sqn Ldrs Derek Tuthill and David Ray (HQ No 18 Group); Air Marshal Sir John Lapsey; Brian Wexham (Vickers); Eileen Norriss (Royal Engineers Library); Jeffrey Pavey (Imperial War Museum); Peter Jones and Steven Smith; Walter Hicks, Donald Morrison, Roger Ramsey, Fred Vening and Wally Watson; and finally, a special thank you to Margaret Hubbard and Jane Livingstone for their assistance and encouragement throughout our project.

All photographs reproduced in this book are British Crown Copyright or British Crown Copyright/AWRE Photographs, unless otherwise indicated.

xi

CHAPTER ONE

Appointed Command

The long 12-month Staff College course was at last coming to an end. It had been a strenuous and demanding time which had certainly caused me, as well as many of my fellow officers, to burn a great deal of midnight oil in order to complete the various exercises set by the Directing Staff. This course comprised selected officers of Squadron Leader and Wing Commander rank, plus three civil servants of equivalent status, and its aim was to provide an advanced service education to officers of senior rank, thereby fitting them for future command and staff appointments.

Looking back, it is now possible to see that 45 Course was sprinkled with a great degree of talent, for it was to supply no less than one Chief of the Defence Staff, in Wg Cdr Andrew Humphrey (later to become Marshal of the Royal Air Force Sir Andrew Humphrey who sadly died during his term of office. This was a great loss to both the Royal Air Force and the nation, for Sir Andrew was a man of tremendous professional ability). Also from this course there were to emerge two other future members of the Air Council.

The policy at Staff College was to announce during the final month of the course all postings for those graduates completing the course. These postings, having been finalised by the Air Secretary, were passed to the Commandant for announcement on a specified day – a date on the calendar eagerly awaited by all concerned, and I was no exception.

Some three months prior to this date all graduates had been permitted to give three preferences for their next appointment; however, we were all sufficiently experienced to realise that in the Air Secretary's Department it is always a question of which vacancies need to be filled that is the most important deciding factor, balanced with the best qualified officer in each case. Therefore, we knew that the chance of obtaining the posting of choice was no more than 50/50.

My own preference was clear; I had previously completed a staff appointment as Personal Staff Officer to the Air Member of Personnel. Therefore I not only desperately wanted to return to a flying appointment, but thought my chances were good; and so I had requested a posting to the newly emerging V bomber force. The flying qualifications necessary to be accepted into this new elite force were high; however, this did not worry me as I had confidence in my abilities.

The date on which the postings were to be announced arrived, and there was an air of excitement and expectancy as we all assembled in the main lecture hall to await the Commandant. When he entered, we all stood up as is service custom, and he gave his usual 'Sit down please gentlemen'. He then said 'As you are all well aware, this is the time we announce your next appointments; I know in some cases there will be disappointment but, in others, there will be delight. However, I am sure that you all appreciate, as officers destined for higher appointments, the Air Ministry is conscious of the need to give you a balance of experience. Therefore, whatever now emerges is for the good of your future careers.'

At this stage, the Commandant asked the Deputy Commandant to take over and read out the postings, which were to be announced in alphabetical order. Therefore, before my name was called there were many exclamations of delight at a flying appointment and groans as somebody got landed with a staff job. At last my turn came and I held my breath as the Deputy Commandant called 'Squadron Leader K. Hubbard – posted to the V Force for Flying Duties'. I released a sigh of relief and felt almost light-headed with joy. Little did I know that this was to emerge as the most exciting and challenging task of my life, a task which was to unfold progressively as the following months passed.

With the excitement of postings concluded on this day in December 1955, we soon settled back to the business of morning lectures and discussion. To ensure we returned to hard reality, the Directing Staff issued the final major exercise, to be completed as usual in a specified time scale; this meant further periods of burning the midnight oil. With the anticipation of my future posting in mind, I really did not mind wading through the final exercise, outlining a possible international situation in which I, as Senior Air Staff Officer at HQ Bomber Command, or perhaps a Senior Planner, would be required to produce a Service Paper outlining with clarity the overall situation, aim to be achieved, possible courses of enemy action, review of our forces available, courses of action open to ourselves, and a final recommendation for the Commander-in-Chief of the best possible course of action to achieve the stated aim.

With this exercise complete, typed and presented to the Directing Staff, I turned my attention to the pleasant aspects of Staff College.

Exercise 'Chicken 55' was a stage show presented by course members in the form of a revue covering the antics of the past 12 months. This was the occasion when the Directing Staff were at the mercy of course members, and any habit or peculiar personality of Staff Members was ruthlessly portrayed, to the delight of the audience. 'Chicken 55' was no exception and when the curtain came down the applause indicated that it had been a great success. On this note, the remainder of the evening was devoted to a social occasion in the bar.

One more formal duty was on the programme, and that was the final interviews where each course member is told by the Commandant or Deputy

Commandant how Staff College considers he has acquitted himself during the course. I had been told that this interview could be very brutal and gave a clear indication of future career advancement – or otherwise.

Knowing that in my own mind I had only just made the grade, for my attention to detail in exercises had not been as precise as the Directing Staff required (and this was borne out by the amount of red ink comments which normally adorned my paper when it came back from the Directing Staff) I was prepared to have a rough ride at interview; however, it was not to be, for when my name was called and I presented myself in the office of the Deputy Commandant, Air Cdre Favell, his words were:

> Well Hubbard, I think it is true to say that you have found the going hard; we liked your determination and application, although you still have a long way to go before you could be termed a really good staff officer. You have made great progress during the course in setting your thoughts to paper in logical order, and as you gain experience this should come more easily to you. You have demonstrated sound qualities of loyalty and we like the enthusiasm displayed.
>
> Staff College is a milestone in the career of a permanent officer if he is to progress further. You have the qualities to succeed and with your enthusiasm and determination should do well in the future.
>
> I am glad you have got your wish and been posted to the V Force, for we know you have the necessary background experience and, in confirming to you that you have successfully graduated with the symbol psa to be added to your name in the Air Force List, we wish you every success in this next appointment.

I duly thanked the Deputy Commandant and escaped, thankful that the final hurdle was over and all of my thoughts and efforts could be concentrated on the next stage of my path to 49 Squadron, within the refresher jet flying programme ahead of me. Before this, with the Christmas period almost upon us, there were to be a few days leave before I reported for duty early in January 1956, to RAF Manby. So, with all formalities complete at Staff College, I packed my bags, watched by my faithful spaniel 'Crusty', who was well accustomed to this performance; when the bags were loaded into the car he commandeered his seat and we headed for Norwich to spend a few days with my parents.

Reflecting on the past 12 months at RAF Staff College, I realised that in this period I had grown in service experience and stature, in a manner which could only have been achieved at such a place of learning. The pressures had been considerable in academic requirement to express oneself clearly and concisely on paper, having marshalled carefully all the factors associated with the problems set. At times, in the early stages of the course, I wondered if I should acquit myself of a high enough standard to justify my qualifications for the psa. However, as time progressed, I found that my approach to a set problem became more disciplined, in marshalling my thoughts, sifting the evidence and then setting this to paper in logical sequence. My knowledge of all three services had been expanded by the liaison visits made during the course and indeed we were also introduced to many of the problems of industrial companies.

All the serious work during the year had been carefully balanced by a social programme which included the now famous Staff College garden party at mid-term, the cocktail parties and end of course Ball. Yes, although the going had been tough, I had enjoyed the course and looked forward to my new appointment.

Wg Cdr KG Hubbard, OC 49 Squadron. *(Author)*

CHAPTER TWO

Refresher Course

The All Weather Jet Refresher Course was located at RAF Strubby, Lincolnshire, although students and staff were accommodated in the Officers' Mess at nearby RAF Manby. The course was designed to meet the Air Staff requirement for returning officers of Squadron Leader and Wing Commander rank to full all-weather flying effectiveness, having spent a period away from flying duties whilst employed in a staff appointment. For many of these officers this would be their first experience of flying a jet, having been previously only accustomed to piston engine operation. Thus for them the course presented an exciting challenge and readjustment of operating procedures. For such a conversion the Meteor Mk 7 was an ideal aircraft, delightful and exciting to fly, but the standards demanded on this course were high and produced a failure rate when it came to all-weather operation.

On the first Sunday in January, with Crusty by my side, I set course for Manby in my Wolseley 'in convoy' with Sqn Ldr John Mason (who also had been on the RAF Staff College Course), he leaving from his married quarters at Bracknell, me from my flat in Windsor. It was a cold but sunny day with a strong breeze, although the weather forecast was for heavy snow showers later in the day; however, at the time I did not anticipate any difficulty in reaching Manby. We left at about 10.00hrs and made good progress, stopping briefly for lunch; as the sky by this time was looking ominous, we pressed on knowing that if heavy snow commenced, we should soon experience drifting with the strong winds, especially on the open Lincolnshire roads.

We encountered snow some 20 miles from Boston and, in a matter of 30 min, it was obvious that these roads would soon be impassable with drifting as the snow swept across the road. Already it was necessary to keep the speed up to avoid getting caught in a drift. By the time we reached Boston it was quite clear that further progress on that type of country road to Louth near Manby would be impossible. I therefore pulled into the Peacock Royal Hotel in the centre of Boston and decided to call it a day as accommodation was available. A check with the AA confirmed that all roads out of Boston were now blocked, so we resigned ourselves to staying the night in the hopes that our journey could be resumed the next day. A telephone call to the Duty Officer at RAF Manby confirmed that conditions were no better at that end. Having informed him of our whereabouts and stating we would try to get through the next day if conditions improved, we settled down to an unplanned stay at Boston. I explained to the hotel manager that my dog was with me; this caused no problems, so we retired to our rooms. By this time the hotel had fitted in other luckless travellers forced to spend the night, so the evening produced a pleasantly relaxed atmosphere in the bar, where most of us were relieved not to have been caught out in a snow drift on the open road.

The following day produced no change in the weather – more snow and the roads still blocked. That evening the snow stopped and there was hope that the snow ploughs would soon have cleared the drifts and we could continue our journey to Manby. The morning was bright and clear but freezing hard, and I hoped we could get under way again if reports indicated the roads were open. Whilst waiting for the up-to-date situation, I gave Crusty a good walk round the town, and by lunch time all indications were that the road through to Louth was open, so we lost no time in setting course. After a difficult drive, we arrived at the Officers' Mess, RAF Manby, by about 17.00hrs.

Coming to RAF Manby was a return to my old home, where I had spent three happy years, initially on the flying staff of the Empire Air Armament School, followed by a spell on the Directing Staff of the newly established Royal Air Force Flying College which amalgamated three Empire Schools (namely the EAAS at Manby, the EANS at Shawby, and the EAFS at Hullavington, which were all disbanded).

Having parked my car and walked into the Mess, it was good to be greeted by the familiar faces of the civilian mess staff. Indeed, my old Batman, Mr Godbold, who was now working in the Station Commander's house, came over to see me the same evening to welcome me back to Manby. He was particularly keen to meet Crusty, as on my previous tour he had cared for my dog Butch, a bull terrier, who sadly died during the final months of my stay. Mr Godbold is still alive today at the ripe old age of 80 and often sends me a card at Christmas.

All peacetime RAF stations during the 1950s were fortunate to be staffed by civilian batmen and waiters who had spent their entire careers in the service of the Royal Air Force. Sadly, as these efficient and loyal men retire there are no replacements. Younger men are no longer prepared to undertake this type of work which entails unsociable hours and is more a way of life than a form of employment. Some of the older men are still serving, but they are a fast declining force who served the Royal Air Force with such devotion and maintained the highest possible standards in Mess routine for all types of functions.

RAF Manby, as the home of the Royal Air Force Flying College, was under the command of Air Cdre Gus Walker (later ACM Sir Augustus Walker) – the all weather Jet Refresher Course also came under his command.

In Air Cdre Walker the RAF had a Commandant of unique qualities; he was one of the finest leaders in the Royal Air Force. During the war, when a Station Commander in Bomber Command, he had approached a blazing Lancaster with a full bomb load in an attempt to rescue the crew, but was caught in the blast as the aircraft and bomb load exploded, resulting in the loss of his right arm. He was a man of great personal leadership ability who was admired and respected by all ranks and renowned for his incredible memory for names.

As the only Wing Commander on the course, I was appointed senior student and duly reported to the Commandant in order to pay my respects. It was good to see the Air Commodore again, for I had last seen him at RAF Manby in 1948 when I was then Deputy OC flying for the Empire Air Armament School. We chatted about Staff College and the V Force and he then gave me a run-down on the all weather course.

In explaining the aims of the course, he stated that most officers on this particular course had been away from active flying for three years because of staff appointments, and in most cases this would be their initial introduction to jet flying. Since the course was very concentrated and would be undertaken over the worst winter period, they would find the transition at times difficult, for there are special physiological aspects to high speed flying, particularly in relation to instrument flying under realistic bad weather conditions. Therefore, since I had kept my flying up to date, he would be looking to me to provide an example for my fellow students.

It is of interest to record that this man, although he had no right arm, never accepted, at any time, that this should affect his flying, and to overcome his disability he had a special artificial arm, complete with clamp which could be attached to the aircraft controls. This allowed his left arm to be free for the throttle controls and in this configuration he flew all types of aircraft as captain. When he wasn't flying he would never wear an artificial arm and the right sleeve of his uniform would be pinned to his side.

The course itself was to comprise 35 flying hours on both the Meteor Mk 7 (the dual control aircraft) and the Meteor Mk 8, which was the single-seat version. Ground school lectures were to cover 62hrs, and the first week was to be devoted to familiarisation of the Meteor inclusive of all fuel, hydraulic and pneumatic systems, emergency procedures, airfield layout and ejector seat drill.

During that first week, weather precluded our flying, so we were forced to concentrate on ground lectures and to get to know the aircraft, which also enabled me to get to know more about my fellow officers on the course. Certainly very few had flown a jet before, and were all excited at the thought of getting back to full flying duties. Some were a little apprehensive of adjusting to the physiological differences between piston-engined medium speed and altitude aircraft, and high speed and high altitude flying, particularly in view of the weather conditions in which we should be operating. At any rate, not having flown one myself over the past four years, I was going to find it hard to produce the results expected of me. Indeed, I was to find this course very difficult from a flying point of view, although I never admitted it!

For those not familiar with the Meteor Mk 7, let me briefly explain that it was a twin engine jet-propelled two-seat advanced trainer, powered by two

Derwent Mk 5 engines. The two pilots' cockpits were in tandem and enclosed by a hinged canopy. No guns were fitted, but a retractable gyro gunsight and camera recorder were mounted in the front cockpit, and neither cockpit was pressurised. The Mk 8 was a single-seat fighter which did have a pressurised cockpit.

During the initial week of lectures, I was impressed by the care taken by the staff of the All Weather Jet Refresher School to learn and retain details of the flying background of each student. This was important, for it allowed them to highlight sensibly the differences in operating medium speed and altitude piston aircraft, and high speed, high altitude jets. These are of course the aerodynamic differences in handling at high altitude and speed, combined with fast climbs and descents.

In this respect emphasis was placed upon physical fitness for improved alertness, due to the shorter reaction times required; optimum resistance to effects of 'G' (force of gravity) on the body, reduced susceptibility to any decompression sickness and fatigue. Following this, the effects of high speed were analysed to stress the importance of pilots' quick reaction and visual alertness. When flying on instruments at high speed, there is a need for an extremely accurate standard to be maintained; in order to avoid false sensation of attitude caused by the part of the middle ear that controls one's balance, physical sensation must always be completely ignored in favour of instrument indication. The misleading sensations are normally over-ridden and suppressed by the visual sense which deduces attitudes from the appearance of the horizon, but problems of disorientation under instrument conditions are more likely to occur when a pilot is suffering from anxiety, underconfidence, fatigue or rough flying. Therefore, to avoid this, a jet pilot must be:

a)   Fit and clear headed.

b)   Confident and fully familiar with instrument procedure.

c)   Relaxed – not concentrating on any one instrument, moving in his seat and avoiding a rigid, tense or hunched up position.

d)   Flying smoothly.

All of these were important points for students to understand before becoming involved in the initial flying programme.

With the first week complete, including a full introduction to the ejector seat for those who were to experience this for the first time, we hoped that weather on the following Monday would allow a full commencement of the flying programme.

The course was scheduled to last 10 weeks and therefore it was essential for the flying programme to get under way if all was to be achieved in such a tight time-scale, bearing in mind likely weather conditions in January and February. For myself, a signal from the Air Ministry stated that my full programme was to be completed before taking up my command of 49 Squadron. Whilst realising that I was destined to command a Valiant squadron, this was the first official indication that I was Officer Commanding 49 Squadron designate. On completion of the Meteor refresher course, I was to undertake a short course at the Bomber Command Bombing School located at RAF Lindholme, to be followed by the short Canberra aircraft conversion course at RAF Bassingbourn, before presenting myself to RAF Gaydon, which was the Bomber Command Valiant Operational Conversion Unit. Here I would meet up with my own crew as well as certain crews destined to serve with 49 Squadron. Now aware of my full programme, I was keen to press on with the Meteor conversion to ensure the various dates arranged by Air Ministry were achieved.

The Monday dawned with heavy overcast cloud, but it was clear and the snow had ceased to fall. After breakfast in the Mess at Manby, we all climbed into the crew bus, complete with flying kit, and headed for Strubby. I was scheduled to fly with a Flying Officer Beard who was to be my instructor; therefore on arrival I quickly changed into flying kit and made my way to the crew briefing room.

The first exercise was to comprise engine starting, taxiing, take-off climb, stalling and rejoining circuit with a roller and final landing. All this was discussed on the ground, including the local Strubby airfield procedure for climb out and rejoining the circuit after let down from altitude. Today we were only going to 20,000ft; therefore it really was medium altitude.

We walked out to dispersal which was adjacent to the crew buildings, and on arrival at the aircraft carefully went through the full external checks, by which time I was thoroughly cold as there was a freezing breeze blowing. However, this was soon forgotten once settled into the cockpit and strapped into my seat – the delight of being at the controls again completely overcame my personal discomfort, for I knew that as soon as the engines were started we would quickly have the benefit of heating.

Having completed all internal checks, we were ready for 'Start engines'. The ground crew signalled clear for starting, and ensuring that the throttle levers were fully closed, high and low pressure cocks ON, we started No. 1 engine, having first selected the low pressure pump to ON and two seconds later pressed the starter button for that engine, releasing it two seconds later. (This procedure was to energise the solenoid which would cause the starter mechanism to be 'wound up', but the starting cycle would not commence until the starter button was released.) The engine accelerated to idling speed, the jet pipe temperature slightly exceeded the idling limit with minor resonance, then settled back to approximately 500°C. The same procedure was then repeated for No. 2 engine. Both engines were now idling at around 3,300 rpm, and with this situation the 'After start' checks were carried out.

All now complete, we were ready to taxi, so Strubby Tower was contacted for clearance to the active runway. This obtained, the ground crews signalled for 'chocks away' and we were on the move, slowly taxiing on to the perimeter track towards the active runway. Once at the Hold Point for the active runway, the final checks for take-off were commenced:

Trim: Elevator and rudder-neutral
Fuel: LP Cocks – ON
        HP Cocks – ON
        LP Pumps – ON
Flaps: ⅓ down
Check pneumatic supply at 450lb/sq in
Air brakes – closed
Canopy – locked

These completed we called for take-off clearance. Once obtained we moved on to the runway, lining up carefully, making sure the nose wheel was straight, then smoothly opened both throttles to take-off rpm and released the brakes, allowing the Meteor to surge forward with an exhilarating sense of power. As the speed built up to 90kt, the nose wheel was eased off the ground; with the speed coming to 125kt the aircraft was rotated by a backward pressure on the control column. When comfortably airborne, the undercarriage retracted before 175kt was attained, the ⅓ flaps taken in, and we settled down to a steady climb at 290kt, reducing revs to approximately 14,100rpm for economical climb. Control was again contacted for clearance to change frequency to Strubby approach. Since I had previously flown the Meteor, my instructor had allowed me to handle the aircraft from the word go, merely reminding me of speed limitations to observe.

We climbed quickly through the heavy alto cumulus cloud, which had a base of 3,000ft emerging into bright clear sunlight at 8,000ft, and reached our altitude for this first exercise, 20,000ft, having changed the millibar setting on my altimeter for the airfield QNH to standard atmospheric setting of 1013 millibar at 3,000ft. We levelled and settled at 20,000ft with the aircraft trimmed. It was possible to admire the panoramic view, for in every direction there was a vast expanse of white cloud tops giving the impression of a massive area of undulating fleecy wool illuminated by a brilliant winter sun. My few seconds of taking in the scene were broken by the voice of my instructor saying 'I have control now and will demonstrate for you firstly a clean stall with flaps and undercarriage up, followed by a stall with flaps and undercarriage down.' He then turned the aircraft through 360° to ensure no other aircraft was in the vicinity or below, and throttled fully back, easing the nose above the horizon, allowing the speed to fall off until, as 100kt was reached, there was slight elevator buffeting accompanied by minor fore and aft pitching with vibration as the nose dropped; any tendency for either wing to drop was not apparent. To recover, full power was applied and the controls were eased forward slightly to regain level flight with minimum loss of height.

The instructor then repeated the same manoeuvre with flaps and undercarriage down. The stall in this configuration was similar except at the point of stall the nose of the aircraft was higher above the horizon, and there was a more pronounced stall warning of elevator buffeting, accompanied by fore and aft pitching with vibration some 10kt before the actual point of stall was reached at approximately 90kt. The stall itself was more positive and the nose dropped sharply with a tendency for one wing to drop. Recovery was again straightforward, with full power, the control column slightly forward, and correcting the wing drop by gentle opposite rudder to recover back to level flight with minimum loss of height.

This complete, I was instructed to repeat the exercise. Fortunately there was a break in the layer of cloud below and, as we anticipated our position to be over Grimsby, I was able to confirm this visually before turning the aircraft through 360° to ensure all was clear for the stalling manoeuvre to commence.

I then placed the nose of the aircraft above the horizon, closed throttles and eased the control column back, allowing the speed to fall off until we attained a complete stalled condition around 100kt, with the nose dropping. Immediate recovery action was applied, the throttles open, the control column forward, checking any tendency for a wing drop by application of opposite rudder, and regaining level flight with minimum loss of height. Having repeated the exercise with flaps and undercarriage down, we turned our attention to spinning. Here, the instructor said he would first demonstrate a spin to the left.

Once again, before spinning it is essential to first establish position, turn the aircraft to the left and right in order to ensure no other aircraft is in the vicinity or below, and check the harness is secure and that there are no loose objects in the cockpit. With all this complete, the manoeuvre was commenced: throttle closed, control column back until the aircraft stalled, then hard left rudder and the aircraft whipped into a tight left spiral. After two turns, my instructor applied the opposite rudder to stop the turn, moving the control column forward, keeping ailerons neutral; then centralising rudder as the spin stopped and gently recovering from the ensuing dive, applying power and settling back to level flight.

With the words 'You have control and when ready carry out a spin to the right, recovering after two turns', I acknowledged and assumed control of the aircraft. After completing a turn to starboard and one to the left to ensure no other aircraft in our vicinity, I placed the nose of the aircraft well above the horizon, closed throttles and, as the speed fell off, moved the control column back until the point of stall was reached. At this point I applied full right rudder and the Meteor whipped into a tight starboard spiral. With two turns complete, I applied hard left rudder and, as the spiral ceased, centralised the rudder, easing the control column forward, with ailerons neutral and progressive application of power until speed built up, and then slowly eased the aircraft back to level flight.

These two exercises complete, it was time to return to base. Since a controlled descent was required, we called Strubby Approach requesting 'Controlled Descent and GCA' in view of the weather. We were quickly identified and given a course to steer; then Strubby gave a course on to the descent safety land and we commenced a rapid descent – throttles closed, air brakes out, speed 250kt and descending at 1,100ft/min – which was continued to the check altitude of 1,500ft where we levelled out with air brakes in and throttle adjusted to maintained speed of 250kt. At this point the GCA Controller turned us on to the runway heading and instructed complete pre-landing checks for final approach talk-down.

We settled at 1,500ft, undercarriage down selected, and speed reduced to 140kt with ⅓ flap; the controller called for descent at 500ft/min. This we continued under control, until the runway could be seen clearly at 400ft, where full flap was selected, and the speed was slowly reduced to achieve boundary crossing at 105kt, a gentle flare out, throttles slowly closed, holding off, keeping the nose up to achieve a smooth touch of the main wheels on the runway. In this position – as we had identified to control – our first landing would be a roller; the throttles were opened to full power and as speed increased to approximately 120kt, a backward movement of the controls produced a rotation and, once safely airborne, undercarriage up was selected and flaps positioned at 1/3. Then, with the airspeed 150kt, a climb commenced and the remainder of flap was selected up. In this configuration a normal visual circuit was flown and then downwind final landing checks were carried out:

Brakes – off and check brake pressure
Undercarriage selected down and three green lights checked.
Flap – to ⅓

On final turn into wind for the active runway, full flaps were selected and Strubby Control was contacted, indicating on 'Finals for full stop landing'. Speed on approach was down to 140kt, the aircraft trimmed and reducing to 105kt for boundary crossing; a smooth flare out and hold off with throttle closed and the aircraft settled gently on to the runway.

With the first flight successfully completed, we taxied back to dispersals, carried out the engine shut down drills and climbed out of the Meteor, well satisfied with this exercise; I was aware however that my performance indicated in places a need for polish and elimination of rust; this I was prepared to work on.

These points were highlighted at debriefing, and I made note of all of them. Having changed out of flying kit, it was time for lectures; then at 17.00hrs we returned to Manby. By this time it was noted with regret that the weather was once again closing in and heavy snow fell all that night. To the dismay of all concerned, this adverse weather continued for some days, and it was not until 27 January that the flying programme could be resumed. However, this period was not wasted, for we settled down to a concentrated lecture programme.

There was much to learn regarding high altitude meteorology and, from the Aviation Medical Specialists, all physiological aspects of high speed/altitude flying – all this in addition to a detailed knowledge of all the technical systems of the Meteor. Furthermore, during this non-flying period, we were given experience in the Aviation Medicine decompression chamber in order to acclimatise ourselves with the discomfort of flying at 40,000ft in an unpressurised cockpit – which was amusing in the extreme, although at times embarrassing. Before embarking on this adventure, the flying Medics gave a good lecture on the use of oxygen and the effects of lack of oxygen (called 'anoxia') which is insidious, for the victim seldom realises he is affected, and is often convinced that he is performing supremely well. When flying above 10,000ft in unpressurised cockpits it is necessary for a pilot to breathe a minimum of oxygen by means of a face oxygen mask, because lack of oxygen above 10,000ft becomes progressively more pronounced with altitude. The classic signs of moderate anoxia are normally:

a)   Inefficiency and over-confidence
b)   Poor performance of simple tasks
c)   Slow reactions
d)   Blueness of ears and lips
e)   Breathlessness on exertion
f)   Numbness and drowsiness

Above 20,000ft these symptoms are more severe and above 30,000ft there is a rapid loss of consciousness.

The lecture dealt with the effect of altitude on the body above 10,000ft or 40,000ft, because this is what we were to experience in the decompression chamber. As altitude is increased above 10,000ft, the atmospheric pressure decreases; thus in an unpressurised cockpit, the pilot experiences extreme discomfort due to expansion of gas in the bowels.

The other problems associated with unpressurised cockpits (which are in fact pressurised to maintain an equivalent atmospheric pressure associated with 8,000ft) is the possibility of decompression sickness. This is caused by nitrogen passing out of the solution in body fluids at low pressure and, by doing so, a collection of bubbles forms in the body tissues. The most common symptom is an aching pain in a limb or joint which, if not severe, can be ignored with perfect safety, and very rarely does the condition cause faintness or interferes with breathing. Should these latter signs be experienced, altitude must be reduced as quickly as possible. Recovery is immediate on descent to lower altitudes. Pilots likely to be over-susceptible to decompression sickness are soon identified by means of simulated test conditions in the decompression chamber.

Our lecture programme in this initial phase of the course also covered the Martin Baker ejection set and operating drills, which we were able realistically to acclimatise ourselves on the Ejection Seat Ground Trainer which did enable a pilot to try the force of G in ejection without having to do this from an aircraft.

With an improvement in the weather, flying was resumed and the next few sorties were devoted to circuits and landings in the Meteor 7. We performed asymmetric flying – which is flying with one engine flamed out – including single engine landings and overshoots, and with all this done to everybody's satisfaction on the Meteor 7, one was sent solo in the Meteor 8.

During the next few weeks, the weather varied a great deal and although we did not have any further heavy snow falls it remained very cold with a mixture of freezing rain and low cloud – the occasional bright clear day was a tonic for all concerned. However, the variation of weather did not prevent the flying programme going ahead. It is to the credit of the Flying Instructor Staff that they knocked the rust off all of us in so short a time as to leave students flying solo in very marginal weather conditions, all of which made one grateful for the efficiency of the Ground Control Approach Staff who were always there to provide a confident talk down through the worst of cloud.

Once at home with the Meteor 8, the next serious phase of the course was concentrated instrument flying, for we were all required to undergo the full instrument rating test by midway through the course before the night flying phase commenced. Indeed, any student not able to cope with the instrument rating test was suspended; if he could not fly a jet with safety and confidence under full instruments conditions, he could not be sent solo at night. During the entire period of the course, ground lectures were blended in with the flying programme, providing the correct balance at all times.

With the instrument flying requirement satisfied, the flying side concentrated on medium level aerobatics and high level handling, including climbs to 40,000ft for high speed runs and maximum rate turns and descents. The dual aspect of this in the Meteor Mk 7 was painful and uncomfortable because of its unpressurised cockpit. However, using the Meteor 8 for the solo exercises, the discomfort was eliminated because of its pressurised cockpit, and these exercises were great fun.

Another pleasant part of the flying programme was devoted to formation flying, and because this was something I had covered during my days as a Flying Instructor it was a delight to go through these exercises again. New to me was formation aerobatics, but provided the leader was smooth in all his manoeuvres and you kept your aircraft well stationed on the leader, it was easy to maintain this position in any manoeuvres, for you were completely oblivious of the attitude of your aircraft to the horizion, because of concentrating on the aircraft with which you were formating.

When descending in formation through cloud it was even more necessary to maintain a close position and concentrate completely on the leader. Under these conditions you do not even look at your instrument panel and it is essential to have absolute faith in the aircraft on which you are formating. It is so easy, under severe cloud conditions when descending in formation, to feel a false physical sensation or illusion and this has to be ignored. This is easy to do when you are in good flying practice, fully familiar with your aircraft, feeling confident and relaxed in your flying.

The final phase of the course was devoted to night flying amounting to a total of 5hr, made up of 2hr dual instruction and 3hr solo in the Meteor 8. Exercises included circuits and landings, single engine landings and overshoots, high altitude, high speed runs, max rate turns and max rate descents; all culminating with a final handling check.

For my dual high altitude exercise, the Meteor 7 was used, and on that particular evening the night was clear but there was a marked mist which made the night visual horizon difficult to discern and could easily give a false impression. However, on the dual sortie all went well, although, as this was conducted at 40,000ft unpressurised, I was glad to reach the point where we commenced a max rate descent with air brakes out down to 1,500ft for a GCA controlled talk down and landing. After landing and taxiing back to dispersal, my instructor and I walked to the Crew Room for debriefing; with this complete I was authorised for a solo flight in a Meteor 8, to go through the same exercises.

Having signed the Form 700, I walked out to my aircraft, completed the external checks, climbed into the cockpit and strapped myself in, thankful that it was a Meteor 8 equipped with a pressurised cockpit, so the climb to 40,000ft would be comfortable.

With engines started and taxiing clearance obtained from control, I taxied out to the active runway. Pre-take-off checks completed, I called the tower for take-off clearance; this was given and I slowly taxied on to the runway with nose wheel lined up for take-off. Take-off clearance was passed and I proceeded with a normal night take-off, quickly settling down to the climb out course, having cleared from local frequency to Strubby Approach.

The climb to 40,000ft was uneventful and having settled the aircraft and trimmed it to fly with no pressure on any control, I had a Mach reading of 0.72. For the benefit of those not accustomed to high altitude and high speed aircraft, I should explain that in all jet aircraft a pilot requires an additional instrument to the Air Speed Indicator, for this is completely inaccurate at high altitudes. Therefore, as the aircraft is to experience compressibility, it is important for the pilot to have an instrument which is capable of indicating its speed in relation to the local speed of sound. For this we had a Machmeter which is graduated to give an immediate indication of the aircraft's true airspeed in relation to the local speed of sound. The mach number is indicated as a decimal.

Since the vertical visibility was good, there was no difficulty in establishing my position before commencing max rate turns; this complete, I turned my attention to the high speed run. For this exercise it is necessary to trim out the aircraft for normal flight and then open up the throttle maintaining altitude. Speed on the Machmeter increased and at Mach 0.76 there was a progressive strong nose up change of trim and slight buffeting was experienced. To overcome this I used trim to ease the pressure on the control column. The Machmeter increased to 0.78 and the nose up change of trim became very pronounced and, as instructed, I resisted the temptation to relieve this pressure by the use of trim. However, I was determined to take it to 0.80 and this was my undoing, for suddenly I experienced a pitching oscillation with 'snaking', then, without warning, a wing dropped.

At this stage I decided it was time for a rapid recovery which should have been simple – both throttles closed and air brakes out, which produced a rapid deceleration. However, I had allowed the wing drop to put me into a dive and in doing so, with little or no clearly defined horizon, I became momentarily completely disorientated. I could see the stars quite clearly and the lights of Grimsby and Cleethorpes were also visible, but I could not discern a horizon to regain level flight.

Whilst this sensation only lasted a few seconds, it seemed a life time as I struggled to reorientate myself. In doing so I released pressure on the controls and slowly adjusted myself to the instrument panel and my artificial horizon which showed me to be in a steep dive to the left. Slowly I levelled the ailerons and then eased the aircraft out of the dive and, as the Mach number dropped back to 0.72, selected air brakes IN and set throttles back to 14,000rpm.

I regained my composure, a wiser man, annoyed with myself for allowing such a situation to occur. I then repeated the exercise, but not beyond Mach 0.76, and recovery was normal. I called Strubby Approach for rapid descent clearance and feed into GCA for final landing. It was good to see the altimeter winding down in the rapid descent.

This aspect of the exercise was completed without incident, and after landing and taxiing back to dispersal I reflected on the carelessness and ineptitude of my handling of a situation in high speed runs which was of my own creation. I learnt a very severe lesson that night, but at debriefing decided 'silence was golden' and somehow those details were not mentioned. This was my last solo exercise and I had only to fly a final night handling test for the completion of the course which, in spite of bad weather, had been achieved in the 10 weeks allocated, taking us to mid-March.

Having completed all end of course formalities, including a pleasant evening in the bar with my fellow students and the staff, I had to report to the Commandant as Senior Officer on the course. On the date of my departure, I walked over to Tedder Block, which housed the Royal Air Force Flying College Lecture Block and Administrative Offices, where the Commandant's office was also located. His ADC ushered me in, and after saluting the Air Commodore asked me to sit down.

We chatted about the course in general and the Commandant wished to know if I had any proposals for its improvement or any criticism to offer. I said that I had found it a very well planned and demanding refresher course; the staff and instructors had gone out of their way to be helpful and showed themselves to be extremely understanding of experienced officers' problems in returning to flying duties.

Air Cdre Walker thanked me for the enthusiasm I had displayed and example set as Course Leader, and wished me success for the future as a Squadron Commander in the V Force. On this note I took leave of the Commandant, and left his office.

I had enjoyed my return to RAF Manby, and was looking forward to a short spell at RAF Lindholme, the Bomber Command Bombing School, where I was to be introduced to the Radar Navigation Bombing System – the Blind Bombing Equipment fitted to all V bomber aircraft.

With all departure formalities complete at No. 3 Squadron – Jet Refresher School, I bade farewell to my fellow course students and the staff, satisfied to have completed this stage of the retread programme, and returned to the Officers' Mess at Manby to pack and once again take my leave of the civilian staff who had looked after me so well.

Somehow, leaving Manby was like departing from an ancestral home where I had spent many happy years and been so very well cared for. I am sure many retired RAF officers today remember their days at Manby, which was one of the oldest stations in the Royal Air Force, with a proven history of service. Sadly, today RAF Manby is no more an active station, for it was made redundant with the 1970 contraction of the Royal Air Force, and many of the station buildings are occupied as part of an industrial estate.

However, the car was packed, Crusty in his position, and with a last look at the majestic mansion we headed for the changing scenery of Yorkshire. It was not a particularly pleasant day, for, as I remember, it rained all the way and I was glad to turn off the A1 and head for the main guardroom gate at RAF Lindholme. Having booked in and registered my car in the usual way, I drove to the Officers' Mess and found that a room had been reserved for me, so Crusty and I settled in.

The Bomber Command Bombing School offered a very academic course on the theory and practical application of bombing and navigation equipment to all navigators coming into Bomber Command who were to be the navigation radar operators, and to the crew members who would be responsible for operating the new radar bombing system.

Lindholme, being a permanent type station, was well equipped with lecture room facilities and Radar Simulation Trainers. To provide navigators with airborne experience of the equipment, the station had available a squadron of Vickers Varsity twin engine navigational training aircraft, specially fitted out as flying classrooms with the radar blind bombing equipment installed.

For pilots like myself, not familiar with this equipment, we were required to undertake a very much shortened version of the main course, during which we were introduced to the theory of this radar system in its broadest terms, allowed to operate the equipment in the ground trainer, and eventually elevated to being permitted to handle it in the Varsity both as a navigator and as the pilot. Normally this was with the navigator who was to be a member of the pilot's crew; for me this was not possible and in the event I did not meet up with my own navigator radar operator (Flt Lt– later Sqn Ldr – Alan Washbrook) until arriving at RAF Gaydon, the Valiant Operational Conversion Unit.

Bomber Command has always had an all weather capability, and indeed it will be remembered that the introduction of H2S Radar Equipment during World War 2 enabled a navigator to see ground features without reverting to visual means, thus enabling targets to be identified and pinpointed when the ground was completely obscured by cloud. Since the radar navigational bombing system incorporated the basic principles of the H2S radar, I will give a few words of explanation of the general principles of H2S radar, for those not familiar.

This equipment was completely self-contained in the aircraft and independent of any ground-based sources for radar information. It therefore had the advantage that when flying in darkness or in or above cloud, accurate flying was still possible. In effect the radar equipment provides the navigator with a picture of the ground beneath and around the aircraft, on a radar screen similar to a map. Interpretation of the radar screen picture by the navigator calls for considerable skill which is only acquired by intensive training and experience. The screen picture is obtained from radar pulses transmitted from the aircraft, which upon striking the ground features, are reflected back to the aircraft. The actual amount of reflection is determined by the nature of the ground feature struck in a manner comparable to that of light. Measurement of the time elapsed before echoes return to the aircraft provides an accurate measurement of the distance of the object from which reflection has occurred. The direction from which the echo comes indicates the bearing of the ground feature from the aircraft.

This bearing is determined by the means of an aerial system on the aircraft rotating through 360°; the system also makes possible the simultaneous solution of both bearing and distance. This information, as mentioned above, is portrayed on a radial screen in a manner similar to their appearance on a map. This basic radar equipment is incorporated into the navigational radar bombing system but provides far more accuracy and detail, enabling detailed target information to be recognised and linked to a bomb aiming system for the accurate delivery of a nuclear or conventional weapon on to any target, under all weather conditions.

Much of this latter aspect of the equipment was new to me and therefore, once again, I was to make the old brain box work overtime in assimilating the vital basic theory and standard operating procedures. However, the atmosphere was relaxed, and the instructional staff experienced in dealing with pilots; they were able to impart information in a manner easy to absorb, for which I was extremely grateful as the basic mysteries of radar and electronics has never been one of my strong subjects! Also included in this course were a number of periods devoted to visual bombing techniques with the British Mk 14A bomb-sight, which was also fitted to the V bombers. I was to be thankful for this aspect of the course, for I was ultimately to discover that the special task allotted to 49

Squadron involved the use of the Mk 14A bombsight for a a highly accurate visual bombing operation.

I do not intend to launch into a detailed description of the Mk 14A bombsight or to delve deeply into the theory of visual bomb aiming; since visual bombing techniques were to play a major role in our future function, certain aspects will be covered in later chapters. Sufficient at this stage to say that the problem of simple visual bombing is to reach a position in space from which it is possible to release a given type of bomb in order to achieve a direct hit on any target. To attain this degree of accuracy, there are five factors which must be studied in some detail. These are the bomb ballistics, the wind velocity at the bombing height, the aircraft's attitude at the point of release, the actual bombing height and the aircraft's airspeed. All these factors combine to make up the actual bomb trajectory. In order to collate this information and project into the correct bomb trajectory for any task under visual conditions, the Mk 14A bombsight was the ideal equipment. It was what is termed a continuously set vector bombsight consisting of three main components; namely, the computer unit, the sighting head and the control panel.

Let us briefly look at these three components. The sighting head is essentially a reflector sight which is coupled to the computer by two flexible drives. When these drives are turned by the computer unit, which in reality is the brain of the bombsight, the correct drift angle and sighting angle are registered on the sighting head, which allows the bomb aimer to sight along the correct line of sight merely by observing an illuminated sword-shaped cross, through a glass panel known as the reflector glass. The computer unit requires information in order to calculate the two angles and this is obtained partially by hand settings and partially by automatic measuring drives contained in the computer unit itself. The control panel consists of two rheostats which control the brilliance of the graticule lamp and the drift scale indicator lamp, both of which are located in the sighting head. At Lindholme the ground lecture programme advanced into a comprehensive explanation of this equipment and its range of applications, which was later included in the flying practice bombing programme.

To me, the period at Lindholme was a pleasant change from the intensity of getting jet refresher flying completed in such a tight time scale, in far from ideal weather conditions. However, I was well aware that the time at Lindholme was limited and not to be wasted as the overall programme allocated to me could not be varied; there was now a firm date for me to assume command of 49 Squadron.

In the Royal Air Force, wherever one is stationed, one always finds familiar faces, and Lindholme was no exception. The Chief Navigation Instructor was Wg Cdr (now AVM) Dougie Bower, an old friend of mine from the first Royal Air Force Flying College Course at Manby. Indeed, we were to meet yet again on Christmas Island where he was the Wing Commander in charge of administration. Also, I found the Station Commander to be no less of a person than

Gp Capt John Palmer OBE, who again had been with me at RAF Manby where he was Station Commander from the first days of the establishment of the Royal Air Force Flying College until he departed to his next appointment, in Jordan.

I had of course on arrival called on John Palmer to pay my respects, and he said then that he would be in touch to invite me to his house for dinner one evening. True to his word, the invitation came and I duly accepted. On the appointed night, as I changed into dinner jacket, I reflected that the evening ahead of me could be a little difficult; for since my days with John Palmer at Manby, he had become divorced from his first wife Anne and had married again a lady he actually met in Jordan. I resolved to be careful in my general dinner chat, for obviously Manby would be mentioned and I must try not to reminisce too much on the hilarious days when Ginger Weir was Wing Commander Flying (later AVM, sadly he died when on the Diplomatic Staff at Washington in 1965). John's first wife Anne was a great party girl, as was 'Moo', the wife of Ginger Weir, and we had all enjoyed a hectic way of life in those days.

I found John Palmer's second wife a very sincere and delightful person who made me feel very much at home, and since she and Anne, John's previous wife, were also friends, there was a completely relaxed atmosphere and I thoroughly enjoyed my evening. We were all to meet again, for when John Palmer retired from the RAF, he settled near RAF Scampton in Lincolnshire, and during my spell as Station Commander, Scampton, 1963/64, I was able to return his hospitality.

On 2 May 1956 I set off from Lindholme on a beautiful morning for Bassingbourn. As I drove along, I was conscious of a wonderful relaxed feeling at the thought of at long last being able to fly a Canberra. This was an aircraft that I had longed to fly ever since it came into service, but since it formed the initial twin jet light bomber coming into Bomber Command, No. 231 Operational Conversion Unit had been heavily committed to keep pace with crew output to match the re-equipment of squadrons with this efficient and delightful aircraft.

My course at No. 231 OCU, RAF Bassingbourn, was scheduled to last five weeks, which would take me into the first week of June and thence at long last on to the Valiant at No. 232 OCU Gaydon. I stirred myself from these pleasant reflections and concentrated on driving as we rejoined the main A1, and headed steadily south, with the usual congestion as Stamford was reached; then past RAF Wittering, our ultimate destination when all training had been completed. Shortly after passing RAF Wittering, I pulled into a lay-by to give the dog a walk and stretch my own legs. It was one of those lovely early spring days, bright sunshine and a scent of freshly cut grass all around as the nearby fields were in the process of being cut for hay; all utterly relaxing and pleasant. But we were soon under way again for I was keen to get settled in at Bassingbourn and commence this short course, because although I should be joining up with a normal full conversion course of pilots and navigators, it was only intended to give me an abbreviated experience of the Canberra, prior to the Valiant.

Just past Alconbury Hill we turned off the A1 onto the A14, through Huntingdon and on to Bassingbourn. As Bassingbourn came into view, it was possible to see the airfield clearly, with Canberra aircraft on dispersals and a certain amount of circuit flying in progress; runway 27 was in use and aircraft on final approach to land came in over the A14.

I turned right into the main entrance and booked in at the Guard Room, then straight on to the Officers' Mess. Here again, Bassingbourn being a permanent type station, the Officers' Mess was of the usual dignified style. Regrettably now, of course, Bassingbourn is no longer a flying station, having become redundant in the subsequent contraction programme, but it has been kept in the military family and is now used by the Army.

That night in the Mess I met the Chief Flying Instructor, Wg Cdr Alan Pickering, over a drink in the bar, and on the following morning, duly presented myself to Ground School, ready to tackle the course.

The first few days were devoted to getting to know more about the Canberra, its various operating systems – such as hydraulics and electrics – as well as cockpit layout and start-up and operating drills. With this complete, I was introduced to Sqn Ldr Holt who was to be my flying instructor, and at last came that exciting moment when we walked out to the dual control Canberra T4 for our first flight.

For those not familiar with the Canberra B2 light bomber, let me include a very brief description. It is a product of the old English Electric Co, and powered by two Avon Mk 1 engines, each of 6,500lb thrust, or alternatively two Avon Mk 101 engines, each of 7,150lb static thrust. The cabin is pressurised and provides accommodation for a crew of three in ejection seats. There is an alternative position in the nose for the air bomber, but there is no provision made for ejection from this position. The aircraft has a well proportioned bomb bay in the belly of the fuselage.

Having completed all external checks, we climbed into the cockpit by means of the side door and I settled myself into the left hand seat, my instructor squeezing himself into the right hand dual seat. I say squeezed, because the Canberra cockpit is extremely compact and comfortable for the pilot in the left hand seat; however, it is not a wide cockpit, being designed for single pilot operation. Therefore the poor instructor, once in, has to settle himself in a very confined space.

Once strapped in and able to take stock of my surroundings, I was aware that everything about the Canberra seemed perfect. With aircraft you get an initial impression that it looks right, and then once seated at the controls it either feels professionally attractive and comfortable or alternatively it feels awkward. The Canberra immediately gives you the feeling that it is a perfect aerodynamic specimen, and it certainly is, for the all-round vision is ideal (because of the bubble canopy) and all the controls are conveniently placed.

That first taste of the Canberra T4 on the morning of 17 May was something special, to recall with pleasure, for at last I was coming to grips with an aircraft that I had longed to fly ever since it was introduced into service. That first dual trip produced no problems and merely confirmed the delightful characteristics of the aircraft. This initial flight gave me an opportunity to familiarise myself with the general take-off and upper air handling, and also my first experience of the approach and landing characteristics.

Following this dual flight there were three more trips in the T4 to cover asymmetric performance, single engine landing and in-flight re-light drills. Then came the long anticipated day when I was let loose in a Canberra B4, on 23 May, with Flt Lt Williams as my staff navigator.

The weather could not have been more favourable; it was a typical summer day with half cloud cover of cumulus cloud, giving broken base of 2,000ft. Therefore the flight was to be under full visual flight rules, and, although at this stage I had 3,900 flying hours under my belt and had flown some 28 aircraft types, I was excited at the prospect of flying that Canberra solo.

Having been briefed on the complete flight profile to be flown, my navigator and I walked out to the aircraft and quickly completed all external checks, before climbing into the cockpit, strapping into the ejector seat and thence on to all checks prior to taxiing and take-off. It was an exhilarating feeling to have the aircraft to myself and somehow there existed a complete atmosphere of controlled confidence, for I felt absolutely at home and relaxed.

This flight was stimulating from the moment of lining up on the runway and opening the throttles for take-off, to the point where I closed the throttles on crossing the airfield boundary, holding off for the final landing, and felt that satisfying sensation of the main wheels touching lightly on the ground. I was absolutely convinced that this was one of the finest aircraft I had ever flown and no subsequent flight ever changed that opinion. The Canberra was a thoroughbred in every sense of the word.

During May and into June, the course progressed at a well regulated pace, balanced with ground school and flying in order to achieve a total of 20hrs by the end of the course on 10 June.

In those five weeks at Bassingbourn the weather on the whole had been extremely pleasant, although there were days when rain and cloud gave ample experience of operating the Canberra under Instrument Flying Rules procedures and realistic Ground Control Radar Approaches, which was a pleasure, for the aircraft trims out so well on an instrument final approach that it was not difficult to produce a high standard of instrument flying for this vital stage of the let down to break off altitude, followed by a visual reference to runway lights and the final landing.

Those weeks passed quickly and once again I was packed and ready to move on to the final stage of my training. This time my destination was to be No. 232 OCU at RAF Gaydon in Warwickshire. Here I was to undertake the full 10-week course with some of the crews that were to be part of 49 Squadron, and I was also to meet my own crew members who were then to go through the entire ground school syllabus with me and then fly every training sortie as my crew, being progressively welded into a fully operational and effective Valiant team.

For me this was to be a very testing period, as I was required to produce the same academic standards in ground school as every other aircrew member undergoing the course, and during those weeks I was well aware that crews destined to serve under my command would be taking stock of me; therefore it was up to me to set the example from day one.

The V Bomber Valiant Course at RAF Gaydon was intensive, because the Valiant compared to any other aircraft flown to date was complicated in its technical systems, flight deck instrument layout and operating procedures. All had to be thoroughly understood on the ground and meticulously practised in the Valiant Ground Simulator before one was even allowed near the aircraft.

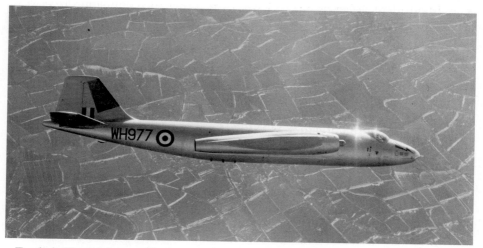

English Electric's superb Canberra. Here a B7 shows her lines to advantage, and 'looks right'.

CHAPTER THREE

Introduction to the Valiant

My arrival at Gaydon was in many ways significant, because this was my introduction to No. 3 Group; Gaydon came under this command, as did RAF Wittering. Thus I was now under the command of AVM K. Cross CB, CBE, DSO, DFC (later ACM Sir Kenneth Cross) and little did I realise at this stage that I was subsequently to serve under his command in various appointments for no less than eight years: as Squadron Commander, as Staff Officer when he was later C-in-C Bomber Command, also as one of his Station Commanders, and finally as Group Captain Training during his period as C-in-C Transport Command. It is appropriate at this stage to comment further on this very famous man, for to him I owe a great debt of gratitude. Under his command, both during my tour as Officer Commanding 49 Squadron and later appointments, he made me, as one of his junior commanders, exercise firm and determined leadership, demanding only the best from myself and those under my command.

AVM Cross as Air Officer Commanding was known as a powerful, determined and dedicated leader with a gallant and distinguished war record; a man who would stand no nonsense from any officer under his command. He set a personal standard both on moral issues and in flying, as an example to all. With this AOC every officer under his command knew exactly where they stood; and those who got on with the job and produced results had nothing to fear. However, those who were not up to the standard required in the V Force quickly found themselves posted elsewhere.

AVM Kenneth Cross had been brought into Bomber Command by the Commander in Chief, AM Sir Harry Broadhurst, who was himself a legend in the Royal Air Force, being highly decorated with the DSO and bar and DFC gained during his time with Fighter Command. When Sir Harry took over as C-in-C, he quickly realised that with the move into the nuclear age and the re-equipping with V bombers, his was to be the elite Command, and the entire attitude and outlook would need reshaping to match the required state necessary for a future deterrent nuclear force.

For his two Operational Groups, Nos 1 and 3, he brought in senior commanders well known to him; men capable of building up this force to the high state of operational perfection demanded. For No. 3 Group which was to have the Valiants and Victors, his choice was AVM K. Cross, and for No. 1 Group, which was to re-equip with the new Vulcans, it was AVM Augustus 'Gus' Walker, the famous one-armed World War 2 bomber ace who I mentioned previously in this book.

I am sure that the history of the Royal Air Force will show both ACM Sir Harry Broadhurst and ACM Sir Kenneth Cross to have been two of the finest Commanders-in-Chiefs of Bomber Command during the post-war years. Thanks to the far-sightedness and stirling qualities of leadership of these men, the new generation of high performance strategic V bombers was matched with crews of well trained and dedicated personnel. Sir Kenneth, when he took over, ensured the Command had nuclear teeth, and was capable of maintaining a constant high state of operational readiness, with crews second to none for their professionalism.

Those of us who had the privilege of serving under these two commanders in the V Force were able to appreciate the contribution both made to maintaining peace by ensuring that Britain's nuclear deterrent force was seen to be effective and constantly at a high state of readiness during the Cold War years of delicate international climate.

RAF Gaydon was under the command of Gp Capt (later AVM) Brian Young, a dynamic and forceful leader whose enthusiasm permeated throughout the Operational Conversion Unit. The Chief Instructor was Wg Cdr (later Gp Capt) Hank Iveson DSO, DFC, an experienced pilot with a brilliant war record. RAF Gaydon was not a permanent type station, therefore all accommodation was of the single storey prefabricated type construction. However, it was very adequately provided for, particularly with Ground School accommodation. The Officers' Mess was comfortable with the sleeping accommodation separate from the main mess.

Having arrived at RAF Gaydon, one quickly settled in; and typical of the excellent station organisation, the course was asked to assemble that first night in the bar, to meet the Station Commander and Chief Instructor for a few words of welcome and a brief introduction to the general scope of the course. This enabled pilots, navigators and air electronic operators to meet each other over a pint, and ensured that by the following day at the commencement of Ground School, we all knew each other. For me, this gave an opportunity to meet all those destined to come under my command and equally it gave crews a chance of making their initial assessment of me.

The course was to be divided into two distinct phases: initially a period of three weeks for Ground School which was to culminate in a written examination; then the second phase, to be devoted to a full flying programme interspersed with exercises in the Valiant simulator.

Having all been given a copy of the ground training programme, we assembled at the Ground School block at 08.30hrs the following morning for the initial introduction lecture by the Station Commander followed by the Chief

VICKERS VALIANT

In January 1955 the Valiant was introduced into squadron service with No. 138 Squadron at RAF Gaydon, the home of the Valiant conversion unit, No. 232 OCU. A total of 104 aircraft was produced, equipping 10 RAF squadrons: Nos 7, 18, 49, 90, 138, 148, 199, 207, 214 and 543. The last Valiant was delivered in September 1957.

The Valiant saw action when in late October 1956 Nos 138,148, 207 and 214 Squadrons were deployed at Luqa, Malta, from where they flew the opening sorties of the Suez campaign. Additionally, for more than eight years the Valiant was a vital part of the United Kingdom's strategic nuclear deterrent. It also gave distinguished service in a number of ancillary roles. During 1959 and 1960 No. 214 Squadron pioneered the use of V-bombers in the flight refuelling role and, in so doing, established several non-stop distance records, including UK to Cape Town (6,060 miles) and Singapore (8,110). A further significant achievement concerned PR Valiants of No. 543 Squadron, RAF Wyton, which, during an 11-week period in 1965, photographed some 400,000sq miles of the Rhodesias, now Zimbabwe.

In the early 1960s studies showed that the V-bombers could not expect to survive at high altitude against improving Warsaw Pact air defences and in 1962, following extensive trials in Canada, the Valiant converted to the low-level role. Three years later the aircraft was withdrawn from service after the discovery of fatigue cracks in the main wing spars.

1   Photo flash recorder
2   Stowage for navigator's folding stool
3   Auto-pilot amplifier
4   Instrumentation recorder No. 1 and thermal recorder
5   Ditching system time and distance unit
6   T4 bomb sight computer
7   Auto-pilot gyro unit
8   Auto-pilot approach coupling unit
9   Auto-pilot power factor unit
10 Rebecca receiver aerial
11 Equipment in radio crate
12 Modifications to rear pressure bulkhead
13 Radio compass junction box. Type 1623
14 Film boxes; two port, two starboard
15 IFF aerial switch unit
16 IFF receiver-transmitter
17 Modifications to panel Z
18 Radio compass loop aerial
19 Panel J (HRC fuses for furnaces and Green Satin inverter and relays for furnaces)
20 IFF aerial change-over switch (ground test only)
21 EM twin fuzing unit
22 Forward snatch plug latch plate
23 Forward port crutch strain gauge connector
24 No. 3 slip position
25 Centre bomb bay camera and lamps

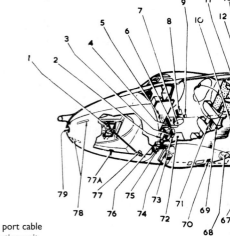

26 Rear port cable retraction unit
27 Rear port crutch strain gauge connector
28 Lanyard pack
29 Port bomb bay film boxes
30 Strain range recorder
31 No. 2 oscillator, transmitter and relay
32 T4 bombsight air supply bottles
33 Green Satin tracking unit
34 Instrumentation in port aileron
35 Port wing camera
36 Equipment in special tail cone
37 No. 2 oscillator aerial
38 Film box
39 Film boxes
40/41 Green Satin transmitter-receiver unit
42 Film boxes
43 No. 1 oscillator aerial
44 Green Satin aerial
45 No. 1 oscillator, transmitter and relay
46 Auto-pilot rudder servo unit
47 Auto-pilot elevator servo unit
48 Port fuselage camera
49 Switch and connector for store crutch strain gauge recorder
50 Rear bomb bay camera
51 Starboard bomb bay film boxes
52 Rear port store crutch

Vickers photograph

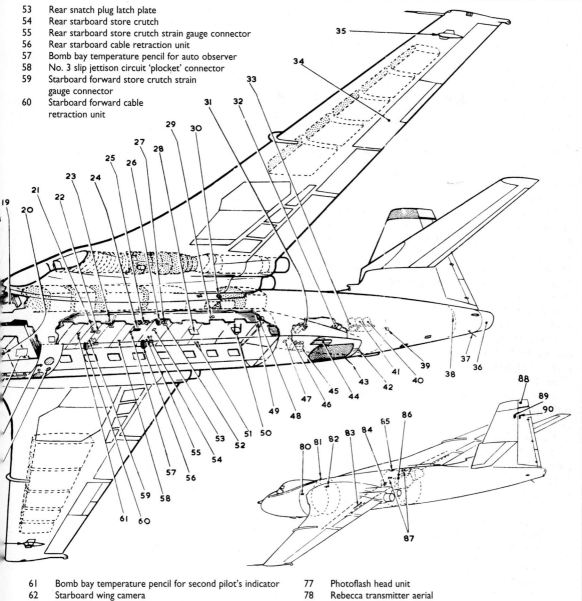

53 Rear snatch plug latch plate
54 Rear starboard store crutch
55 Rear starboard store crutch strain gauge connector
56 Rear starboard cable retraction unit
57 Bomb bay temperature pencil for auto observer
58 No. 3 slip jettison circuit 'plocket' connector
59 Starboard forward store crutch strain gauge connector
60 Starboard forward cable retraction unit

61 Bomb bay temperature pencil for second pilot's indicator
62 Starboard wing camera
63 Air mileage unit
64 Outside air temperature pencil for auto observer
65 Equipment at forward end of bomb bay
66 Radio compass sense aerial
67 Radio compass sense amplifier
68 Instrumentation recorders' junction box
69 Film box on cabin floor
70 IFF aerial
71 Instrumentation control panels
72 Instrumentation supply distribution box
73 Extra crew member's seat
74 T4 bombsight head unit
75 Rebecca transmitter-receiver
76 T4 bombsight amplifier

77 Photoflash head unit
78 Rebecca transmitter aerial
79 Rebecca homing aerials
80 Thermal detector
81 Film boxes (two), port
82 IFF aerial
83 Film boxes (two), starboard
84 Strain range transmitter (port rear spar)
85 Auto-pilot aileron servo unit
86 Thermal detector head
87 Strain range recorder
88 Film boxes, two port, two starboard
89 Rudder tip aerial, used for Gee H Mk 2-C or Decca Aerial change-over relay (Gee or Decca)
90 Aerial amplifier unit

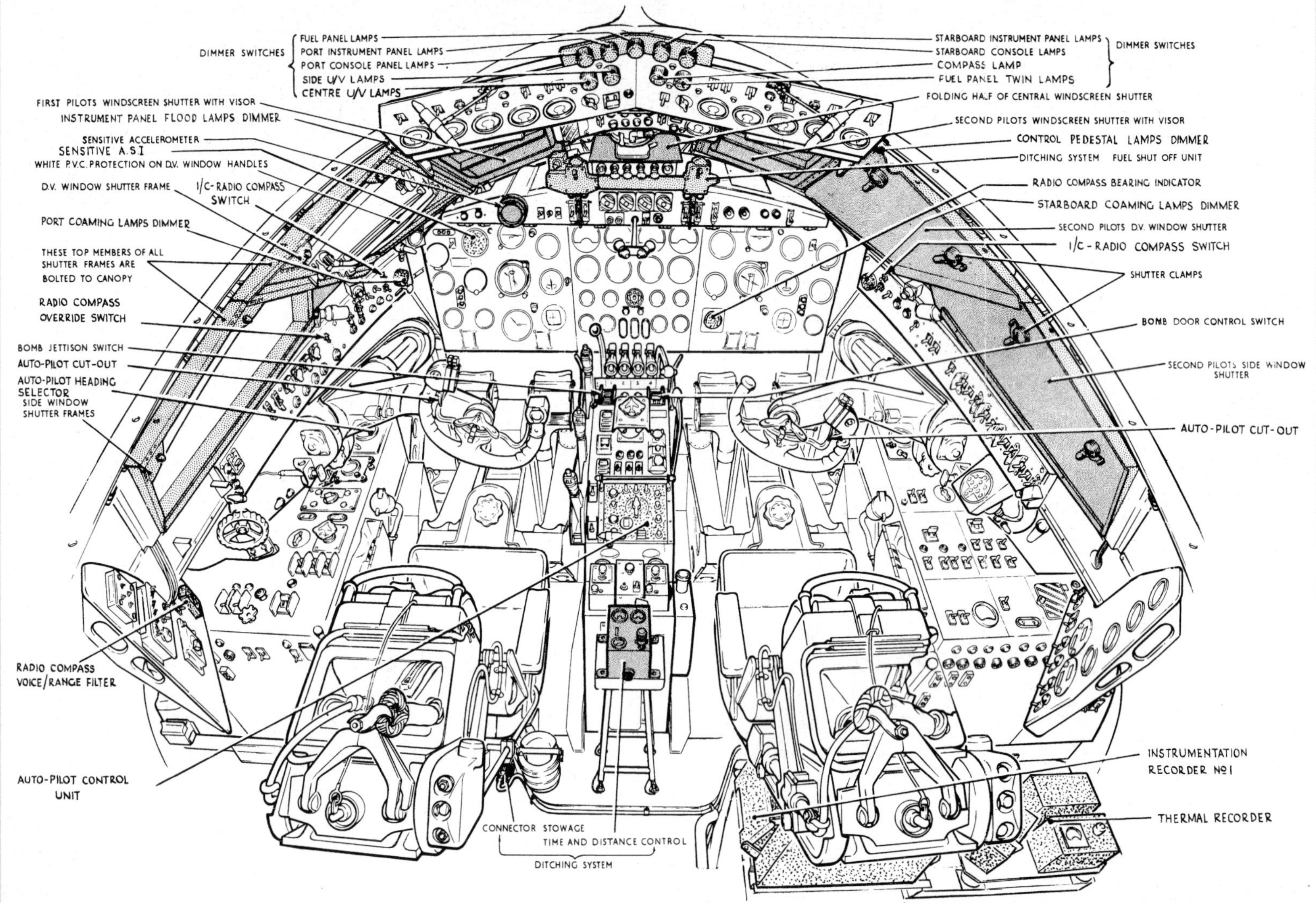

The Cockpit layout of a Valiant (Not a 'Grapple' type). (Author)

Above: Equipment in a 'Grapple' type Valiant

Labels (clockwise/around diagram):

- DIMMER SWITCHES
- FUEL PANEL LAMPS
- PORT INSTRUMENT PANEL LAMPS
- PORT CONSOLE PANEL LAMPS
- SIDE U/V LAMPS
- CENTRE U/V LAMPS
- FIRST PILOTS WINDSCREEN SHUTTER WITH VISOR
- INSTRUMENT PANEL FLOOD LAMPS DIMMER
- SENSITIVE ACCELEROMETER SENSITIVE A 51
- WHITE P.V.C. PROTECTION ON D.V. WINDOW HANDLES
- D.V. WINDOW SHUTTER FRAME
- I/C-RADIO COMPASS SWITCH
- PORT COAMING LAMPS DIMMER
- THESE TOP MEMBERS OF ALL SHUTTER FRAMES ARE BOLTED TO CANOPY
- RADIO COMPASS OVERRIDE SWITCH
- BOMB JETTISON SWITCH
- AUTO-PILOT CUT-OUT
- AUTO-PILOT HEADING SELECTOR
- SIDE WINDOW SHUTTER FRAMES
- RADIO COMPASS VOICE/RANGE FILTER
- AUTO-PILOT CONTROL UNIT
- CONNECTOR STOWAGE
- TIME AND DISTANCE CONTROL
- DITCHING SYSTEM
- INSTRUMENTATION RECORDER Nº1
- THERMAL RECORDER
- AUTO-PILOT CUT-OUT
- SECOND PILOTS SIDE WINDOW SHUTTER
- BOMB DOOR CONTROL SWITCH
- SHUTTER CLAMPS
- I/C - RADIO COMPASS SWITCH
- SECOND PILOTS DV WINDOW SHUTTER
- STARBOARD COAMING LAMPS DIMMER
- RADIO COMPASS BEARING INDICATOR
- DITCHING SYSTEM FUEL SHUT OFF UNIT
- CONTROL PEDESTAL LAMPS DIMMER
- SECOND PILOTS WINDSCREEN SHUTTER WITH VISOR
- FOLDING HALF OF CENTRAL WINDSCREEN SHUTTER
- FUEL PANEL TWIN LAMPS
- COMPASS LAMP
- STARBOARD CONSOLE LAMPS
- STARBOARD INSTRUMENT PANEL LAMPS
- DIMMER SWITCHES

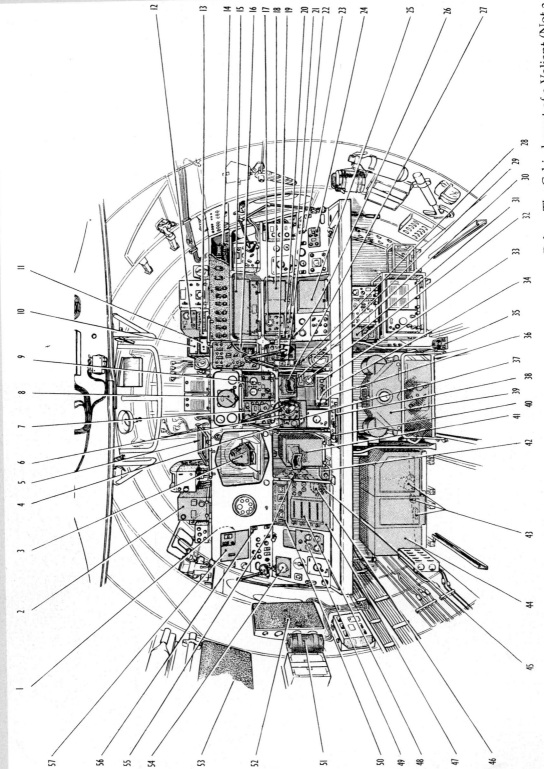

Above: Equipment in a 'Grapple' type Valiant cabin. *(British Aerospace)*

Below: The Cabin layout of a Valiant (Not a 'Grapple' type). *(Author)*

1	Photo cell supply relay, Type 9	30	Air mileage indicator
2	Fuze control unit, Type 1	31	Radio compass receiver (transformer Type 1343 is behind this item)
3	Gamma dosimeter		
4	Radio compass loop controller	32	Decca lane indicator
5	Mounting tray for Gee MK 2-C receiver	33	Air mileage control panel
6	Radio compass control unit (time and distance junction box is behind this item)	34	Radio compass dc supply switch
		35	Film box
7	GPI MR4	36	Navigator's I/C - radio compass switch
8	G4B compass master indicator (junction box is behind panel)	37	Radio compass bearing indicator
		38	Decca flight log
9	Green Satin indicator, Type 101	39	Instrumentation recorder No 2
10	Radio compass power factor transformer, Type 1571	40	Decometers and ground reference switch and indicators
11	Radio compass voltage regulator, Type 1555A	41	Loran receiver (or Gee Mk 2-C indicators)
12	Decca power unit	42	Loran aerial loading unit
13	Decca power relay and HRC fuse	43	Pitch and roll inverter, suppressor and junction box
14	Panel G fuses	44	Auto observer
15	Decca receiver	45	Pitch and roll inverter relay N, Type S2
16	Power distribution box fuses	46	Telemetry junction box
17	Flight log control unit Type 750	47	Instrumentation control panel
18	Decca computer	48	Switch bank cover
19	Rebecca control unit, Type 525	49	Alternative store auxiliary display panel
20	Decca power switch	50	Telemetry control panel
21	Decca receiver control unit, Type 356	51	Second Navigator's ration heater
22	Rebecca switch unit	52	Supply distribution box
23	W/T operator's I/C - radio compass switch	53	Panel F fuses
24	IFF control unit	54	Cabin altimeter
25	Decca velodyne unit	55	Switch bank relays
26	Decca/Gee selector switch	56	Jettison test isolating switch
27	Rebecca indicator	57	Bomb control unit, Type 1
28	Bomb release Instant/Delay switch and type Q1 relay		
29	Bomb release time delay switch unit		

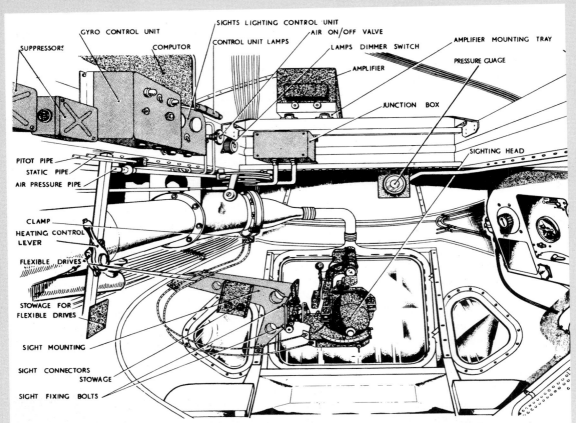

SUPPRESSORS
GYRO CONTROL UNIT
COMPUTOR
SIGHTS LIGHTING CONTROL UNIT
CONTROL UNIT LAMPS
AIR ON/OFF VALVE
LAMPS DIMMER SWITCH
AMPLIFIER MOUNTING TRAY
PRESSURE GUAGE
AMPLIFIER
JUNCTION BOX
SIGHTING HEAD
PITOT PIPE
STATIC PIPE
AIR PRESSURE PIPE
CLAMP
HEATING CONTROL LEVER
FLEXIBLE DRIVES
STOWAGE FOR FLEXIBLE DRIVES
SIGHT MOUNTING
SIGHT CONNECTORS STOWAGE
SIGHT FIXING BOLTS

Top: The T4 Bombsight installation, in a 'Grapple' type Valiant. *(British Aerospace)*

Bottom: Mk 14A Bombsight in a non 'Grapple' type Valiant.

Instructor. Having completed these formalities, we got down to a general lecture on the Valiant, including operational performance figures; and in the afternoon we concentrated on the fuel system. By the end of the afternoon, I fully realised that we were required to have a detailed knowledge of this aircraft, and that proof of having absorbed this information would need to be demonstrated by examination before any flying began.

The overall lecture programme was divided into subjects special to pilots, including all operating systems in the aircraft, electrical systems of alternator and inverters, high level meterology, high level navigation, flight deck layout and operating procedures. There were separate specialised lectures for both navigators and air electronic operators but for quite a number of subjects we all attended the same lecture.

During the first two weeks course members were allowed to sort themselves out as to with whom they wish to be crewed. On this course there were three crews in addition to myself, destined for 49 Squadron. I was particularly impressed by Flt Lt (later Sqn Ldr) A. Washbrook, a very experienced Radar Navigator, and Flt Lt T. Laraway, an experienced Air Electronics Officer. Alan Washbrook was a short, well-proportioned officer with hair that was disappearing fast; he had a superb sense of humour and it was soon obvious that his navigational ability rated well above average.

Ted Laraway seemed to team very well with Alan Washbrook; he too possessed a lively sense of humour, and here again from a professional point of view his knowledge of electronics was of a high standard. Both enjoyed a glass of beer but knew how to balance things so that this would never affect their duty. I decided that these two experienced officers should join my crew if they so wished. Therefore, one evening over a glass of beer, I asked them if they would like to form part of my crew. They accepted with delight, so that was agreed. I then asked Alan who he wished to have as his navigation plotter, for these were the less experienced and younger navigators. He suggested that we should invite Flg Off Eric Hood to join us as he had already told Alan Washbrook that he would like to be considered. Eric Hood was therefore contacted and he agreed at once to join the crew. Eric was a young and smart officer, highly rated for his navigational accuracy, neatness and application in work. These were qualities I rated extremely highly, for only the best from every member of my crew would be good enough.

There was now only the co-pilot's position to be filled and here I had been watching the progress in lectures of Flg Off Bob Beeson, who impressed me as a keen, knowledgeable and level-headed young officer, smart in appearance and very sober in his habits. Bob Beeson therefore appeared to be the right man for me and as he also got along well with my other crew members I invited him to join the team, and he accepted.

My crew was now complete; this was necessary by the third week because we commenced exercises in the Valiant simulator during this period. The remaining crews were also teamed up by this time – and therefore I knew the composition of the three crews which were to come under my command. The lecture programme progressed well, but I must confess that it taxed my academic ability, particularly when we tackled the complex Valiant electronic system. This had never been my favourite subject and now to be required to understand such a complex matter of inverters, rectifiers etc, made me stay up late swotting; in this respect Bob Beeson proved his worth for he knew the subject well and did much to iron out my weak spots.

At last we were ready to be introduced to the Valiant simulator – which is virtually a working complete flight deck of a Valiant – where the captain and co-pilot can become familiar with the general cockpit layout and where all controls and electrics work, complete start-up, take-off, climb, upper air work and let-down procedures can be rehearsed. All types of emergencies can be fed into the system by the simulator controller in order to give crews experience of every possible emergency procedure.

The Valiant simulator programme was controlled by Sqn Ldr (later AVM) D. Hall, a charming person who took a dedicated interest in his work but nevertheless demanded precision flying by crews in the simulator.

There was a separate programme of study for the captain and co-pilot, to enable them to work progressively through a concentrated series of exercises and prove that they knew every instrument and switch on that flight deck and could handle the Valiant simulator in instrument flying accuracy. These same standards applied to every type of emergency procedure the Simulator Controller could devise.

Similarly the Rear Flight Deck Simulator existed for the two navigators and the AEO, ensuring that they not only knew how to operate every piece of the complex navigation equipment and Valiant electrics, but could perform to a very demanding standard in simulated flight exercises.

The simulator programme was to extend for the entire period of our stay at Gaydon, but before the actual Valiant flying programme began, a laid down syllabus of exercises had to be completed to the satisfaction of Sqn Ldr Des Hall.

The flying phase was scheduled to start by the end of June with a short refresher period on the Canberra to polish up instrument landing system blind approaches, for this would be a standard all weather landing procedure for the Valiant. This comprised one dual sortie and solo flights where I flew with my co-pilot, Bob Beeson.

The last few days of July saw us at long last reporting to 'A' Flight under the command of Sqn Ldr Doug Chopping, an experienced flying instructor and already well experienced on the Valiant. On 27 July, with Flt Lt R. Wareham as my instructor and an OCU staff crew, I enjoyed my first experience of flying this magnificent aircraft.

Having spent so much time in the simulator, I was no stranger to the general cockpit layout and operating procedures. The old days of memorising the various drills were things of the past in the new generation of aircraft, for they were all too complex, and every phase of pre-take-off checks was read out by the co-pilot and each one checked back by the captain as being completed. This also applied to all after take-off and pre-landing checks. It is when you are seated in such a new type of aircraft that the time spent in the simulator is appreciated; the exact location of every switch and control is known to all and one's attention can be devoted to the task of flying the aircraft without diversion of attention to searching for any particular switch.

I had been much impressed by the Canberra, but that first experience of flying the Valiant was something always to be remembered, for here was a pedigree type in every respect: take-off, climb, upper air handling, rapid descent and circuit handling were a sheer delight. In every phase of flight the aircraft could be trimmed out to give a stable platform; the controls were delightfully responsive and whilst being power assisted, the artificial feel system produced a realistic and comfortable control loading – over-sensitive controls make an aircraft tedious and tiring to fly. I was also impressed by the stability of this aircraft with undercarriage down and 20° flap, for the final turn of the approach to land; trimmed out and then with full flap selected, the change of trim was easily countered and speed steady aiming tor 125kt at the boundary crossing. The final round out and reduction of power, holding the nose up and achieving a gentle touch with those eight main wheels, gave the final feeling of stability; then a steady lowering of the nose wheel onto the runway, and steering with the nose wheel steering (to the left of the controls on the captain's side) brought this first flight to a satisfactory conclusion.

This truly was one of the finest aircraft I had flown and must be the best design configuration ever produced by George Edwards (now Sir George) of Vickers. I could not wait for my next sortie which was to be some four days later; however, today after taxiing back to dispersal and going through the extensive shut down drills, my Instructor, Reg Wareham, went through a full post-flight briefing.

For the next two instructional flights with Reg Wareham, we flew with all of my crew with the exception of Bob Beeson. This gave us the initial opportunity of working together in the air; in these two sorties emphasis was placed upon handling at 40,000ft, including high speed runs to Mach 0.84, steep turns, then max rate descent and concentration upon circuit work covering three and two-engine landings and overshoots. At the conclusion of this second dual trip Reg Wareham decided the time had come to allow us, as a complete crew, to embark upon our first solo exercise. Therefore with Bob Beeson in the co-pilot's seat and Alan Washbrook and Eric Hood in the rear flight deck navigation positions, plus Ted Laraway in the air electronics seat, we taxied out as a complete crew for the first time. It was a stimulating experience, and we were now to be flying as a team for no less than 800hrs over the next two years.

This first solo sortie in a Valiant took place on 7 August 1956 and as we roared down the runway I had no doubt we all felt that this was the achievement of something every member of the crew had worked so very hard over the past months to achieve. We were on the threshold of membership of a new generation of Bomber Command crews destined to be the guardian of our freedom through the medium of a long term nuclear deterrent capability. Even on this first trip I was delighted with the efficient performance of every crew member and quite obviously those days spent in the simulator were paying dividends. Having carried out so many simulated airborne exercises as captain and co-pilot, Bob Beeson worked smoothly and efficiently with me, anticipating correctly every phase of the flying exercise, and from that very first flight we operated as a well trained and disciplined team. During all of our ground training I had made it clear to my crew that when flying no idle chatter would be accepted and communication between crew members was to be restricted to essentials.

The initial flight with my entire crew enabled every member to demonstrate their qualities, and in particular it placed the emphasis on me to demonstrate that I could handle the aircraft with precision and smoothness and establish the foundation of complete confidence in my own capability.

During this sortie we carried out a climb to 40,000ft, one high speed run and a max rate descent back to the local airfield area for circuit and landing practice. On the final landing, our airborne time had been 1 hr 5min, and as we taxied back to dispersal I felt a glow of satisfaction with our initial performance and a sense of gratitude to think that I was to be privileged to command 49 Squadron equipped with these superb aircraft.

Training at Gaydon progressed smoothly and by the third week of August the night flying phase commenced. For the introductory flight this was to be a dual sortie with Flt Lt Reg Wareham who put me through my paces in night circuit and landings. Here again, the Valiant was a splendid aircraft to handle at night and not difficult to land. After just over 2hr of dual flight, we taxied back to dispersal. Reg Wareham got out and Bob Beeson then occupied the co-pilot's seat and we proceeded back to the active runway for a period of 50min on night take-off and landings. With this complete and the aircraft returned to dispersal, we walked to the crew coach and were taken back to the Flight Office. A very satisfactory evening! As we chattered over our evening dinner, I could sense that we were quickly becoming a well balanced and co-ordinated team. I returned to the Officer's Mess and to bed as the bar had been closed long ago. That night I slept the sleep of contentment.

Following the night solo sortie we flew two more night exercises, each of 4hr duration, during which we carried out a high level cross country exercise followed by a period in the circuit for instrument landing system practice. The final night exercise of the course was to be the renewal of my Master Green Instrument Rating; for this my examiner was to be the Flight Commander, Doug Chopping. During the proceeding night exercises we had been able to practise the instrument pattern required, in which great accuracy is demanded in maintaining a set height at specific compass headings; therefore I was well prepared for this final night test. Being an instrument rating examiner myself,

A Vickers Valiant B1 V-bomber.

I was required to carry out a full instrument take-off, climb to a given altitude and then fly a precise instrument pattern to defined limits of accuracy. This was followed by Doug Chopping putting the aircraft into unusual attitudes, and when control was handed back, the aircraft then had to be returned to level flight with minimum loss of height by instrument interpretation. This completed the upper air work, and still under instrument conditions we carried out a max rate descent, followed by a feed into the instrument landing system pattern with two engines on one side flamed out. The ILS approach was made down to 350ft followed by overshoot on two engines and once back at 1,500ft the two engines flamed out were relighted and a final four-engine ILS approach and landing carried out. We taxied back to dispersal and when all engines were shut down and we climbed out of the aircraft, I realised that my flying overall was soaked in perspiration. Such a flight profile was extremely hard work, for at no time could there be any relaxation if accuracy was to be maintained.

We were now at the end of August 1956 and No. 8MB Course, as we were termed, was at an end. It had been a stimulating but demanding experience for all concerned and I was delighted to be taking with me to 49 Squadron two very fine crews under their captains. The first was Sqn Ldr Bill Bailey, who had already demonstrated to me his stirling qualities of positive leadership, and from the reports given to me by the staff it was obvious that he had acquitted himself well in all subjects during the course. The other captain destined for 49 Squadron with his crew was Flt Lt 'Tiff' O'Connor, an experienced pilot who had shown himself capable of converting to this new generation of four-jet aircraft and had distinguished himself by results achieved in Ground School.

These two crews throughout the course had impressed me by their enthusiasm and determination to succeed. Having spent a considerable number of hours in their company during those 10 weeks at Gaydon, I was also convinced of their loyalty and genuine belief in the Command's deterrent policy. Throughout the 2½ years these crews served under my command, this initial impression of their ability and personal qualities was not to change.

Before departing from Gaydon, we as a Course organised a final 'End of Course Farewell Cocktail Party' on the Saturday prior to us leaving for RAF Wittering. Here I was pleased to note that everybody made arrangements for wives and girl friends to attend and they all stayed the night in nearby Stratford-on-Avon. Thus I was able to meet some of the wives of my own crew as well as those of the other two coming with me to Wittering. For me this was very important as I always believe a squadron is one large family and if the men are to get support at home, then the wives must be involved. This policy I applied to 49 Squadron from the moment of taking over, and I am convinced it proved a vital asset to morale, particularly with the long separations to which we were all to be subjected during the next two years.

With the farewell party successfully concluded, there merely remained for me to take my formal leave of the Chief Instructor, Wg Cdr 'Hank' Iveson and of the Station Commander, Gp Capt Brian Young. Thus on 31 August 1956 I took my leave of RAF Gaydon and headed for RAF Wittering to take up command of 49 Squadron and embark upon the most fascinating period of my life in the subsequent involvement in Operation Grapple.

CHAPTER FOUR

Arrival at Wittering

M y appointment as Officer Commanding 49 Squadron was effective from 1 September 1956, and it was on this day that I walked into the squadron office accommodation of No. 1 Hangar at RAF Wittering. I had arrived the previous afternoon in order to settle into my own quarters at the Officers' Mess, to make the acquaintance of my batman and, perhaps of greater importance, to ensure the temperamental Crusty settled in without creating a diplomatic situation at such an early stage. I feel sure that during my tour as OC 49 Squadron the fact that the squadron motto was *Cave Canem* (beware of the dog) did much to create a rather superior canine complex in Crusty as he gradually became accepted as a form of Squadron mascot.

The 49 Squadron badge. *(Author)*

I certainly felt proud to be entrusted with this famous squadron that could boast such a proud battle record as can be seen by the honours displayed in the Squadron Standard. No. 49 Squadron had seen service since 1917 and it was only after the climax of the war with Mau Mau in Kenya in 1955 (where the squadron was equipped with Lincolns), that it was disbanded and the squadron colours laid up, until '49' was re-formed to full squadron status. That day had arrived and the task of rebuilding was to commence with effect from 1 September.

The first day in the office was a busy one. I met my Squadron Discipline Senior NCO, Sgt (later Warrant Officer) Wally Cressey; he was a smart and cheerful individual with what I detected to be an impish sense of humour. I was immediately impressed by his open enthusiasm and ability to answer every question I put to him regarding those airmen we already had with us in the squadron, the barrack block accommodation and the petty crime rate. Having explained to Sgt Cressey that I was a great believer in SNCOs being capable of effectively admonishing any airman guilty of some minor offence, I made it clear that any airman before me on a charge would be dealt with firmly; however, I did not wish to see airmen on minor charges that could have been dealt with effectively by their own SNCO in a variety of ways which enhanced an SNCO's authority. With any squadron there are a multitude of tasks for which extra hands are required, particularly in off-duty hours. Therefore, any petty offence could be punished by assigning the offender to a spell on such tasks.

One further requirement I made of Sgt Cressey: in order to ensure that I knew every officer, SNCO and airman, I wanted him to produce a notice board for my office that would show the name and photograph of all squadron personnel. This would enable me gradually to absorb every name, for it is vital for any officer to be able to address those under his command by name, which ensures that every man feels he is part of a very personal team – and that was my aim for '49'. Indeed, Sgt Cressey produced this within a week and as both aircrew and ground crew were posted in over the next few weeks, their names and photographs were added to the ultimate strength of the squadron; by the end of the month I had memorised the faces and names.

After my meeting with Sgt Cressey, I drove over to Station Headquarters for my initial meeting and briefing by the Station Commander, Gp Capt John Woodroffe (who was later killed in a B-47 flying accident in America). We had known each other previously at the Royal Air Force Flying College, RAF Manby in 1950, when he was then Wing Commander Admin and I was the Squadron Leader in charge of the Bomber Instructional Squadron. John first of all outlined to me what had occurred over the past few months for the re-forming of 49 Squadron with Valiants, starting as a detached Flight No. 1321 under Sqn Ldr (later Gp Capt) David Roberts with a total of four crews and three standard Valiant B1 aircraft.

This flight was formed in order to provide two aircraft and crews for partici-pation in Operation 'Buffalo' at Maralinga in Australia, where Britain's first live nuclear device in the kiloton range was to be dropped from a Valiant. Indeed at this time there were two of the 49 Squadron crews in Australia for this operation, namely Sqn Ldr Ted Flavell and crew plus Flt Lt Bob Bates and crew. As will be mentioned later, a live device was dropped by Sqn Ldr Ted Flavell and his crew on 11 October 1956 at Maralinga.

Since this in reality was the spearhead operation of Operation Grapple in the South Pacific, I should briefly outline the scope of Operation Buffalo, for although very little was known of this special operation throughout the Royal Air Force, it did in many ways mark the entry of the new generation of V bombers of Bomber Command into the 'Nuclear Club'.

The operation in South Australia was under the overall command of Air Cdre 'Ginger' Weir (later AVM and sadly now deceased) with Gp Capt (later AVM) Stewart Menaul as Air Task Group Commander.

Initially, to meet the operational requirement, Sqn Ldr Dave Roberts and crew were posted to RAF Wittering with one Valiant and operated as No. 1321 Flight; they were then joined by two more crews under their captains, Sqn Ldr Ted Flavell and Flt Lt Bob Bates. Training was concentrated on visual bombing over the Orfordness bombing range and this included the dropping of special bomb shapes to establish their aerodynamic qualities for housing the nuclear device.

The overall responsibility over this period for preparing the two crews destined for participation in these trials rested with Dave Roberts, who worked out the operational drop procedures and escape manoeuvre to be adopted for this particular test. There was a training period in South Australia for these two crews with their aircraft and this came under the control of Gp Capt 'Paddy' Menaul. The Scientific Director for the entire test series was Sir William Penney; the tests included ground detonation of some devices, culminating with the live drop from a Valiant B1 under its captain, Sqn Ldr Ted Flavell, with his very experienced bomb aimer, Flt Lt Eric Stacey, on 11 October, 1956. A number of delays had been experienced before this actual date became a reality because Sir William Penney had the very difficult task of balancing carefully the need for speed, as each day added enormously to the cost of the operation, with his duty towards the Australian Government, which he had assured that no dangerous degree of radioactivity would fall on any type of residential area. Therefore, with the need to meet these requirements and not jeopardise our right to lose the use of the Maralinga range, he was forced to make no less than nine post-ponements, for the winds had to be just right for the drop – 11 October was that perfect day and the results delighted the entire scientific team. Both Ted Flavell and Eric Stacey were later awarded the AFC for their part in this operation.

This then was the dress rehearsal for the forthcoming megaton range thermo-nuclear trials to be held in the South Pacific in the following year.

My briefing with the Station Commander was now to introduce me to the task for which I had been assigned. Having explained how this initial work-up had been achieved under the control of Dave Roberts and his experienced crew (at the time of this briefing of course the live drop had not taken place), he told me Ted Flavell and crew plus Bob Bates and crew were already in Australia at this time. I had not of course met them, neither had Dave Roberts been able to brief me on the current situation. Therefore John Woodroffe was taking pains to fill me in with every detail, for which I was most grateful.

He explained that at the moment I possessed only a nucleus of a squadron with two aircraft in Australia and a further two standard Valiant B1s at Wittering. There was also a complement of squadron ground crew in South Australia to provide technical support for our two aircraft. He outlined the plans for progressive build-up to full squadron strength of new Valiants being produced at Vickers – these would be to a special 'Grapple' specification to cater for the full scientific requirements and to a standard considered to be necessary for protection against flash in the initial detonation of these very large weapons.

Until the new aircraft were available, I would be required to initiate an intensive training programme with the existing squadron of Valiants, concentrating on visual bombing, all-weather flying capability and extensive use of the Valiant simulator to ensure all crews were fully familiar with the various let-down and holding patterns in use at the Canadian and American airfields that we would be using on route to Christmas Island in the South Pacific.

My terms of command were that I should operate with normal direct responsibility to the Station Commander, but as 49 Squadron was to be assigned to Operation Grapple Task Force, I would also have a direct line responsibility to the Task Force Commander, AVM W. Oulton, who was at this time located with his Headquarters staff in the old underground Air Ministry Buildings near Whitehall Gardens. My operational task and general training requirement would be issued by Grapple Task Force Headquarters and I was therefore authorised to set up a very close liaison with it at all times. It was suggested that I arrange my first visit to meet all personalities as soon as possible. This I agreed made sense and so promised to fix this initial meeting for the following week.

It was obvious that John Woodroffe was not aware of any precise details of the forthcoming Operation Grapple; and since I was soon to discover that everything relating to this operation was in the highest level of security, all information would be on a need to know basis, which had to be observed meticulously in all future air training.

The Station Commander paid tribute to the work carried out by Dave Roberts, and I got the distinct impression that John Woodroffe would have preferred to see Dave Roberts promoted rather than have a fully blown Wing Commander posted in; if this was the case, it never presented any problems in our future relationship for I always found John Woodroffe a tower of strength.

Certainly it is to the great credit of David Roberts that he never ever displayed any resentment at having to hand over Command and work as my deputy. He gave me absolute loyalty from our first meeting and I could not have had a more professional and highly dedicated Flight Commander during our entire tour together. The value of his knowledge and that of his crew, in preparing for the Australian trials, coupled with his extensive experience on the Valiant gained during his previous tour as the Valiant liaison officer at Vickers, were all factors that I cannot overemphasise. To this day I am eternally grateful to have had the privilege of such an officer being my deputy and for the experience his crew was able to pass on to all of the new crews as they came to us.

Having covered all these points, I left John Woodroffe with a more detailed knowledge of the broad parameter of my responsibilities as OC 49 Squadron. I was to find that with our special responsibilities there was no interference, and upon my shoulders fell the unfettered task of producing within 49 Squadron a team capable of meeting a very stringent operational requirement, both in ground and air crews. These aspects were all covered in some detail by AVM Oulton in our first and subsequent briefings and introduction to the detailed task required of the squadron – all this later.

By the conclusion of our meeting it was time for lunch, and afterwards my first task was to have a full session with Dave Roberts whom I had not met before. As it so happened, Dave was in the bar when John Woodroffe and I arrived, so we made our first acquaintance over a glass of beer and after lunch went back to my office together.

Sqn Ldr David Roberts was a very smart officer of pleasant appearance, a quiet but firm manner and a lively sense of humour. We talked for about an hour in the office, during which time he impressed me by his detailed background knowledge not only of the Valiant but of the training required to bring crews to the level of proficiency in the operating procedures we should need to adopt for the forthcoming megaton weapon trials. I could see that the build-up training phase for Operation Buffalo had demanded a careful examination of present visual bombing techniques in order to modify this to meet a specific scientific requirement. His experience to date was going to be vital in the forthcoming months and I was delighted to have this modest and very capable officer as my deputy, I felt sure we could work well together and was determined to ensure that having carried out all the hard slog training responsibility for the Australia test, he should play a prominent part in the tests we were destined to undertake in the South Pacific.

Having thoroughly discussed operational matters, he next gave me a run down on the quality of all aircrew that were with us at the moment. In this respect, when we analysed the experience level of each crew member, I could see that we were indeed fortunate and when this was added to the two crews who had been through the OCU at Gaydon with me, there was a sound nucleus of experience balanced with youth. Turning from aircrew to ground crew, I asked for his opinion of the various technical SNCOs, and in particular the Crew Chiefs. (In this latter trade with the V Force, each aircraft has its own Crew Chief with a rank of Chief Technician, which is equivalent to a Flight Sergeant. These men are highly qualified in all technical aspects of the V bomber and are an integral part of the aircraft crew, always flying with it whenever the aircraft is away on detachment or required to operate away from its home base). Here again, Dave gave me a comprehensive summary, certain aspects of which I noted for future reference. With this complete I returned to the subject of aircrew, for with the build-up of crews over the next few weeks it would be necessary to appoint the various specialist leaders. In this respect it would be only right to appoint by seniority of rank and from what was already apparent, this would equate with experience. These appointments I intended to make by the end of the week after I had made my visit to 'Grapple' Headquarters in London. Having confirmed to Dave that he would be my senior Flight

Top: Valiant WZ366 (49 Squadron) was the first RAF aircraft to drop an atomic bomb, on 11 October 1956 at Maralinga, Australia, during Operation 'Buffalo'. The aircraft was captained by Sqn Ldr T Flavell. *(F. Vening)*

Right: 49 Squadron ~~air~~ground. crew at Maralinga – note the different positions of the radiation counters worn by the men. *(F. Vening)*

Bottom: Sqn Ldr Arthur Steele, third from left, and the crew of Valiant XD823.

Commander, he departed leaving me to sort out one or two matters of administration and to ring 'Grapple' Headquarters and speak to AVM Oulton, who was delighted to know that I had at last arrived at '49'. We quickly agreed a date for our first meeting, which was to be Friday of that week. This allowed me the next three days to settle in to my new appointment and meet up with the aircrew and ground crew. I intended to speak to all aircrew in order to let them know exactly what was required of them and the standards that would be expected both on the ground and in the air. Having decided upon this, I quickly fixed a time with Dave Roberts, requesting him to have all aircrew assembled in the Operation Block Briefing Room for 14.00hrs the following day.

Although I wanted to speak to every aircrew officer, I did not want the flying training programme changed. I told Sgt Cressey to have all ground crew assembled in their respective Flight Dispersal Crew Rooms at 11.00hrs the following day for me to speak to them individually. Here again I wished to make it clear to all concerned that I viewed ground crew with equal importance to aircrew, for they were all part of one team and since we had been selected for a very special task, I would be demanding extremely high technical and personal standards.

A squadron must realise from the start that its Commanding Officer has every man's interest at heart and is prepared to lead by example. From my own personal experience I have always found that provided men understood what was required of them and they felt involved because they were kept in the picture regarding the task ahead, they would respond.

During this first day my own crew had been busy with the usual arrival procedures, which meant getting a documented arrival card signed by every section and drawing any specialised equipment required. When I saw them come into the squadron offices, I called them into my office to see how they had settled in. They all appeared to be in fine spirits and had completed the arrival procedure, so were ready to get down to squadron matters the following day.

I told Alan Washbrook that since he was the senior Radar Navigator, he would be appointed Radar Navigation Leader later that week and I hoped he would be able to work well with the Radar Navigator in Dave Roberts' crew. Alan assured me there would be no problems as they had trained together. I also told Ted Laraway that as he appeared to be the senior Air Electronics Officer and certainly the most experienced, he would in all probability be the AEO Leader. The Nav Plotting Leader would probably come from Dave Roberts' crew. Other appointments to be made in the squadron over the next few days would include a senior pilot as Training Officer, and a Flight Safety Officer.

Whilst all this had taken place on our first day, Crusty had decided that his place in my office was to be the window ledge just to the rear of my desk chair, where he could survey all that occurred outside and, from a point of vantage, could see everybody who came into the office. This seat he retained for our entire tour, although he did vacate it whenever he knew I was taking my service car over to dispersals for inspection.

That evening in the mess I had drinks with a number of my officers including my own crew, for they had not as yet moved into married quarters. After a few pre-dinner drinks we moved into the dining room and settled down to a quality dinner and some good humoured conversation. I was to find that whenever my crew and I dined together one could guarantee a great deal of amusement, for when Alan Washbrook and Ted Laraway were together, the humour was spontaneous. Without a doubt, I could see that I had inherited two great characters, and time was to prove this to be fact.

After dinner I decided to retire early, so first of all having given Crusty his evening meal, we went for a stroll across the mess garden and on to the sports field. On return to the mess I returned to my quarters and, before turning in, sat down and reflected upon all that had occurred on this my first day as OC 49 Squadron. I was now fully conscious of the fact that ahead of me lay a special task that must be carried out to the highest possible service standards.

From what I had seen on this first day, I was convinced that the men were of a high standard and to shape them into a first rate team would depend entirely on my own capability of command and leadership. I turned in that night confident that I could build, mould and lead this team to meet any operational demands placed on us. With these thoughts in my mind, I fell asleep.

On the following day I awoke early, as is my usual custom, and by the time my batman brought me a cup of tea I was already up and about and ready to take Crusty out for his morning walk.

My quarters in the Officers' Mess were situated at the front and looked out upon the mess garden and the sports field; they consisted of a bedroom and sitting room comfortably furnished. Also living in the mess with quarters next to mine was Wg Cdr Murray who was the Wing Commander Operations, and I was thankful that he had already been asked to take on the duties of President of the Messing Committee, which normally falls upon the senior living-in officer.

Perhaps this is the correct place to explain briefly the general organisation of a V Bomber base. The standard Royal Air Force station organisation comprised a Station Commander of Group Captain rank and under him there were three Wings, each commanded by a Wing Commander: the Administrative Wing which contained all personnel, general administration, accounts, education, equipment and medical departments; the Technical Wing, which commanded all aircraft, motor transport and special equipment servicing and repair sections; and the Operations Wing, covering all airfield services including air traffic control, flight safety, fire fighting, briefing facilities and meteorological services. These three Wings on a bomber station provided the necessary support facilities for the operational squadrons to enable them to carry out their appointed role with the maximum efficiency.

At RAF Wittering the personalities at Wing Commander level for these three Wings were Wg Cdr (later Gp Capt) H. Cundall DSO, DFC, AFC as OC Admin Wing; Wg Cdr K. Murray DFC as OC Operation Wing and Wg Cdr (now

Gp Capt) D. Seabrook as OC Technical Wing. These were the major people responsible for all squadrons based at Wittering. At squadron level, in addition to 49 Squadron, there was No. 138 Squadron of Valiants under the command of Wg Cdr Rupert Oakley DSO, DFC, AFC. Here I hasten to say that 138 Squadron held the proud record of being the first Valiant squadron to be formed and in Rupert Oakley had the most experienced Valiant pilot in the RAF. He gave me a great deal of assistance in those early days, and if I had a problem relating to any operating aspect of the Valiant, I never hesitated to consult him, for he had a great deal of experience to draw upon.

Also based at Wittering was the Bomber Command Development Unit, under the command of Wg Cdr Ivor Broom DSO, DFC (later AM Sir Ivor Broom). Ivor and I were old friends from RAF Manby days and his offices were on the first floor of the office accommodation directly above that of 49 Squadron. Ivor Broom not only had a distinguished war record, but had built up a tremendous reputation for himself, and in commanding BCDU he dealt direct with the Operational Requirement Department of HQ Bomber Command. The work this unit carried out was vital to the future operational improvement of the V Force, for the assessments and reports rendered by OC BCDU finished up on the Commander-in-Chief's desk.

The atmosphere at RAF Wittering was a happy one, because all Wing Commanders had the ability to co-operate with each other and, although there was keen competition between all three operational flying units, there always remained the tremendous willingness to help each other with any problem.

On my second day a great deal of time was spent in getting to know the station layout and meeting the various Wing Commanders. However, this did not interfere with the meetings already arranged with my own aircrews and ground crews. At the meeting with my aircrew, all of whom were officers, I gave them a general indication of the task ahead of us, emphasising the high standards of airmanship and crew discipline that would be necessary. The training schedule ahead of us would be a heavy one, during which the major aim was to achieve consistent high level visual bombing accuracy. They would be briefed more thoroughly on this following my meeting with the Task Force Grapple planning team later that week. I further highlighted the high personal standards that were expected of every officer and the need for them to involve themselves fully in all mess functions. In this respect I said we would hold regular squadron parties to ensure that wives and girlfriends were involved, for I felt it important that a wife should feel part of the squadron team.

Finally, I told crews that it was my intention to keep them fully briefed on all aspects of the forthcoming weapon trials and the delivery schedule of our new aircraft. Since our squadron aircraft strength would be eight and crew strength also eight for the 'Grapple' task, each crew would be allocated its own aircraft and crew chief. Whatever information was given to them as officers would be within the terms of the Official Secrets Act and would not be discussed outside the squadron crew room. I concluded by letting them know that a number of officers would be given secondary duties within the squadron organisation and these would be known by the end of the week.

For the airmen and SNCOs I outlined my aims for the squadron and reminded them that they had all been specially selected and security cleared for the special weapon task ahead of us. There would be no room for any weak links and I expected the highest possible technical standards at all times; in addition, personal standards of discipline, both on and off the station, were to be of the highest order. Any misconduct would be detrimental to the squadron's image and where this happened I would deal with the culprit severely. I impressed upon them all the need to participate in station activities, particularly sport, and in this respect I wanted 49 to have a first class football team.

Not only would I be paying close attention to the high technical standard required, particularly with the new aircraft as they arrived, I should also be devoting a great deal of my attention to all matters affecting welfare and morale.

My aim was to create a squadron team second to none, in which every man was a vital part and as such must give all of his efforts; the hours would be long because our flying training task had to be achieved at all costs. I also made it clear that it would be my intention to give talks at regular intervals in order to ensure that, within the bounds of security, everybody was kept fully informed of what we were doing.

With these two meetings complete, I had met all squadron personnel and they all knew exactly what would be required for the future. Of course at this stage we had two aircraft and crews in South Australia participating in Operation Buffalo; they were supported by a team of ground crew headed by our Squadron Technical Officer, Flg Off W. Budden BEM; all of whom I would not meet until their return, which was to be in October.

My attention was now to be concentrated upon deciding upon the appointment of specialist air crew leaders, Squadron Training Officer and Flight Safety Officer. These resolved themselves quite simply, for I was already impressed by the very sound qualities of one senior captain, Sqn Ldr (later Air Commodore) Arthur Steele, a very experienced pilot, qualified flying instructor and whom I judged by our conversation and discussion of training tasks to be a man capable of great detail, of untiring energy and a thorough knowledge of the Valiant and with an engaging personality. I decided Arthur Steele was the ideal man for this task, for he possessed the ability to put a complex programme together in complete liaison with the specialist leaders. My choice in this appointment was proved to be sound and no man could have devoted more time, energy and expertise to this task, which was the dominant factor related to our future success. Neither could I have wished for a more loyal officer who commanded the admiration of every member of the squadron.

With the leaders, it was obvious that Alan Washbrook should be Navigation Radar Leader; here I had a most experienced expert in visual bombing. Ted Laraway was to be the Air Electronics Operation Leader; and here again there was nobody more experienced or knowledgeable. For the Nav Plotting Leader I turned to Flt Lt Ted Dunne from Dave Roberts' crew; Ted was an extremely experienced navigator and just the man to provide a mature lead to the younger navigation plotters.

These three officers I knew would work well with Arthur Steele and should make a first rate team. For the appointment of Flight Safety Officer, as a secondary duty, I turned to Sqn Ldr Bill Bailey, another experienced pilot, who possessed very positive qualities of leadership and a forceful personality. Ideally, Bill Bailey was suited to be a Flight Commander, but these two posts were filled by Dave Roberts for 'A' Flight and Ted Flavell (who was in Australia) for 'B' Flight. However, Bill Bailey was able to stand in for Ted Flavell until his return, which gave Bill some experience in this field.

Normal squadron administration kept me busy over the next day and then of course it was time for me to catch the London train at Peterborough for my appointment with the 'Grapple' team in the Air Ministry underground headquarters.

I arrived at the Air Ministry by about 11.00hrs having found the underground headquarters entrance (for I did not realise this existed although it had been used during World War 2) and identified myself to the security desk by my Form 1250 identification card. This was carefully checked and when cleared I was escorted to the office of the Task Force Commander, AVM W. Oulton CBE, DSO, DFC who explained that Air Commodore C. T. Weir DFC (later AVM but now deceased) was still in South Australia supervising the Operation Buffalo tests.

I had never met AVM W. Oulton before and was very soon impressed by the calm and articulate manner in which he outlined the aims of Operation Grapple and the organisation under his control for this formidable operation. Certainly, in those early days I had not stopped to consider the scope of the overall task necessary to mount such a vital scientific exercise some 9,000nm from the UK on a South Pacific island, where little or no facilities existed, including a suitable airfield. One thing that struck me throughout this fascinating briefing – which involved the parts to be played by the Royal Navy, Army, Royal Air Force and the Scientific Team – was the constant emphasis on good teamwork and the need for whole-hearted and unrestricted co-operation between all elements of this joint force.

The aim of Operation Grapple was to test the performance of thermonuclear weapons in the megaton range, dropped from V bomber aircraft of the Royal Air Force.

All previous British atomic tests had taken place in Australia, either at Maralinga in the South Australian desert or in the small uninhabited Monte Bello Islands off the northwest coast. However, for testing weapons of the yield involved in Operation Grapple, there could be no question from the safety point of view of using the Australian proving grounds. Therefore a completely new base had to be located which could conform to certain essentials. The base had to be remote from any inhabited area, have favourable wind and weather con-

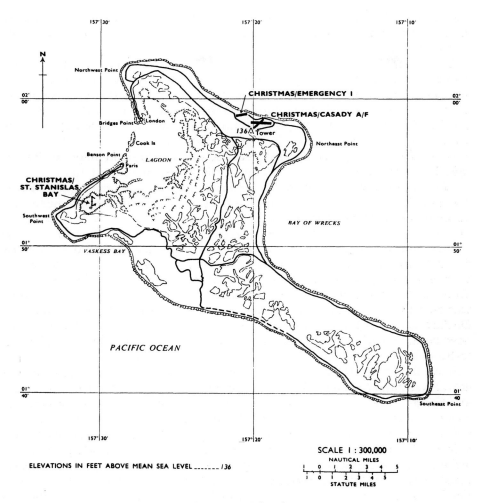

Christmas Island.

ditions for air and sea operation, and, even though distant, be accessible from a source of supply and have a suitable harbour for landing these supplies. Finally, it had to be suitable for the construction of an airstrip which could be used by the Valiant V bomber.

In order to meet these criteria, an area in the Pacific seemed to be the inevitable choice and after careful consideration, and in the light of surveys made by a ship of the Royal New Zealand Navy and by a joint service air reconnaissance from an RAF Shackleton in the autumn of 1955, Christmas Island was selected as the main base island, and Malden Island some 400nm distant as the instrumentation island for the weapon drop.

Christmas Island is the largest coral atoll in the Pacific, although its dimensions are only about 35 miles east and west by 24 miles at its greatest width. From the map it will be seen that the shape of the island roughly resembles a large lobster claw. In general the island elevation is only about 10ft above sea level, but to the east there are sand dunes rising to approximately 20ft. Surrounding the island is a fringe of coral reef, several hundred yards in width. There are coconuts and bush in the west but merely tough prickly grass and low shrubs in the centre. The climate does not encourage the growth of vegetation as the island is subject to severe droughts which may last many months. At such times only 6in of rain may fall in the whole year, but in other years over 100in have been recorded. Day temperatures vary between 70° and 100°F, but the easterly trade winds exert a cooling influence so that despite the high humidity, the heat is not oppressive; no hurricanes have ever been experienced in the area. This then was to be the main base for the operation.

Those interested in history will wish to be reminded that Christmas Island was discovered by Captain James Cook (then a Lieutenant RN) on Christmas Eve 1777, in HM Ships *Resolution* and *Discovery.*

Malden Island, some 400nm south of Christmas Island, is a flat triangular coral island about five miles in length from east to west and about 4½ miles at its greatest breadth. As at Christmas Island, rain fall is variable, prolonged droughts occur at intervals and vegetation is sparse. Malden Island was discovered by Captain the Rt Hon Lord Byron of HMS *Blonde* on 29 July 1825.

So much for the location of this forthcoming operation; how was this to be achieved? The next part of my briefing outlined the parts to be played by the Royal Navy and Merchant Navy, the Army, Scientific Team and lastly the Royal Air Force.

This surely was to be the largest joint service operation since the last war, for on to barren Christmas Island was to be transported every item of equipment required for the operation – and then the base had to be constantly supplied. Here the Royal Navy and Merchant Navy had a vital part to play. Their task, broadly, was two-fold; first the provision of seaborne support, involving not only the shipping equipment, stores, provisions and fuel into the area, but also the provision of port facilities for off-loading. Secondly, when into the operational phase, naval units would be required to act as weather ships and to provide technical and operational control facilities in the Malden Island forward area.

Following the preliminary overall planning for Operation Grapple, the first task was to transport all the necessary men and mass of equipment over the 9,000nm from the UK to Christmas Island.

The Naval Task

The only means of achieving this mammoth task was by a fleet of ships. The responsibility for providing this fleet and co-ordinating the requirements of all services involved in the operation fell upon the Naval Staff of the Task Force under Cdre P. W. Gretton DSO, OBE, DSC (later Adm Sir Peter Gretton).

The first members of the 'Grapple' team led by the Deputy Task Force Commander landed on the disused World War 2 airstrip in an RAF Shackleton on 19 June 1956. Four days later *Fort Beauharnois* of the Royal Fleet Auxiliary arrived to establish the first bridgehead for logistic support and to act as a temporary Headquarters ship. This was quickly followed by other Royal Fleet Auxiliary ships and the troopship *Devonshire*. Thus the stores and personnel began to build up. By November 1956 over 20,000 tons of cargo and all the Army Engineers had landed.

To maintain this force, which had the task of undertaking all the initial construction, ships capable of supplying fresh provisons and fuel oil had to be brought into action.

HMS *Messina*, an LST (landing ship tank), arrived at Christmas Island by August 1956 and was to be used as the headquarters ship for the Senior Naval Officer in the area, and also in general support of the landing operations. She had been specially fitted out to make up to 100 tons of fresh water per day for consumption both afloat and ashore, and with large refrigerators in the tank deck for storage of fresh and frozen provisions until required on the island. HMS *Messina* also had specially fitted wireless transmitter equipment to enable her to act as the main communication link between Christmas Island and the United Kingdom. She in addition had transported all the plant and special equipment on Malden Island, using her LCMs and DUKWs to land them.

By early March of 1957 it was intended to complete the complement of the Naval Task Force by the arrival of HMS *Warrior* and HMS *Narvik*, together with two frigates of the Royal New Zealand Navy, HMNZS *Pukaki* and *Rotoitic*. This date was to coincide with the arrival on Christmas Island of the 49 Squadron detachment of four Valiants. HMS *Warrior*, a light fleet carrier of 14,000tons displacement, would act as the operation control ship in the target area, wearing the pennant of Cdre P. W. Gretton DSO, OBE, DSC as Commodore 'Grapple' Squadron. We were subsequently to work closely with HMS *Warrior* during the training work-up period and the actual live drops. Her radar would be used to keep track of all aircraft in the operational area, particularly of the Valiant dropping the live weapon. In addition she was also destined to act as a weather reporting station while her aircraft would be available for search, communication and air/sea rescue in conjunction with the RAF Shackleton aircraft. HMS *Warrior's* aircraft comprised an Avenger (a single-engine American aircraft carrying a crew of three), and Westland Whirlwind helicopters. During my various subsequent detachments to Christmas Island over the next two years I was to enjoy a great deal of hospitality from the crew of this ship.

HMS *Narvik*, another LST and sister ship of *Messina*, was an 'old hand' in atomic tests, and at, the time of my briefing was acting as Headquarters and Control Ship for the Monte Bello tests in Australia. She was to be fitted with up-to-date accommodation and scheduled to be the Scientific Technical Control and

Top: RFA *Fort Beauharnois*, which arrived at Christmas Island to establish the first elements of the new base. *(Royal Engineers)*

Centre: The light fleet carrier HMS *Warrior*, which acted as the operations control ship during the test series. *(Wright & Logan)*

Bottom: HMS *Narvik*, the scientific monitoring ship. *(K Barks)*

Monitor ship which would remain in the Malden Island target area. She would be equipped with special aerials, air conditioned scientific work rooms and photographic dark rooms. Additionally she was fitted with a wooden helicopter deck with facilities for operating two helicopters. I shall refer to HMS *Narvik* a great deal in later chapters, for during every training flight in the target area we would be working closely with *Narvik* as her telemetry equipment was directly linked to the special telemetry fitted into the Valiant.

In concluding the naval and merchant navy role, mention must be made of the detachment of Royal Marines comprising two officers and 53 other ranks, for they played such an important part in providing crews for the landing craft in their amphibious role.

Thus it will be seen that the Naval side made a mammoth contribution to Operation Grapple long before we even reached the operational stage. Their task was to continue throughout the entire period of the tests then, at their conclusion, there would be the requirement of transporting every item of equipment and men back to the United Kingdom.

I make no apology for taking up so much space in covering the Naval role, for when I eventually arrived on Christmas Island and was able to see the extent of the entire operation, my admiration for all that this entailed was considerable, and I never ceased to respect the Naval men's contribution through each and every detachment.

The Role of the Army

Having outlined the Naval role, reference should be made to the role played by the Army in converting a relatively barren island into an effective operational base capable of receiving and maintaining all the forces involved. This meant building up from scratch a considerable township with its own seaport and airbase, a road system and transport service, mains electricity, a fresh water distillation plant, and providing sewage and hygiene services and cold storage, as well as taking responsibility for catering, petrol and other supply depots, and general maintenance and house-keeping for a population that at its peak was to reach 3,000. All had to be planned and executed by the Army element of the Force under the command of Col J. E. S. Stone OBE, as Commander Army Task Group.

To carry out these vast tasks a group of Army units was formed, with 28 Field Engineer Regiment, Royal Engineers as its nucleus and main element. Incidentally, I should mention at this stage that the Christmas Island Garrison Commander working closely with the Army Task Group Commander was Col J. C. Wollett OBE, MC, RE. (later Major-General.)

Thus within the broad outline of tasks mentioned above, the Royal Engineers had to construct a complete airbase on the island, together with all its necessary attendant facilities required for modern aircraft. This alone involved first the clearing, excavation, compacting, levelling and surfacing of a main runway, 2,150yd long by 60yd wide to a specification suitable for the Valiant V bomber. In addition, 8in concrete paving had to be laid to provide runway ends, taxiways and aircraft dispersals. Some 20 miles of access roads had to be constructed and approximately 700,000sq yd of scrub cleared for airfield approach zones. New airfield buildings needed to be erected and existing ones reconstructed. At the Port area installations had to be built up and a camp constructed. In a very short time after the Engineers began work there were well over a hundred tents and marquees plus some 7,000sq yd of buildings. Twelve 105,000gal fuel tanks for storing aviation fuel, diesel and petrol were assembled and pumping station, pipes, roads and protective banks for the tank farm constructed. For the Port and Camp such amenities as light, power and fresh water, showers and ablutions also had to be provided. A second camp nearer to the airfield and known as Main Camp – for the Headquarters and the majority of Force personnel (including all squadrons to be involved in the task) – was constructed. This comprised over 700 tents and marquees as well as about 40,000sq ft of hutted accommodation.

All of this work had to be complete prior to the arrival of the main operational flying squadrons. It is to the credit of the Army and in particular 28 Field Regiment Royal Engineers that by March 1957 we were able to land our Valiants on a first class runway and find accommodation waiting for us.

Mention must be made of No. 51 Port Detachment Royal Engineers, which provided the nucleus of skilled labour for the discharge and loading of vessels in the Port area.

No. 504 Postal Unit, Royal Engineers, which had its main detachment at Christmas Island plus a small team at Honolulu Air Force Base, was responsible for organising the receipt and despatch of all mail. In this respect I must comment that under the dynamic control of Postmaster Maj A. Fancourt it made a contribution to morale throughout the series of tests completely out of proportion to the unit's small size. No. 2 Special Air Formation Signal Troop, Royal Signals provided all communications for the Port, the engineer construction sites at the main airfield and island administrative area. It also built the operational line communication system providing multi-position exchanges at the Joint Operations Centre and Main Airfield.

Then there was a special Royal Army Service Corps Services Unit organised into an amphibious vehicle platoon. This unit was also responsible for a butchery, cold storage and field bakery section. Also formed for 'Grapple' was a special RADC unit responsible for stores and laundry.

Finally, mention must be made of another Army unit formed specially for this operation. This was the Special Engineers Regiment Workshop, Royal Electrical & Mechanical Engineers, to give all workshop support for the RE Army equipment.

In evaluating the colossal contribution of the Army to Operation 'Grapple', it must always be remembered that the most difficult aspect was that it was

Top: The main camp on Christmas Island.

Centre: Royal Engineers constructing the main runway. *(Royal Engineers)*

Bottom: The Christmas Island airfield: note the weapon assembly area in the right foreground, and the Shackleton, Dakota, Canberra and Valiant aircraft.

undertaken 9,000nm from England in such a normally inaccessible area. The planning for every item of equipment had to be right from the word go; once the force had been established on the island, no further regular supply line existed.

The Scientific Task

The next stage of my education was to be directed towards the main purpose of Operation Grapple, which in reality was the scientific task, before looking at what Royal Air Force units were needed to enable the scientific task to be achieved.

The scientific task was embodied in the aim of Operation Grapple, which was to test the performance of nuclear weapons in the megaton range to be dropped from RAF Valiant V bombers. In this connection the scientists from the Atomic Weapons Research Establishment, were under the control of Mr W. R. J. Cook CB (later Sir William), the Scientific Director.

The main scientific effort was to be directed towards the assembly of the weapon, loading it into the Valiant, and the measuring and recording of the magnitude of the explosion. In order to carry out these tasks the scientific party was to be divided into a number of groups, each group having a specific task.

The **Weapon Groups** would be responsible for the preparation and assembly of the explosive and radioactive components of the weapon. Once assembled into the weapon, comprehensive tests were made before it was loaded into the

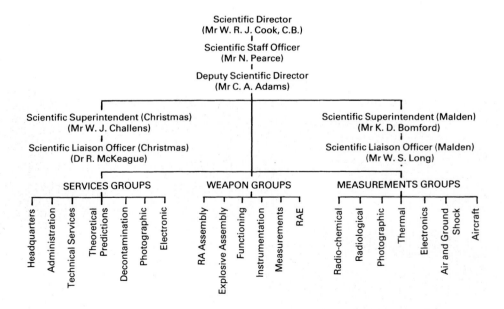

Top: Sir WRJ Cook, the
Scientific Director. *(Author)*

Bottom: The main camp of the
scientific teams on Malden
Island.

aircraft, then further tests carried out after loading as well as checks on the bomb release mechanism and other installations in the aircraft. Only after everything had been subjected to rigorous test schedules was the complete apparatus handed over to the captain of the aircraft. Responsibility for this vital work came directly under Mr Charles Adams, who was Deputy Scientific Director.

Next there were the **Measurements Groups** under the joint control of Mr Ron Bamford as Scientific Superintendent (Malden Island) and Mr Wally Long as Scientific Liaison Officer (Malden Island). This was to provide instruments and apparatus to record and measure the many effects of the explosion. To achieve this, installation and telemetering equipment would be positioned on the ground, in Naval ships and RAF aircraft, particularly the Valiant dropping aircraft. The effects to be measured would include blast, nuclear and heat radiations and residual radioactivity. The object was of course to find out how well the bomb worked.

The other groups were termed the **Services Groups** under the control of Mr Bill Challens as Scientific Superintendent (Christmas Island) and Dr R. McKeague as Scientific Liaison Officer (Christmas Island). These groups were to have a number of commitments. Firstly there was the Headquarters, responsible for the direction and planning of the scientific element of the operation and for liaison with the Task Force. Other responsibilities included technical services, theoretical predictions and decontamination, including health and safety of personnel against radioactivity.

This then was the scientific organisation and I will outline how it operated in later pages when we discuss the flight profiles to be flown by the designated dropping aircraft prior to the actual live drop.

The Role of the RAF

Finally, I was to be acquainted with the overall role of the Royal Air Force, and for the subsequent pages of the book to be understood it is important to outline the responsibilities of all RAF units involved, for each gave support to the others within the complex operation. The Royal Air Force responsibilities within Operation Grappple were many and varied. Not only was there the specialised task of actually dropping the weapon itself, but there was also a requirement for high and low level meteorological reconnaissance flights to assist the weather forecasters, cloud photography and sampling after burst. Also there were the general and perhaps less exciting – though just as vital – duties of communication and ferrying men, materials and mail between various islands, together with such jobs as air/sea rescue and pest control. To undertake all of these commitments a wide variety of aircraft were required and included detachments of Hastings, Shackletons, Canberras and Valiants.

To control this air task group No. 160 Wing was formed. The various RAF Commands providing the aircraft required selected the necessary squadrons.

Coastal Command selected three: Nos 206 and 240 equipped with Shackletons for Maritime Reconnaissance and 22 Squadron equipped with Whirlwind helicopters for communications, air rescue and insecticide spraying. Transport Command provided a service of Hastings aircraft to be based on Christmas Island for transport duties between the island and Hickham AFB, Honolulu, and also a flight of Dakotas for duties between Christmas and Malden Island.

Bomber Command provided 76 Squadron equipped with the Canberra B6, which was to be specially equipped and used to take samples of the mushroom cloud after weapon explosion. Also there was 100 Squadron equipped with Canberra PR7s for high level meteorological survey work. Finally, selected to carry out this all important task of dropping the live weapons, was 49 Squadron equipped with new Valiant B1 aircraft, all specially modified to meet the 'Grapple' scientific requirement.

This then was the background and complexity of the requirement; next I needed to know exactly what was involved in the task assigned to 49 Squadron in order to meet the scientific specification, for it was becoming increasingly clear that there would be a combination of operational techniques to fit in with the scientific telemetric recording equipment and a guarantee of accuracy to ensure that precise measurement of all the weapon characteristics and yield could be recorded.

The final phase of the briefing outlined to me details of the special equipment that would be installed in the new Valiant, to the 'Grapple' specification, and gave me an explanation of the operational procedures to be adopted for the live weapon drop in order to ensure a high airburst 1½ miles over the sea from the target aiming point at the south promontory of Malden Island.

With each operational drop, there would be a set pre-live drop procedure involving several rehearsals to ensure that everyone on the ground and in the air knew his job, for there could be no room for error; this was to be an occasion for teamwork and perfection. First of all there would be flyover trials, where the Valiant would be required to take off from Christmas Island and fly to the target area carrying a dummy weapon, some radio and electronic equipment, and once in the target area to fly the full operational procedure as for a live drop, complete with escape manoeuvre after simulated bomb release. On the ground the weapon measurements and electronic services groups would check all transmissions from the aircraft. This complete the Valiant would be required to return to base, and once on the ground the results of the flyover trial would be examined by the Weapons Groups. Any deficiencies in the equipment, either in the aircraft, on the ground, or in the ship from which the scientific part of the operation was controlled, had to be corrected; and, if necessary, a further flyover trial flown and analysed.

With the flyover trial satisfactorily completed, there followed a requirement to drop practice weapons, again to enable the Weapons Groups and certain scientists of the Measurement Groups to test their equipment. However, this is where the selected Valiant dropping crew would have to prove its bombing accuracy to the scientific limit laid down. At this stage the nominated crew must have proved over a very extensive training period its ability to achieve a consistently high standard of accuracy.

Next would come a full operational rehearsal, when all personnel on the island and ships in the force would take up positions they would occupy when the live drop took place and where all equipment had its final check. The Weapons Group would carry out the procedure of assembly and loading the bomb into the aircraft, the Valiant crew following the full pre-weapon loading checks and then accepting the aircraft back after weapon loading was declared complete, followed by final pre-start checks, to take off at the designated hour.

During this period in the target zone and in the ships, scientists and members of the services would make any final adjustments to their equipment and then take up their allotted station. All had to proceed to a very carefully laid down timetable, with everyone being checked to ensure they were in the right place at the correct time. Once the Valiant arrived over the target area the full operational pattern would be flown, and when all weapon telemetering and equipment was declared to be satisfactory, clearance for the live bombing run would be given, although on the dress rehearsal the weapon would be of similar shape but containing only a high explosive charge. The Valiant crew would follow the full operational procedure, with all metal anti-flash shutters in the cockpit in position; therefore, the entire flight would be on instruments except for use of the bomb aimer's window. Once the weapon left the aircraft the bomb aimer would close his shutter. The captain then had to roll the Valiant into the escape manoeuvre on to a set heading which accurately pointed the tail cone cameras on to the burst point and allow a period of 10sec between roll-out from the manoeuvre to actual bomb burst. With this complete, the Valiant would return to base.

The next flight would be the live drop and for this both the Task Force Commander and the Scientific Director had to ensure that the live nuclear weapon was dropped only when weather conditions were perfect. In getting this absolutely right, a heavy load would rest upon the scientists of the Theoretical Prediction Group for they, in close collaboration with the Meterological Staff, had to study weather reports and from these predict the fall-out pattern. Once the Prediction Group decided that forecast conditions were favourable, the Task Force Commander and the Scientific Director would give the order to begin the pre-firing phase which meant that the weapon would be dropped 24 hours from then. All personnel then had to carry out the final checks and adjustments just as in the dress rehearsal. The Decontamination Group, with the RAF, then had to make final preparation to the Canberra cloud sampling aircraft, and the Health Physics Team had to ensure that all was ready for subsequent contamination checks, including the provision of protective clothing for personnel detailed to enter any radioactive areas.

During the last few hours before the pre-firing phase ended, final weather reports were to be scrutinised. Should the weather still be favourable, the Task

Force Commander and Scientific Director would agree to order the commencement of the firing phase and this meant that the Valiant carrying the live weapon was cleared for take-off.

This discussion had put me completely in the picture and I now left the Task Force Commander for a more detailed session of my own training requirements from Gp Capt Freddie Milligan and Wg Cdr Butch Surtees, the RAF Air Staff Planners. Here we discussed the bombing accuracies to be achieved, details of the operational procedures to be adopted, including more precise limits of the escape manoeuvre to be practised and the special visual bombing technique to be adopted in order to provide the weapon release position 1½ miles from a specific aiming point, for a burst altitude of 8,000ft. This was designed purely to meet the scientific requirement and was never a Command operational weapon release procedure. I could see that in order to comply with the full telemetering parameters for recording weapon and firing mechanism as well as feed back by telemetering of all aircraft instrumentation on the bombing run in line, a very high degree of accurate instrument flying would be required of the aircraft captain: this, combined with a well-oiled understanding with the bomb aimer, to ensure the dropping aircraft could be kept over a geographical bomb line, to achieve the correct bomb sight graticule coincidence at the actual aiming point, on the correct heading, precise Mach number and accurate height. This condition was then to be held with no variation in height, airspeed or heading for the pre-calculated period necessary to give the 1½-mile factor before the weapon was released.

I also realised that crews would need adequate practice at the escape manoeuvre for it meant flying the aircraft under full instrument conditions to limits which were close to the point of high speed stall. All of this merely highlighted the need for experience and a very high, consistent standard of instrument flying and high level bombing capability. Even with so little experience of the crews with me in 49 Squadron, I had no doubt that to achieve these exceptionally high standards would present no problems.

We then discussed the delivery programme of the new Valiant aircraft, all completed to the special 'Grapple' standard.

This meeting at Task Force HQ was to be the first of many, but already the essential liaison was established and I was extremely impressed by the detailed planning of the vast operation and even more so by the tremendous team spirit that was so evident and by the attention being paid to safety for all concerned.

Throughout my entire involvement with all the live weapon tests carried out in the 'Grapple' series of tests, I was always most impressed by the meticulous care taken to ensure safety for each and every phase of the operation. This covered all aspects of personnel protection against the slightest risk of any radiation contamination. I highlight this in view of some of the misleading statements made in recent television interviews regarding the risks involved in the Christmas Island tests. Whilst I sympathise with those who feel their later ill-health can be attributed to their experiences on Christmas Island, I do not

believe that any man of Operation Grapple was exposed to any radiation contamination during or after these tests, both my crew and I being present for every
test series.

On completion of my initial full introduction to the entire 'Grapple'
operation, I emerged from the underground headquarters just after 17.00hrs
into the usual rush of commuters heading for the various tube stations on their
way home. I headed for Liverpool Street station and having settled into my seat
on the train, sat back and reflected upon all that had been explained to me that
day. I was acutely conscious of the size of the operation and of course very
aware of the privilege of being involved with my squadron.

As the train sped along *en route* for Peterborough, I spent the time making
mental notes of the type of training programme that must be instigated to
achieve the consistent bombing accuracy that would be necessary. I also realised
that with UK weather factors it would be difficult to achieve very many days
each month when clear skies allowed visual bombing from 40,000ft. In addition,
certainly there were no ranges where the special technique required could be
practised; therefore, this meant there must be an adequate training period allocated to the squadron once we arrived on Christmas Island. However, I knew
that once a regular pattern of consistency in visual accuracy had been achieved
using the standard release methods, there would be no difficulty in crews

AVM WE
Oulton,
the Task Force
Commander.

becoming accustomed to the time delay release system, once we could drop a few practice bombs on the Malden Island target range.

Should we run into a real patch of bad UK weather, it might be necessary to take a detachment of aircraft out to El Adem in Libya, where we knew we could guarantee clear skies and there was a good bombing range available. Indeed, El Adem was a regular training camp for the RAF. However, these thoughts would need to be discussed with HQ 3 Group if it became necessary. As it turned out, although we did experience many frustrations due to UK weather, we did not have to resort to an overseas detachment prior to departing for Christmas Island. In view of the constant modification programme to our special aircraft, it would have been difficult to have had a detachment away from Wittering during the forthcoming pre-departure training period.

All my thoughts and reflections came to an abrupt end as the train pulled into Peterborough station, and I got out to find my car and drive back to Wittering with the weekend ahead of me. On Monday I would plan out the programme in detail with Arthur Steele and the specialist leaders, for we now knew exactly what was required of the squadron.

CHAPTER FIVE

Squadron Preparation

H aving briefed Arthur Steele and the specialist leaders, I left them to insti-
tute a training programme aimed to achieve maximum utilisation of our
aircraft to give crews high level visual bombing practice balanced with
all weather let-down procedures, particularly concentrating on simulated exercises in American beacon holding patterns as would be required in our transit
through the USA to Christmas Island.

Over the next few weeks training progressed well and we were already
working with the scientific team, the Weapon Groups having set up an arrange-
ment with the Orfordness bombing range to enable us to carry out one or two
special weapon drops on the groups' behalf. One of these I carried out with my
own crew in Valiant 378, which was a non-'Grapple' modified aircraft.

During this period I was able to get to know my crews and meet their wives,
an essential part of building this squadron into a team. Additionally, it was
important for me to make myself memorise names and faces and to ensure that
the technical side was working well.

Each day was a full one – paper work, meetings and flying – and once a week
the Station Commander held a meeting at which all Wing Commanders were
expected to attend and I, in turn, always held a weekly meeting of my Flight
Commanders and Training Officers to discuss and evaluate every aspect of
training carried out during the week and to enable me to put them in the picture
regarding any changes in plans received from 'Grapple' HQ.

By mid-November our first new 'Grapple' Valiant arrived; it was Valiant
XD818, destined to become the Squadron Commander's aircraft and one in
which I was to fly no less than 600 hours over the next two years.

Officially, training for the forthcoming Operation Grapple began on 1
September 1956, but of course a considerable amount had already been under-
taken by Dave Roberts and his crew in order to prepare for the weapon trials in
South Australia, to which 49 Squadron contributed two crews. This specialised
training was in accordance with Directives issued by Headquarters Bomber
Command dated June and August 1956.

One of my first tasks on assuming command was to study the directives in
great detail, for they were to form the basic structure of our subsequent training

programmes, which all crews were required to complete before they could be considered as potential 'live drop crews'.

Following my very comprehensive briefing at 'Grapple' Task Force Headquarters, my attention over the next few weeks was concentrated upon ensuring, with the aircraft we had available, that crews completed an intensive phase of high level visual bombing from both 25,000 and 40,000ft using 100lb practice bombs. In this respect we were accorded priority on the use of Orfordness bombing range where the Weapon Groups from AWRE under the control of John Challen had set up its own telemetering equipment, to be used when we were required to drop special inert weapons, to test aerodynamic qualities; these would be the case size and shape of the live weapons to be used in the forthcoming scientific trials.

For all practise bombing on the Orfordness range, normal standard direct aiming visual bombing was practised, for the ranges were not equipped to cater for the special time delay techniques we were required to adopt once in the South Pacific. By now we had the 'Grapple' specification T4 bombsight, a modified version of the standard Mk 14A sight with the time delay mechanism, but experience for crews of this special scientific requirement could not be acquired until we arrived at Christmas Island. At this initial stage, my requirement for crews was consistent accuracy.

In this respect the results of every bombing sortie were examined in great detail by the Bombing Leader, Alan Washbrook, and the Training Officer, Arthur Steele. Any inconsistency had to be pinpointed, for with high level visual bombing it was essential for the bomb aimer to be able to guide the captain accurately to achieve graticule coincidence in the T4 bombsight at the aiming point and to achieve this it was essential for the aircraft captain to fly with precision on instruments and to react to the bomb aimer's corrections immediately and with smoothness allowing no variation of altitude or airspeed. Any variation of either at point of release would automatically feed in bombing errors.

All results were critically reviewed at my weekly conference, where the following week's flying programme would then be discussed. The training directive called for visual bombing to be carried out both by day and night, and indeed we found that it was necessary to take advantage of every opportunity to fly, for with the average UK weather, visual bombing from 25,000 or 40,000ft was only possible on occasions, and so our training requirement demanded that flying programmes must be sufficiently flexible to take advantage of weather.

In addition to the main priority of visual bombing, crews had to be exercised on long range sorties over the Atlantic and, where necessary, every captain and co-pilot's instruments rating had to be renewed. Being a qualified Master Instrument Rating Examiner, I carried out these renewal tests. This, as it turned out, gave me an ideal opportunity of flying with every one of my co-pilots in the squadron, invaluable in my assessment of them for recommendations as future

Excerpts from the 'Grapple' type Valiant technical manual

GENERAL

1 Certain alterations have been made to these aircraft to cover the requirements of the operation. These include precautionary measures to protect the aircraft and crew, instrumentation for scientific observations and the addition of extra and special equipment for navigational and bombing requirements. The aircraft carry the following serial numbers: XD818, XD822, XD823, XD824 XD825 XD827, XD829 and XD857.

PRECAUTIONARY MEASURES

2 Precautionary measures have been taken to protect the aircraft from the effects of heat and radiations from the explosion of the special store These fall into two categories: those measures built into the aircraft during manufacture and those applied just prior to the special sortie.

Special Treatment

4 Special protective treatment has been applied where necessary to aircraft parts, electrical wiring and items of equipment. The treatment varies according to the size, shape and degree of probable exposure and this should be borne in mind when carrying out external checks on the aircraft when it may be noticed that some items have been treated whilst similar items have not . . .

6 Structure seals have been changed. The new seals are made of white silicon rubber. However, some of these seals may be of black rubber due to non-availability of the white rubber seals for certain positions (particularly for the engine door to fuselage seal) and these will be painted white. It is important that this paint is in good condition before the special sortie, if in the slightest way suspect the seals should be repainted . . .

8 The air spoilers have been modified so that when they are extended, only the minimum of radiations can penetrate the aircraft.

9 The external finish and bomb bay of the aircraft has been changed and is now white. Extreme care has to be taken to avoid damaging the paint which should be cleaned down at regular intervals. A minimum paint thickness of .003 inches is necessary for protection from radiations. The anti-dazzle area is painted matt white on top of the glossy white finish. Service markings – registration

(Author)

letters, roundels and flashes – together with some of the ground servicing instructions have been painted with special paint mixtures and it is NOT necessary for these to be painted out before the special sortie.

Extra precautions for special sortie
10   Special reinforced ailerons, elevators and rudder will be fitted for the special sortie together with their respective tabs. The rudder tab will be of a shorter span . . .

INSTRUMENTATION
14   Instrumentation has been fitted to aircraft to record various aspect of the explosion including the effects of radiation on representative parts of the aircraft structure. An auto-observer is fitted in the cabin to record the various aspects of the store control and its release.

15   The instrumentation includes:
  (i)   A photoflash recording apparatus in the nose; the detector protrudes through the bottom of the nose fairing.
  (ii)   Strain gauges, resistance thermometers and accelerometers in the inboard section of the port aileron.
  (iii)   A camera in the port side of the fuselage to photograph the behaviour of the port aileron when the store explodes.
  (iv)   Two cameras in the bomb bay and one in each wing at the landing lamp positions to photograph the release slip and the store as it leaves the aircraft (two lamps are provided for the centre bomb bay camera to illuminate the release slip).
  (v)   A gammo [sic] dosimeter in the cabin to record the amount and intenstiy of gammo [sic] radiation penetrating the cabin.
  (vi)   Film boxes containing sensitised film strip in various parts of the aircraft (including the bomb bay and cabin) to record radiation intensities.
  (vii)   A strain range counter on the rear spar of the port wing.
  (viii) Accelerometers on the rear spar at the aircraft centre of gravity.
  (ix)   A special tail cone containing two cameras arranged so that they will 'look' directly at the explosion, samples of various materials each sample containing thermocouples and six thermal detector heads.
  (x)   Eight thermal detector heads are fitted to record radiation temperatures, as follows: One facing forward, in the extreme nose. One facing upwards, in the fuselage top near the rear spar Two facing downwards, in the tail cone Four facing directly at the explosion, in the tail cone.
  (xi)   The access panels in Nos 2 and 3 flaps port and starboard, will be replaced by reflectivity panels made of pure aluminum and these may be treated by RAE personnel for temperature and radiation measurements.
  (xii)   The inside of some of the windscreen shutters may be treated by RAE personnel for temperature and radiation measurements.
  (xiii) In addition to the auto-observer, three sets of recording gear will be fitted in the cabin: Two instrument recorders, one under the radio crate and one behind the 2nd pilot's seat on the NBC crate. One thermal recorder, with associated equipment mounted behind the starboard console on the NBC crate.
  (xiv)   Two radio release signal oscillators are fitted in the rear fuselage, each having its own VHF transmitter and aerial system. The aerials are mounted one on the lower starboard side of the rear fuselage and one at the extreme tail just forward of the special tail cone.
  (xv)   A control panel is mounted on the radio crate for the instrumentation together with the telemetry control panel.
  (xvi)   A telemetry installation is fitted to the aircraft in connection with the store controls, metering instruments being fitted on the telemetry control panel in the radio crate.

SPECIAL INSTALLATIONS
Rebecca Mk 4
1   A Rebecca Mk4 installation is fitted to the aircraft, the control unit, swtich boxes and indicator being mounted at the 1st navigator's position on the radio crate. The transmitter-receiver and port aerial switch unit are mounted above the bomb aimer's nacelle and below the pilot's platform . . .

17   Four aerials are fitted, one (receiver aerial) on the port side of the nosewheel bay, one suppressed in each side of the metal nose fairing (homing

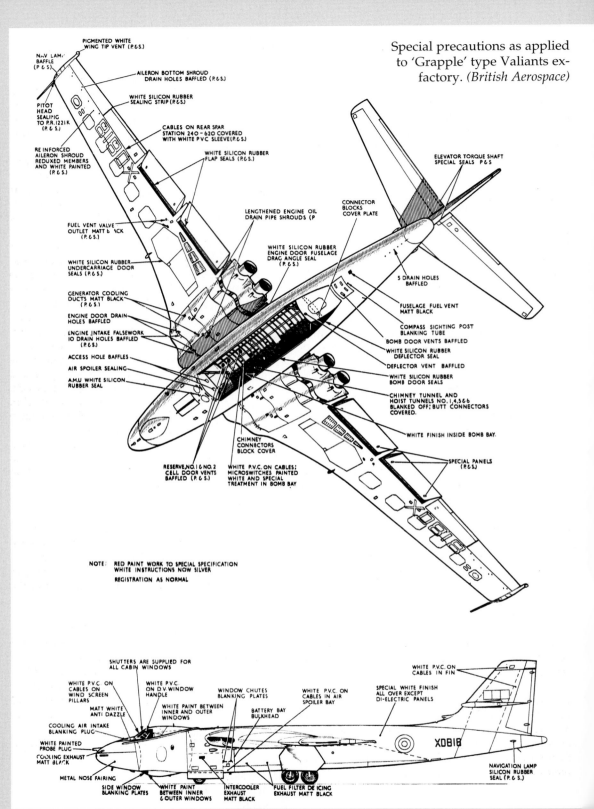

Special precautions as applied to 'Grapple' type Valiants ex-factory. *(British Aerospace)*

PIGMENTED WHITE WING TIP VENT (P.&S.)

NAV LAMP BAFFLE (P.&S.)

AILERON BOTTOM SHROUD DRAIN HOLES BAFFLED (P.&S.)

WHITE SILICON RUBBER SEALING STRIP (P.&S.)

PITOT HEAD SEALING TO P.R.1221K (P.&S.)

CABLES ON REAR SPAR STATION 240~620 COVERED WITH WHITE PVC SLEEVE (P.&S.)

REINFORCED AILERON SHROUD REDUXED MEMBERS AND WHITE PAINTED (P.&S.)

WHITE SILICON RUBBER FLAP SEALS (P.&S.)

ELEVATOR TORQUE SHAFT SPECIAL SEALS P&S

LENGTHENED ENGINE OIL DRAIN PIPE SHROUDS (P

CONNECTOR BLOCKS COVER PLATE

FUEL VENT VALVE OUTLET MATT BACK (P.&S.)

WHITE SILICON RUBBER ENGINE DOOR FUSELAGE DRAG ANGLE SEAL (P.&S.)

5 DRAIN HOLES BAFFLED

WHITE SILICON RUBBER UNDERCARRIAGE DOOR SEALS (P.&S.)

FUSELAGE FUEL VENT MATT BLACK

GENERATOR COOLING DUCTS MATT BLACK (P.&S.)

COMPASS SIGHTING POST BLANKING TUBE

ENGINE DOOR DRAIN HOLES BAFFLED

BOMB DOOR VENTS BAFFLED

ENGINE INTAKE FALSEWORK IO DRAIN HOLES BAFFLED (P.&S.)

WHITE SILICON RUBBER DEFLECTOR SEAL

ACCESS HOLE BAFFLES

DEFLECTOR VENT BAFFLED

AIR SPOILER SEALING

WHITE SILICON RUBBER BOMB DOOR SEALS

A.M.U WHITE SILICON RUBBER SEAL

CHIMNEY TUNNEL AND HOIST TUNNELS NO. 1,4,5&6 BLANKED OFF; BUTT CONNECTORS COVERED.

WHITE FINISH INSIDE BOMB BAY.

CHIMNEY CONNECTORS BLOCK COVER

SPECIAL PANELS (P.&S.)

RESERVE, NO.1 & NO.2 CELL DOOR VENTS BAFFLED (P.&S.)

WHITE P.V.C. ON CABLES; MICROSWITCHES PAINTED WHITE AND SPECIAL TREATMENT IN BOMB BAY

NOTE: RED PAINT WORK TO SPECIAL SPECIFICATION
WHITE INSTRUCTIONS NOW SILVER
REGISTRATION AS NORMAL

SHUTTERS ARE SUPPLIED FOR ALL CABIN WINDOWS

WHITE P.V.C. ON CABLES IN FIN

WHITE P.V.C. ON CABLES ON WIND SCREEN PILLARS

WHITE P.V.C. ON D.V. WINDOW HANDLE

WINDOW CHUTES BLANKING PLATES

WHITE P.V.C. ON CABLES IN AIR SPOILER BAY

SPECIAL WHITE FINISH ALL OVER EXCEPT DI-ELECTRIC PANELS

MATT WHITE ANTI DAZZLE

WHITE PAINT BETWEEN INNER AND OUTER WINDOWS

BATTERY BAY BULKHEAD

COOLING AIR INTAKE BLANKING PLUG

WHITE PAINTED PROBE PLUG

COOLING EXHAUST MATT BLACK

METAL NOSE FAIRING

SIDE WINDOW BLANKING PLATES

WHITE PAINT BETWEEN INNER & OUTER WINDOWS

INTERCOOLER EXHAUST MATT BLACK

FUEL FILTER DE ICING EXHAUST MATT BLACK

XD818

NAVIGATION LAMP SILICON RUBBER SEAL (P.&S.)

aerials) and one (transmitter aerial) mounted centrally under the nose fairing.

Loran APN-9

18 A Loran APN-9 installation is fitted to the aircraft, the receiver unit and serial loading unit being mounted at the 1st navigator's position on the radio crate. The VHP aerial at the top of the fin is used for this installation, as well as for the VHF system . . .

Decca navigator Mk8 (Mod 2410)

19 A Decca navigator Mk8 installation is fitted to the aircraft, the receiver, torque amplifier, power unit and velodyne unit being mounted at the W/T operator's position on the radio crate. The receiver and flight log control units are mounted on the radio crate below the radar panel and the flight log, decometers and ground referencing switch and indicators are recessed in the radio crate table top at the 1st navigator's position. Care must be taken when opening the table top not to damage these instruments.

20 The Gee Aerial at the top of the rudder is used for this installation, the Gee H Mk2 installation not being required for this exercise. A DECCA/Gee change-over switch is provided on the radio crate for switching the aerial as required.

Gee Mk2-C

21 The Gee HMk 2 installation has been removed from these aircraft and the spaces on the radio crate thus provided have been used for other equipment
22 It may be necessary, however, to use Gee during training flights in the UK in which case a Gee Mk2-C installation will be fitted,the receiver being mounted on the Gee H Mk2 receiver tray.

Bomb release time delay switch unit

33 A time delay switch is provided at the 1st navigator's position in the radio crate. This switch provides a time delay, variable between 8-20 seconds, between the time that the bomb release switch is operated and the time that the bomb release operates . . .

General handling

76 The general handling of the aircraft has not in any way been affected by the preparations for this operation. The handling of the aircraft will, therefore, be as laid down in the standard Valiant Pilots' Notes with the following exceptions.

Windscreen shutters

77 Special frameworks have been clamped to all the cockpit window frames to which metal shutters can be fitted. The frame works are so arranged that the canopy may be jettisoned with the shutters in position. The shutters are necessary to prevent the flash from the explosion of the store from entering the cabin.

78 The central windscreen has the top half of its shutters bolted in position because of its complex shape to protect the compass and to allow for its adjustment. The bottom half of this shutter is hinged about its bottom edge and is not normally removed.

79 The shutters are fitted into grooves in the bottom horizontal members of each framework; these grooves each have two dowels for locating the shutter sideways. With the shutter in position, it is locked by two locking handles, one in each top corner, light sealing being completed by white silicon rubber gasket seals attached to each shutter.

80 The individual pilot's windscreen shutters each have a sliding visor which may be used at the pilot's discretion when the shutters are up. These are retained in the open position by a spring catch. When the visors are shut, a welder's glass panel in each shutter is exposed so that the pilot may have some vision when the store explodes.

81 The shutters are stowed in canvas containers in the crew compartment and have to be handed up to the pilots. The recommended sequence for fitting the cockpit shutters is as follows. . .

CREW WINDOW SHUTTERS

82 Shutters, similar to those for the pilots' windows, are supplied for fitment to the crews' windows. The cabin side windows are located by vertical flats on one side and are retained in position by clamps, one at the top and one at the bottom.

111 A bomb loaded indicator on the observer's control panel is controlled by a micro switch touching the bomb casing and will show red at all times when the bomb is loaded until the bomb is released. It is used as an indication of the unlikely event of the bomb dropping off the slip hooks when the bomb doors are closed; no other indication of this occurrence is given and it may not be sensed in the cabin as the bomb has only to fall about 1 inch.

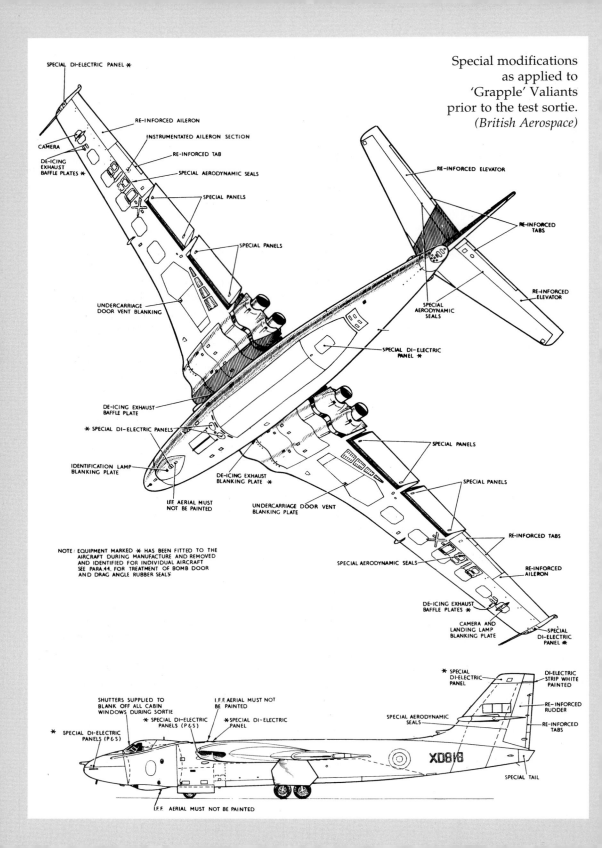

Special modifications
as applied to
'Grapple' Valiants
prior to the test sortie.
(*British Aerospace*)

SPECIAL DI-ELECTRIC PANEL ✳

RE-INFORCED AILERON

INSTRUMENTATED AILERON SECTION

CAMERA

RE-INFORCED TAB

DE-ICING
EXHAUST
BAFFLE PLATES ✳

SPECIAL AERODYNAMIC SEALS

SPECIAL PANELS

SPECIAL PANELS

RE-INFORCED ELEVATOR

RE-INFORCED
TABS

SPECIAL
AERODYNAMIC
SEALS

RE-INFORCED
ELEVATOR

UNDERCARRIAGE
DOOR VENT BLANKING

SPECIAL DI-ELECTRIC
PANEL ✳

DE-ICING EXHAUST
BAFFLE PLATE

SPECIAL PANELS

✳ SPECIAL DI-ELECTRIC PANELS

IDENTIFICATION LAMP
BLANKING PLATE

DE-ICING EXHAUST
BLANKING PLATE ✳

SPECIAL PANELS

I.F.F. AERIAL MUST
NOT BE PAINTED

UNDERCARRIAGE DOOR VENT
BLANKING PLATE

RE-INFORCED TABS

NOTE: EQUIPMENT MARKED ✳ HAS BEEN FITTED TO THE
AIRCRAFT DURING MANUFACTURE AND REMOVED
AND IDENTIFIED FOR INDIVIDUAL AIRCRAFT
SEE PARA.44. FOR TREATMENT OF BOMB DOOR
AND DRAG ANGLE RUBBER SEALS

SPECIAL AERODYNAMIC SEALS

RE-INFORCED
AILERON

DE-ICING EXHAUST
BAFFLE PLATES ✳

CAMERA AND
LANDING LAMP
BLANKING PLATE

SPECIAL
DI-ELECTRIC
PANEL ✳

✳ SPECIAL
DI-ELECTRIC
PANEL

DI-ELECTRIC
STRIP WHITE
PAINTED

SHUTTERS SUPPLIED TO
BLANK OFF ALL CABIN
WINDOWS DURING SORTIE

I.F.F. AERIAL MUST NOT
BE PAINTED

✳ SPECIAL DI-ELECTRIC
PANELS (P&S)

✳SPECIAL DI-ELECTRIC
PANEL

SPECIAL AERODYNAMIC
SEALS

RE-INFORCED
RUDDER

✳ SPECIAL DI-ELECTRIC
PANELS (P&S)

RE-INFORCED
TABS

XD818

SPECIAL TAIL

I.F.F. AERIAL MUST NOT BE PAINTED

captains. It also enabled me to assess the degree of instruction and guidance being given by their own captain.

These were extremely busy but pleasant weeks, during which my crew and I flew a great deal, because the high standards required applied to all alike and my own bombing results came under the same critical scrutiny, for I was determined to set standards in flying for all to follow; in this respect, no one was more critical than myself of my own performance on each training sortie.

By mid-October the two crews detached to South Australia for the nuclear trials in Operation Buffalo returned to Wittering after completing a successful air drop of a nuclear weapon in the kiloton range on 11 October 1956. The crew flying the Valiant aircraft was captained by Sqn Ldr Ted Flavell and his bomb aimer was Flt Lt Eric Stacey; both were awarded the Air Force Cross for their efforts. The support Valiant was captained by Flt Lt Bob Bates.

On the day of their arrival at Wittering, they were welcomed back by Air Cdre (later AVM) Mickie Dwyer, the senior Air Staff Officer No. 3 Group, representing the Air Officer Commanding, by the Station Commander John Woodroffe, and by myself. For me their return was of great importance, because their recent experience was invaluable and of course it gave me two more aircraft and crews to feed into the 'Grapple' training programme. Additionally it gave me on return our Squadron Engineering Officer, Flg Off W. Budden BEM. However, their homecoming was not without its problems. Once the crews had been greeted by their families, Sqn Ldr Flavell said he would like to talk to me about a problem he had experienced with his crew. Having arrived back on the Friday, I knew the crews all wanted a weekend to recover with their families. Therefore, I asked Ted Flavell if he would prefer to leave his crew problem until the Monday, and he agreed.

On that following Monday Ted Flavell gave me a detailed report of the operation from a squadron point of view and also put me in the picture regarding the reservations he had regarding his Air Electronics Officer who had apparently been smitten by the moral rearmament bug. Having fully briefed me on all aspects, I asked Ted to send his AEO over to my office for interview – this he did.

My adjutant came in to announce that the officer concerned was waiting so I told him to show him in. I had only met this officer on the arrival back last Friday, so he was not an individual that I had any background knowledge of in any way. My first impression was of a rather highly strung young man, and this opinion was borne out in the subsequent interview.

Having told him to sit down, I said that his captain had reported to me that he now held some very extreme views regarding the use of nuclear weapons and was involved in the moral rearmament organisation. I then allowed him to expand his own views, which quite obviously were contrary to the concept of a nuclear deterrent force and indeed extreme to the point of being subversive. Such views were completely unacceptable in any Royal Air Force Officer and certainly there was no room for them in the V Force, particularly in 49 Squadron with our special task. I was extremely surprised to think that a man with these views could have come through a positive vetting, and had no intention of allowing him to taint any of my crews. Having told him that his attitude and beliefs were completely unacceptable, he was suspended from duty and instructed to report back to the Mess and stay away from the squadron until his future was resolved.

Having concluded the interview, I rang John Woodroffe and asked if I could come over to see him about a personnel problem. Having put the Station Commander in the picture, he then spoke to the Senior Personnel Staff Officer at HQ 3 Group, who would then brief the AOC.

By the following day a signal arrived, posting the officer concerned to a holding unit and he was off the station on that same day. I subsequently learned that he was released from the Royal Air Force as his services were no longer required. A replacement AEO was quickly posted into Sqn Ldr Flavell's crew and the entire matter was quickly forgotten as we had more important things upon which to concentrate. Certainly I have never come across another example of any crew member in the V Force becoming affected in this manner.

By the end of October, the ground crew who had been detached to South Australia in support of our two Valiants had returned to the fold and both 'A' and 'B' Flights were now at full strength in ground and air crew. The training programme was in full swing by both day and night, but, in spite of taking every opportunity to get aircraft in the air under all types of weather, it was apparent that the visual bombing requirement was falling rapidly behind the planned schedule due to weather factors which ruled out visual bombing. This was a great worry, for I knew that our first detachment to Christmas Island was planned for the late spring of 1957 and that November, December, January and February would be difficult weather months from a high altitude visual bombing point of view. Fortunately, the Task Force 'Grapple' Headquarters was also thinking along the same lines and was beginning to plan on a reasonable pre-drop training period at Christmas Island.

Balanced in with the intensive flying training programme were social and sporting diversions, including a squadron party staged in Stamford, and I personally enjoyed the occasional invitation to dinner at the Station Commander's residence, and Mess activities included a regular monthly guest night.

I am a great believer in squadron parties, for this gives a Squadron Commander a real opportunity to test the morale of his squadron, and the opportunity to talk with the ground crew in particular, who contribute so much in a quiet and unpretentious manner. The quality, reliability, technical expertise and enthusiasm of the ground crew are vital for the operational efficiency of any squadron.

The month of November was to bring our greatest moments of excitement, for midway through the month our first all-white brand new Valiant to the full 'Grapple' special equipment specification arrived. This was Valiant XD818, which was to be my own aircraft. XD818 was then quickly followed by XD822, XD823, XD824 and XD825; all these were allocated to specific air and ground crews. As the new aircraft arrived, we were required to prepare our existing Valiants for transfer to 214 Squadron, which was in the process of being re-equipped at RAF Marham, under its Squadron Commander, Wg Cdr Alan Boxer (later AVM Sir Alan Boxer), an old friend from RAF Staff College days who was later to become Station Commander RAF Wittering, following the tragic death of John Woodroffe. By Christmas 1956 I was able to report that the squadron was at full strength with aircrews and ground crews.

Considerable progress had been made with the training programme regarding special inert weapon drops, Atlantic long range sorties, bad weather instrument let-down procedures, and visual bombing accuracy, but because of weather factors we were way behind the training requirement in the number of practice bombs dropped as laid down in the Bomber Command Training Directive. Exercises in the Valiant simulator by crews were up to date, and these were important, for only in the simulator could we practice the American beacon holding and let-down patterns. Emergency drill training had progressed well, including wet dinghy drills, with crews dropped from a helicopter over the Channel and being required to get into the dinghy and finally winched back into the helicopter. Most of us carried out this phase of our training in November and I do not think I have ever been so cold in my life!

By this time I had thoroughly assessed every aircrew in the squadron and was more than satisfied with the all round standards. Similarly on the ground crew side, I was much impressed by the quality of the crew chiefs and in general with the standard of airman, with one or two exceptions.

Thus, without being complacent, I felt we were all settling down to become a really effective operational team; every officer and airman was now pulling his weight and each felt that they were part of something special. This atmosphere and dedication is something that remained with '49' all through the next two years and has indeed remained to this day in the form of the '49 Megaton Club' (I shall mention more of this club in the concluding pages of this book). So, looking back on this first three months, we now found ourselves with a total establishment of five Valiant B1 aircraft to the 'Grapple' modification. Since mention has been made of special modifications to meet the requirements of our future task, it is appropriate to explain what these comprised.

Firstly, all aircraft were treated with a special anti-flash finish, capable of withstanding 72 calories of heat energy per square centimetre. All control surfaces were strengthened to withstand the over pressurisation wave, which follows the flash on detonation of a nuclear device or weapon. Each aircraft was fitted with metal anti-flash screens, for the flight deck and bomb aimers position, to provide complete crew protection. The aircraft were also provided with special scientific equipment, including tail cone cameras to record the actual weapon detonation and fire ball development. There were bomb bay cameras to record the initial ballistic characteristics of the weapon on leaving the aircraft's bomb bay, and provision was also made for cameras in each wing tip to focus on the weapon's initial rate of fall. Strain gauges to record the over pressurisation experienced after weapon detonation and gauges to record thermal temperatures were included. A special automatic observer was also fitted to record, with great accuracy, vertical velocities experienced after the bomb doors were opened and at the actual point of weapon release from the aircraft. Every aircraft was also provided with a radio release tone system on VHF which transmitted the moment of weapon release. Finally, these aircraft were not fitted with the radar navigational bombing system which was standard for all Bomber Command V Force aircraft. Instead, in this position a special scientific weapon switching panel was installed, and responsibility for operating it rested with the Air Electronics Officer, who was to work to a special bombing procedures check list.

We were also at full strength for aircrews including the following captains and their crews:

> Sqn Ldr D Roberts
> Sqn Ldr T. Flavell
> Sqn Ldr A. Steele
> Sqn Ldr B. Millett
> SqnLdr W. Bailey
> Flt Lt T. O'Connor
> Flt Lt R. Calliard
> Flt Lt A. Chambers
> Flt Lt R. Bates

Flying continued up to the day prior to Christmas Eve, when we stood down for a well earned rest over the Christmas period. For myself and faithful Crusty it meant a few days at home with my parents in Norfolk and a chance to drive to the lovely East Coast beaches where we could walk for miles on unspoilt sand, with Crusty enjoying every moment.

On one particular day, as I strolled along the beach, wrapped up against the cold east wind, my thoughts ranged over the past three months, for they had been extremely stimulating. In this time I had had the opportunity to assess the air crews and felt convinced that they were some of the finest in Bomber Command, the ground crews had settled in well, and there was already a first class squadron feeling of pride, everyone knowing they were to be involved in something very special. Everybody was looking forward to the forthcoming detachment at Christmas Island, although of course nobody knew who would be the lucky ones to go. This for the aircrews would depend upon bombing results over the next few months, and for the ground crews about half would remain at Wittering to support the back-up aircraft, which would be used in the courier role.

I had already been informed by Task Force HQ that the detachment for

'Grapple' would involve five months on the island, and was looking forward very much to the experience of having the squadron on overseas detachment. At this stage my visions of life on a coral island were a little idealistic – visions which were to change after the first five months experience!

Turning to more serious thoughts, I reflected upon the importance of the outcome of these future trials tests. What would they achieve for the effectiveness of the V Force and Britain's independent deterrent? What were the requirements from a Command point of view, from a megaton nuclear warhead? They seemed to fall into four categories: firstly, it could be used as a free falling weapon; secondly, with the increase of Russian defences, there would be a need to adapt it to a stand-off powered type guided bomb, for by this time Blue Steel was in the design stage. It could also be applied to a medium range ballistic missile; and lastly of course it could lead to a multi-megaton warhead.

As these thoughts filled my mind, they brought home to me the importance of these forthcoming tests, for neither the Americans or Russians had carried out a live air drop of a megaton nuclear device; Britain and the Royal Air Force would be chalking up a first, and 49 Squadron was to be honoured by being the squadron to whom the task was to be entrusted.

On Boxing Day I again drove to the coast with my dog, and as we strolled along the hard sand, left by the tide as it receded, I allowed my thoughts to reflect upon the qualities of the crews, as I had been able to assess them over the past three months. Firstly, from the indications given to me by Headquarters Bomber Command, I was aware that the actual detachment of 49 Squadron on Christmas Island was to be four aircraft and crews, which were those selected to carry out the live drops. Secondly, I had been told that the duration of our stay on the island would be approximately five months; and thirdly, there was a further requirement to have another four Valiants and crews available for courier duties between the UK and Christmas Island. Therefore, the selection of the four crews to form the actual bombing element was of vital importance. What then was my assessment at this stage, based on a number of factors?

At all costs I wanted Sqn Ldr Dave Roberts and his crew to be included; their experience to date was considerable and in view of all the background training given to preparing the two crews for Operation Buffalo, there was no doubt in my mind that this crew must be included. Its bombing results to date were first class, showing every proof of consistency; therefore this crew was a certainty.

Already, I had been much impressed by Sqn Ldr Arthur Steel and his crew; not only was Arthur Steel an above-average captain who flew the Valiant with great precision, but he possessed in his crew a very experienced bomb aimer in Flt Lt Wilf Jenkins (since deceased), and here again this crew was already demonstrating consistent bombing accuracy. Furthermore, as Squadron Training Officer, I certainly required the services of Arthur Steel to co-ordinate the initial training phase once we arrived. Therefore it looked a certainty for this crew to be included.

Another crew that had impressed me by its quiet efficiency was that of Sqn Ldr Barny Millett; once again, its results to date on both accuracy and consistency justified inclusion.

Finally of course, there was my own crew, and with such a steady and experienced bomb aimer as Alan Washbrook, our results to date met the full accuracy and consistency criteria. This was vital, for I knew we would be carrying out the first live drop.

This then appeared to be the bombing team, with the remainder of the squadron crews allocated to the courier role, for the fast transit of sensitive parts of the weapon to Christmas Island. However, these crews were also required to be capable of being phased into the bombing team as and when required, so their bombing training results had to meet the full operational accuracy criteria.

With crews of such high calibre as those mentioned above, I already felt confident in meeting the task ahead of us, in spite of weather difficulties to date which had severely curtailed our visual bombing training programme.

On completion of the Christmas stand-down I returned to Wittering, and the training task was resumed. Naturally we took time off to celebrate the coming of the New Year which, as time proved, was to be a momentous one, although none of us at the time fully appreciated the historic significance of the operation ahead. Having seen the New Year in, we got down to the next stage of our serious training programme, which included a requirement from every crew to become proficient in the escape manoeuvre to be carried out after release of the weapon.

Our new 'Grapple'-modified aircraft were all fitted with the sensitive accelerometer which measured the positive G force pulled in a steep turn. The escape manoeuvre called for a 60° banked turn to port, through 130° at a constant measurement on the sensitive accelerometer of 1.7G. This to be a purely instrument turn by the captain, for on the occasion of a live drop the entire cockpit windows would be blacked out by metal shutters. I am sure that experienced pilots will recognise this as a highly delicate manoeuvre, for any gross inaccuracy at 46,000ft can easily result in a high speed stall. Therefore it was vital that crews practised this in every bombing detail to ensure they became both proficient and confident under these instrument conditions.

By the first week of January the Headquarters Bomber Command operations order, specifying the Command task in Operation Grapple, arrived. This then provided me with the overall relevant situation and our own commitment, from which I was able to make our final training and courier support plans. Additionally, with this information, I was able to set out our own detailed operations order.

We had now reached the stage where five 'Grapple' standard aircraft had arrived and the aircrew complement was complete; from these 10 crews six had been fully cleared for visual bombing above 40,000ft and the other four were on the point of being cleared.

Exercises had been completed with HMS *Warrior* at Portland, to test her radar control. This had followed a conference the previous November at Wittering with Air Cdre C. T. Weir DFC, the Deputy Task Force Commander and Gp Capt L. E. Giles OBE, DFC, AFC from HQ Bomber Command, at which we also discussed the current training state of the squadron and I was able to indicate the further training required once at Christmas Island necessary for crews to perfect the special overshoot technique to a consistent accuracy before they could be cleared for a live drop.

At this meeting I was also able to outline the plan for the next stage of training prior to departures, and press my claims for a speeding up of further modifications required by the scientists, and also the need to take urgent action for priority on the fitment of Decca navigation equipment which still had to be installed in all 'Grapple' Valiants prior to departure. In all these matters action was promised, and there was understanding of the problem being experienced in achieving the visual bombing programme due to the UK weather, and a promise to consider carefully my request to detach aircraft and crews to RAF El Adem in Libya, where we could have unrestricted use of the bombing range and guarantee visual conditions.

Thus it was as a result of this conference that the next stage of the training programme was designed; January saw us concentrating upon all the special drills necessitated in co-ordination with the scientific team, for the constant monitoring of the weapon before and after release.

At a meeting with Brian Trubshaw, Deputy Chief Test Pilot at Vickers, prior to Christmas, he was able to confirm that the final three 'Grapple' Valiants would have completed their post production acceptance flight tests and be with the squadron during January. In this respect he was as good as his word and by the end of January XD827 and XD829 had arrived; in early February our establishment was completed by the arrival of XD857.

Now, being fully aware that the first four Valiants were required to depart for Christmas Island at the beginning of March 1957, a great deal had to be achieved during January and February in order to:

1 Complete the next stage of training;

2 Ensure that all aircraft special fit modifications including the Decca equipment were complete;

3 Balance aircraft hours into the technical servicing programmes to ensure each aircraft had available sufficient flying hours for the period at Christmas Island without requiring a minor inspection. In this respect both my Squadron Technical Officer, Flg Off Budden, and the station technical wing were to be congratulated on the priority given for this task;

4 Assemble the necessary spares backing considered essential to maintain the detachment at Christmas Island over a five-month period.

In order to achieve all the objectives outlined above, my first task was to issue a detailed squadron operation order in accordance with the overall directive contained in the Bomber Command operation order. The squadron operation order had to cover every detail of the pre-departure for both aircrew and ground crew, and set out the aircraft and ground crew departure and route transit arrangements, and spell out the responsibilities of the rear detachment remaining at RAF Wittering, for continued training and preparation of Valiants required to be employed in the fast courier support role, which necessitated positioning of crews at selected airfields between Christmas Island and RAF Wittering. This was duly completed following a detailed conference with my Squadron Training Officer, the two Flight Commanders, all the specialist leaders and the Squadron Technical Officer.

During January I attended two more conferences at HQ 'Grapple' in London to discuss special equipment and procedure drills. There was also a detailed technical programme conference at Wittering in February, attended by Gp Capt P. Brousson OBE from HQ 'Grapple', Gp Capt J. Bruce from HQ 3 Group, Gp Capt Vic Otter OBE, and Sqn Ldr W. Collins from HQBC. At this conference the accent was on the availability of the Decca equipment and it was obvious that a certain amount of this work would have to be undertaken when we arrived at Christmas Island.

Also during January and February, all non-'Grapple' Valiants had been re-allocated to other Bomber Command squadrons so that at last we were self-contained as a fully-equipped 'Grapple' Valiant squadron.

By mid-February I was satisfied that in spite of a shortfall in visual bombing hours, the selected dropping crews had achieved the high standard of consistent bombing accuracy for 40,000ft and were fully proficient at the escape manoeuvre, completely exercised on all aspects of the bad weather let down procedures for the American airfields we were scheduled to stage through, had completed the full emergency drills including a thorough knowledge of the special 'destruct' modification fitted to the automatic pilot system, were fully conversant with the scientific bombing procedure, and that all instrument ratings were current.

On the technical side, the programme of minor inspection had been carefully adjusted to allow all aircraft detailed for detachment to have the necessary hours available as specified in the squadron operation order and planning was well in hand to cover the courier requirement.

It had been decided that for the first detachment, the ground crew in 'A' flight should go to Christmas Island, as the first four aircraft and crews were coming from this flight. Thus all 'A' flight ground crew under Flt Sgt Wally Asprey were issued with their tropical kit, plus Sgt Wally Cressey who was also included as the Squadron Discipline SNCO. This, as will be seen in later chapters, was a task that Wally Cressey carried out with great success and much humour. All aircrew, including myself, were issued with lightweight tropical flying overalls and helmets.

There now remained the detailed pre-departure briefing of both aircrew and ground crew, which were carried out independently.

Firstly, all ground crew were to proceed by civil charter aircraft to Christmas Island, under the control of Sqn Ldr Myers, the Squadron Specialist Navigation Leader; they were assembled in the main operation briefing room by Sgt W. Cressey and I gave them a detailed briefing on all aspects of their departure including the route timing, and the knowledge that the long journey would be broken at New York to give them a full night stop, which met with general approval. I also briefly outlined the tasks ahead of them once they arrived on the island in order to prepare for the arrival of the four Valiants. They were also warned of the rather primitive living and feeding conditions we could all expect. However, they were all delighted to be taking part in the forthcoming operation and a great air of excitement prevailed.

Having covered all the essential points, I stressed the importance of conducting themselves at all times in a manner which was a credit to the Royal Air Force and 49 Squadron in particular – in which they did not let me down.

Thus the ground crew departed a few days ahead of the planned take-off date for the Valiants in order to give them time to complete pre-aircraft-arrival tasks on Christmas Island. The main briefing for aircrews was scheduled for 1 March and all assembled in the operations briefing room on this date at 11.00hrs.

Firstly the Station Commander, Gp Capt John Woodroffe, gave a brief general talk on the forthcoming task. I followed his address as Squadron Commander, explaining that this briefing would cover in some detail the transit route for the main bombing force, to be followed by certain aspects of the courier commitment. There then followed a full route navigation brief by the Navigation Leader, the radio briefing by the Air Electronics Leader, and a full meteorological briefing covering present weather over the route, with particular accent on the inter-tropical front situation that could be experienced over the South Pacific. Finally, the Bombing Leader covered the operational procedure at Christmas Island.

With this complete, I then resumed a general briefing to remind captains and co-pilots of bad weather let-down crew drills, and action to be taken regarding emergency procedures if experienced *en route*. I then turned to the all important courier task to be undertaken by the 'B' Flight crews and aircraft covering the highly sensitive nature of the cargo being carried, the special procedures to be adopted in the event of any accident to the cargo, and the action to be taken by crews in the event of a major emergency in the air.

The other important aspect of the courier task, bearing in mind that the cargo was radioactive, was crew and aircraft positioning in accordance with the operation order, to a very tight and precise time scale. The responsibility for ensuring that this programme was activated in accordance with the schedule laid down in my squadron operations order was vested in Sqn Ldr T. Flavell who was to remain at Wittering as acting Squadron Commander.

Finally, I covered general administrative matters at Christmas Island and gave all crews a broad picture of what they could expect on the island and what they would have to put up with in the way of personal discomfort, and the need for absolute security at all staging posts *en route*. Our task was Top Secret, and although Parliament had been informed of the forthcoming tests by the Prime Minister on 5 June 1956, the general public was not aware of our task.

The planned departure schedule for the bombing aircraft from RAF Wittering was:

> 2 March 1957 – XD818: Wg Cdr K. G. Hubbard and crew, plus Crew Chief Tech W. Caple
>
> 3 March 1957 – XD822: Sq Ldr D. Roberts and crew plus Crew Chief Tech S. Small
>
> 4 March 1957 – XD823: Sq Ldr A. Steele and crew plus Crew Chief Tech W. Quinlan
>
> 5 March 1957 – XD824: Sq Ldr B. Millett and crew plus Crew Chief Tech C. Mathers

The Valiants at this stage were not fitted with underwing fuel tanks; therefore there prevailed certain limitations to be imposed *en route* which was selected in order to meet this criteria.

The route selected by HQ Bomber Command was as follows:

> RAF Wittering to Aldergrove in Northern Ireland for a top-up of fuel prior to the Atlantic crossing
>
> Aldergrove to Goose Bay in Newfoundland
>
> Goose Bay to Namao
>
> Namao to Travis AFB in California
>
> Travis to Honolulu
>
> Honolulu to Christmas Island

With the strong westerly winds prevailing at this time of the year over the Atlantic at flight levels of 40,000ft, it was necessary to land at Aldergrove in Northern Ireland to top up with fuel. Crews also had to be aware of the strong westerlies prevailing over the Pacific, for the leg from Travis AFB in California to Honolulu; the distance on this leg was 2,100nm, and therefore only a head-wind of up to 30kt could be accepted, to allow for sufficient fuel to be available for diversion.

The meteorological briefing on 1 March showed that Goose Bay was experiencing extremely bad weather, with snow reducing visibility to nil; and the weather pattern at Aldergrove was also extremely poor, with low cloud, rain and vertical visibility below limits.

Final meteorological briefing for my own crew would be 08.00hrs on the following day, 2 March; but, with the extreme bad weather prevailing at Goose Bay, this was then delayed until 3 March. The following day at Met briefing it was clear that the weather was now within limits at Aldergrove, although there was little change in the situation at Goose Bay. It was decided therefore that we should proceed to Aldergrove in the hopes that there would be sufficient clearance at Goose Bay on the following day.

I was pleased to be on the move, for hold-ups such as these are so very frustrating for all concerned. Everyone's bags were packed, the aircraft was fuelled, the bomb bay panniers loaded with spares; the previous weekend I had already taken Crusty to stay for the duration with my parents.

On the morning of 3 March my crew and I left the Operations Block and were taken out to Valiant XD818 in one of the station crew buses. On arrival at the aircraft we were met by my Crew Chief, Bill Caple, who had ensured that all ground checks were complete, and the aircraft fully serviceable for departure. We loaded our heavy baggage into one of the bomb bay panniers, having previously made sure that no toiletry bottles, etc were in our bomb bay baggage which would be subjected to unpressurised conditions at 45,000ft.

Bob Beeson and I duly carried out the lengthy external checks on XD818, whilst Alan Washbrook, Eric Hood and Ted Laraway took up their positions on the rear flight deck. External checks complete, the co-pilot and I climbed in and strapped ourselves into our ejection seats. With the master switch on and power from the ground power unit, we then progressed through the complicated pre-start-up checks, which are read out by the co-pilot and acknowledged by the captain or appropriate crew member as each drill or switching is completed.

With the Crew Chief plugged into the intercom from his ground position, I indicated being ready to start engines and called for clearance – this means the Crew Chief checking all ground crew clear of the jet efflux. With this clearance we started engines in the following order – 3,2,1,4. All engines running, jet pipe temperatures and pressures were checked and the full after-start drill then carried out to check all electrics, operation of flaps, air brakes, bomb-bay doors and fuel pumps.

All checks now complete, I indicated chocks away and told Chief Tech Bill Caple to come aboard, for he was flying out with us as a full crew member. With him aboard, the exit door was closed and permission to taxi out obtained from flying control.

As I opened the throttles and felt the powerful surge of the engines the Valiant moved forward; I think we all experienced that wonderful feeling that at last the long awaited adventure was beginning.

We slowly taxied to the holding point of the runway in use and, as always with XD818, I had a great feeling of pride to be at those controls. The aircraft was spotlessly white in its anti-flash colours, contrasting greatly with the drab weather conditions prevailing. With all pre-take off checks complete, we were ready to move on to the runway and line up for take-off.

Clearance was given and, as we rolled on and lined up the nose wheel, the tower wished us luck and gave take-off clearance. I acknowledged and warned the crew to be ready for take-off; the co-pilot gave the acceleration check point and unstick speeds; then with brakes held on I called for 7,000rpm, and as engine temperatures and pressures were confirmed as normal, the brakes were released and I called for full power.

XD818 surged forward under this power and initial directional control was maintained by nose wheel steering until 80kt was indicated, then the nose wheel was raised and directional control maintained by use of rudder. As the unstick speed was attained, the aircraft was rotated by a backward pressure on the control column and we were airborne.

Once comfortably airborne I called for undercarriage up, at the same time applying the toe brakes to stop all wheels rotating; I reduced power to 7,400rpm, with speed now building to 150kt and the co-pilot reporting all undercarriage lights out and the doors closed. I called for flaps up and allowed the speed to increase to 170kt. The co-pilot having reported flaps up, he selected cabin air and bomb bay heat on and commenced his fuel cycling programme.

Airfield clearance was obtained and we turned on to our course, climbing, for Aldergrove; having settled into the climb, revs were set at 7,800rpm and speed for the climb increased to 275kt. All rear crew members reported service-ability of equipment at 10,000ft oxygen check and we continued our climb to 40,000ft allowing speed to progress to Mach 0.75 indicated; this was maintained until we levelled at the top of the climb. At this point autopilot was selected and I settled back to reflect that we really were on the way to our very special detachment.

As the flight to Aldergrove was a short one of approximately an hour, we were soon checking with Aldergrove approach on the weather conditions and began a maximum rate descent commenced to feed into the field's instrument landing system. An instrument approach was necessary as weather conditions were low cloud at 400ft with rain. At 1,500ft we levelled from our descent and soon picked up the ILS localiser, then as the glide path needle was intercepted a steady descent commenced with undercarriage down, 40° flap selected and all pre-landing checks complete.

Valiant XD818 trimmed out comfortably (as always) and settled on the glide path; during this descent, as was our normal bad weather procedure, the co-pilot flew the approach on instruments and I monitored, ready to take over the controls as we emerged from cloud and the runway approach lights came into view. As we passed 450ft on the airfield QFE, the approach lights were visible; I selected full flap, took control, re-trimmed the controls and carried on to make a normal landing.

We cleared the runway as instructed by control and taxied in to our dispersal position. We were scheduled for a night stop at Aldergrove so there was ample time for refuelling and a visit to the meteorological section to check on the latest weather at Goose Bay. Because of the security classification of the aircraft, we were given a secluded dispersal and a 24hr guard.

Having completed all drills and shut down engines, we tidied up the flight deck, removed our overnight kit and locked up the aircraft. We were all then transported to the station operations centre where we made the necessary arrangements for refuelling and our overnight accommodation. Our visit to the Met Office was disappointing, for it was obvious that there had been no improvement in the weather at Goose Bay and the met forecast was not optimistic.

However, the Met Officer promised to obtain further information by signal regarding actual conditions for us by early next morning, so really there was little else, at this stage, to do, other than accept the situation and review things in the morning. Little did I realise that my patience was to be tested to the utmost, for another three days were to elapse before we could depart for Goose Bay.

Checks with the Met Office and a close study of the synoptic charts the following morning showed little change and it was obvious that we were to be delayed another 24 hours. I duly signalled my intention to RAF Wittering, copying to HQ 3 Group at HQ Bomber Command, suggesting XD822, XD823 and XD824 be rescheduled for departure in order to maintain the planned separation.

Bill Caple, the Crew Chief, organised some local assistance and an aircraft cleaning service was put in hand. The crew and I spent our time on the flight deck cleaning up and then had a session of practice drills.

That evening we again visited the Met Office to look at the latest weather reports from Goose Bay, more in hope than anger, for we had already been informed that there was little hope of any improvement for at least 48 hours. I was determined to press on if there was the slightest chance of a change in the weather.

We returned to the Officers' Mess resigned to another night at Aldergrove; that evening we enjoyed a quiet drink with the Station Commander, then had a pleasant meal and an early night, for we would be up and about the next morning ready for a planned take-off if the weather at Goose Bay permitted. However, once again on visiting the Met Office, it became apparent that we were destined for yet another night at Aldergrove.

On the third day, 6 March, we again reported to the Met Office, only to find little change in the way of actual conditions at Goose Bay, but the synoptic chart gave some indications of improvements over the next 24 hours. I told the crew we would check again after lunch, for if Goose Bay was likely to come within limits by evening, we would make a night crossing. On the afternoon checks this was ruled out, but it did look hopeful for the following day. That night over dinner Alan Washbrook, Ted Laraway and Eric Hood were in good humour for we all felt confident that we should be resuming our journey in XD818 on the following morning.

Our optimism was justified and at an early morning briefing on 7 March, it was apparent that the weather at Goose Bay had improved to within instrument landing conditions. Bill Caple had the aircraft all ready and we were soon aboard and strapped in ready to start engines. With all engines running, and after start checks complete, Bill Caple came aboard and we were ready to taxi out to take-off position having been cleared by Air Traffic Control. To be once again at the controls of the XD818 and on the move was a wonderful feeling and enjoyed by every member of the crew, for an atmosphere of good humour prevailed.

We lined up on the runway and with clearance for take-off given, XD818 roared down the tarmac, rather like ourselves delighted to be on the move again. Normal rotation was achieved with ample runway in hand, and with undercarriage up we quickly settled into the initial climb; then with flaps up and power adjusted we turned on to our course for Goose Bay and headed out across the Atlantic, set for a climb to 40,000ft.

On the climb each crew member quietly proceeded with his own equipment checks, Bob Beeson was busy with his fuel cycling charts and I set the autopilot in for a cruise climb. The weather as we left Aldergrove had been far from good, but we soon climbed through the layers of stratus and alto stratus to break into clear skies by 20,000ft, continuing to 40,000ft cruising height. The aircraft was levelled at this altitude, all temperature and pressures checked, having completed all crew oxygen checks on the climb.

The view from 40,000ft was magnificent, for ahead and below, as far as one could see, it was a picture of undulating cotton wool mixed with miniature mountains of large cumulus cloud protruding to great heights.

The four Rolls-Royce Avon jet engines of Valiant XD818 purred on an even note, indicating that all was well, and the co-pilot confirmed that fuel consumption was as per flight plan. Eric Hood, the Nav Plotter, reported we were on track, with the Green Satin equipment giving a clear ground speed confirmed by the ground speed indicator. The AEO reported he had HF contact with Area Control and that we should soon be making contact with ocean weather ship 'India'.

Our planned flight time was 5hr 10min, and since Goose Bay, Newfoundland, is 4 hours ahead of GMT and our take-off time from Aldergrove was 13.00hrs GMT, we should in fact be landing at Goose Bay at 14.10 local time. Thus having enjoyed one lunch at Aldergrove prior to take off, we should arrive at Goose Bay in time to join them for a second!

About half-way across the Atlantic the weather pattern below changed and slowly the cloud began to thin until the weather ahead cleared completely, although the Atlantic looked angry with large white horses indicating a very rough sea.

We now had contact with ocean weather Ship 'Bravo' and by this time the AEO was in HF contact with the Newfoundland control zone. The weather pattern below us had changed again and we could see the deep depression which had caused all the problems at Goose Bay and produced such heavy falls of snow. The weather report coming through from Goose Bay was good: a cloud base of 3,000ft, 3nm visibility, but with temperatures below zero and a warning that although the runway in use was clear, braking action would be poor and care must be exercised on landing due to high banks of snow on either side of the runway.

Control gave permission to commence descent from 40,000ft to 25,000ft over Goose Bay beacon for a visual flight rule approach to the airfield. So 30min from our estimated time of arrival, we carried out pre-descent drills and commenced our maximum rate descent at Mach 0.72 phasing to 240kt with air brakes out. We broke cloud at 3,000ft on an area QNH set on the altimeter and levelled at 2,000ft.

As we approached the Newfoundland Coast, the panoramic view of lakes and huge forests covered in a mountain of snow really defied all description; it was a most beautiful picture.

Shortly after crossing the coast, we were in VHF contact with Goose Bay Approach Control and our position was confirmed by their radar approach. We were instructed to make a straight in approach on to runway 27 and cleared to descend to 1,200ft. At this point we were now some 20 miles from the airfield, so pre-landing checks were carried out. By 5nm the airfield was visible, undercarriage down, 40° flap selected, and we were steady on the glide path for landing, with all pre-landing checks complete. The runway could be seen clearly as well as the towering banks of snow to either side. With airspeed steady, full flaps selected and the aircraft trimmed, we made our final approach. On crossing the boundary, power was slowly reduced and we made a neat touch down on the main wheels with the nose wheel held off, and then gently lowered on to the runway where direction could then be controlled by nose wheel steering. We had landed dead on time and came to a stop; local control gave taxi instructions, and with all after landing checks complete, I taxied into our dispersal point and shut down engines.

After a very frustrating start we had arrived at Goose Bay three days late, and as I surveyed the scene from the flight deck, it was apparent that over the past three days several feet of snow had fallen.

On climbing down from the aircraft, I was met by our Bomber Command detachment Commander, who was a Squadron Leader, and I introduced my crew. In order to provide facilities for both Canberra and Valiant aircraft in transit to Christmas Island and to service the fast Valiant courier phase later on, HQ Bomber Command had positioned small detachments of ground engineers at Namao, Travis AFB and Honolulu, under a detachment commander, in co-operation with both the RCAF and USAF.

We were quickly transported to the Station Operations Centre where we were welcomed by the Royal Canadian Station Commander who displayed a great interest in the Valiant, and I agreed to show him around prior to take-off the following day. Whilst I duly completed the arrival signal to be sent to HQ Bomber Command, HQ 3 Group, HQ 'Grapple' and RAF Wittering, Alan Washbrook made arrangements for a full meteorological briefing covering the next stage of our route to Namao, which is also in Canada, for our planned take-off was to be 10.00hrs local time.

The distance flown from Aldergrove to Goose Bay was approximately 1,905nm and the distance again from Goose Bay to Namao was 1,890nm; therefore the flight time for the next stage would be in the region of 5 hours. However, the leg from Namao to Travis AFB in California was only 980nm and the thought was already going through my mind that if the weather was within limits, it might be a sound idea to make a quick refuel at Namao and then press on to arrive Travis that same day, thus at least catching up one of the days lost. This would mean a very long day for all of us; 8 hours flying duty plus pre-flight planning time involving a total of about 11 hours non-stop duty.

I called the crew together and explained what was in my mind; they all agreed that providing the weather was suitable, this extended duty should not produce any unacceptable fatigue. Before leaving the Operation Centre for a meal, I sent a signal back to HQ Bomber Control, informing it of my intentions. We then departed for a well-earned meal and tasted, for the first time, the delights of Canadian food. Since Goose Bay is a very isolated station, and indeed during the winter months can only be resupplied by air, it, by necessity, has to be self-contained in all respects. Thus both service and civilian personnel live on the station, which is rather like a small town. In addition, part of the station was used as a forward base for USAF Strategic Air Command B-52 aircraft, and as is always the case with the Americans on their side of the station, every luxury facility was provided.

The Canadians are very hospitable people and the RCAF was no exception; that evening the Station Commander invited us to go over to his house for pre-dinner drinks and to meet his wife and family. Indeed, as we subsequently staged through Goose Bay so many times during the next two years, I became very friendly with these delightful people.

Dinner that night was in the Mess and I for one was more than ready to turn in early, for the following day would be a very long one if we were to complete the next two legs to Travis. Incidentally, the only reason that the Valiant needed to fly via Namao to Travis was that without underwing fuel tanks, the direct route was beyond its range. Unfortunately, these were not available until later on, when we were then able to by-pass Namao and fly direct from Goose Bay to Travis.

Planned take-off the following day was 10.00 local, which meant Met briefing and pre-flight planning at 08.00hrs. After a very attractive breakfast, and the Crew Chief having confirmed by telephone beforehand that Valiant XD818 was fuelled and completely serviceable, we were transported to the Operation Centre. The weather from Goose Bay to Namao was good and the tentative outlook for Travis was acceptable, although there was a weather front hanging around, which probably meant we should be required to carry out a beacon homing and let down into the base's ground controlled approach pattern.

All pre-flight work complete we climbed into our transport and drove to

XD818; no sooner had we arrived than the Station Commander drove up in his car and I duly gave him the promised conducted tour of the aircraft. That done, he wished us luck with our forthcoming task and departed. With all external checks complete, we climbed into the aircraft and proceeded with pre-start and start up drills. Control cleared us for taxi and also for a direct climb out of its airspace on course for Namao. I once again taxied very carefully because the taxiways were slippery and the huge towers of snow on either side spelt disaster if there was any lack of concentration.

With 818 duly lined up on the active runway and take-off clearance obtained, we commenced our roll dead on 10.00hrs as per flight planning, and once airborne with undercarriage up turned on to our course of 270° for Namao and settled into a cruise climb for 40,000ft aiming for Mach 0.76 speed.

For the first few hundred miles the cloud was well broken and the views below and all round were magical to see, particularly the great lakes, including Lake Eon, Knob Lake and later on the Great Whale River. Although everywhere was well covered in snow, it was possible to confirm our position visually by map reading, which gave sound pin-point positioning, particularly in the Hudson Bay area.

Our flight continued without incident; all engines were performing well, no problem was experienced by the co-pilot with his fuel cycling, and the AEO obtained bearings from the Winnipeg Broadcaster at 500nm range. The flight was now coming to within 150nm of Edmonton and I was relieved to hear the AEO confirm we had picked up the Edmonton range, for our procedure into Namao called for a homing to overhead Edmonton at a height dictated by Namao Approach Control.

Throughout the flight we maintained contact with the various flight information regions and defence areas, and changed our altitude and course accordingly, concluding with a let down to 25,000ft over Edmonton. From this point a further descent was made without difficulty, feeding into the Namao Ground Control Radar Approach for a direct approach landing. Bob Beeson, the co-pilot, flew the descent pattern and I took over for a visual landing as we approached our break-off altitude and the runway ahead could be seen clearly. The procedure of the co-pilot flying the let down descent on instruments, with the captain monitoring and ready to take over for a visual landing, was our standard bad weather technique and one used regularly.

It is of interest to comment at this stage on the quality of the ground radar control at both Goose Bay and Namao, for in the Royal Air Force our ground radar controls for all weather talk-down for instrument landings are of an extremely high standard and a pilot follows the instructions of the controller with absolute confidence. Regrettably, I cannot say the same for the radar controllers at either Goose Bay or Namao and most crews felt that they would leave much to be desired in really bad weather conditions. This to some extent was borne out by our own experience with XD818 when coming in for final landing at Travis AFB.

We had landed precisely 5hr 10min after leaving Goose Bay and taxied into dispersal as instructed by Control. Although Namao was an RCAF station, it also accommodated a USAF B-52 bomber wing; therefore, there were a considerable number of aircraft based on the airfield. Since the ground visibility was good, it was possible to see the massive Rocky Mountain range in the distance shrouded by cloud; this was always an impressive warning that any gross navigational errors in instrument flying conditions could prove disastrous.

There was very little snow at Namao, and since the zone time was 3 hours behind Goose Bay where we departed at 10.00hrs, the local time here at Namao after 5hr 10min was 12.10; we would therefore be in time for lunch.

Having shutdown all engines, we climbed out of the aircraft to be met by our Bomber Command detachment commander, who quickly organised a fuel tanker. I briefed Bill Caple the Crew Chief that we would aim for a take-off at 14.30hrs local, which allowed ample time for an after flight meal and pre-flight planning for the route to Travis AFB, a further distance of 980nm, entailing a flight time of approximately 3½ hours. Thus we should be landing at 18.00hrs local, because Travis was on the same time zone as Namao.

With all arrival signals completed, we enjoyed a good meal and then turned our attention to pre-flight planning and a study of the meterological reports for the route to Travis AFB in California, which was only 10 to 12 miles from San Francisco. The weather in general was reasonable, with cloud cover for most of the route and the possibility of Travis being affected by warm front conditions at the time of our intended arrival.

We returned to XD818 and quickly worked our way through the usual lengthy crew checks, and by 14.30hrs the Valiant was moving down the active runway for take-off. We were smoothly airborne and had power adjusted for a steady cruise climb to 40,000ft at a speed of Mach 0.76.

The navigational side of the flight was uneventful and the co-pilot and myself took turns in flying, to ensure we were both fresh for the let down and approach should the weather be particularly difficult. Contact *en route* was maintained by VHF to various designated reporting points and one deviation to track was necessary in order to avoid the American Western Defence Area. Perhaps the most disappointing aspect of this leg was the fact that solid cloud cover prevented us being able to view the majestic beauty of flying over the famous Rocky Mountains, although we were well aware that we were flying over these great heights because of the turbulent conditions that prevailed during our transit over this area. Knowing the close proximity of Travis to the west side of this high ground, my concern was that we should position accurately for the let-down into Travis under positive radar control. Our destination for let-down into the Travis airfield approach control was Dixon beacon some 15 to 20nm out. Contact prior to Travis approach was with the Oakland flight information region, which cleared us to descend to 25,000ft and maintain this height on the regional QNH milibar setting, for a holding pattern over Dixon beacon.

With this we complied and, with Dixon beacon tuned to our radio compass, began a let-down from 40,000ft; at 25,000ft we were in solid cloud experiencing medium to severe icing. Levelling out at that altitude we reverted to our bad weather procedure let-down and the co-pilot flew the aircraft at 240kt to a prescribed American holding pattern as we had practised back at Wittering in the Link Trainer.

By this time we were in VHF contact with Travis Approach Control, which informed us that there would be a delay before we could be accepted into the radar let-down pattern. This was duly acknowledged and the holding pattern and height maintained; after 30min I was beginning to become impatient at this delay, for there was no major exercise in progress and Travis only handled USAF military aircraft. I therefore found it difficult to accept, and when we had been waiting 45min, suggested to control that it cleared us with the pattern otherwise my fuel state would be below that required for a mandatory diversion.

After a further delay, approach control confirmed it had identified us on its radar screen and gave instructions to commence descent on a precise heading. I was particularly concerned to know the control had positive identification because this would be a fully blind instrument let-down to final approach, as cloud base over Travis was 700ft in rain. We could not afford to lose radar contact because there were extremely high hills just to one side of the airfield.

With pre-descent checks complete we let down at 240kt with air brakes out, on the course given by the controller; during this descent there were long periods of silence from the controller giving me the impression that either he was losing our radar blip on his screen due to clutter caused by rain, or the control ground procedure was slack or casual. Several times it was necessary to request confirmation that the present compass heading was to be maintained. We levelled at 1,500ft on the airfield millibar pressure setting, still in solid cloud, and the controller then instructed us to turn to port on to a course which was the base leg for final approach. By this stage all pre-landing checks had been completed, undercarriage down and 20° flaps selected, with airspeed 150kt.

After what seemed like an eternity, control gave a turn on to the runway heading and handed us over to the Ground Control Approach radar talk-down. Identification completed, he stated we were now at 12 miles from touch down, coming on to the glide path and should commence our descent. This we did with 40° flap selected, and here again the talk down was not constant, there being long breaks in transmisson. At approximately seven miles I was astounded to hear the controller say he had lost contact with us on his radar screen; as we were still in solid cloud at 1,200ft, this was not very reassuring.

I immediately instructed Bob Beeson to maintain the standard descent on the present heading; if radar contact had not been regained by 400ft, we would initiate an overshoot. As we passed 600ft the controller came back saying he had us again on the screen and that we were well lined up and on the glide path; I briefly acknowledged and concentrated on the approach. By 500ft we came out

The crew of XD818. From left to right: Wg Cdr KG Hubbard, Flg Off Bob Beeson, Flt Lt Ted Laraway, Flg Off Eric Hood, Flt Lt Alan Washbrook and Chief Tech Bill Caple.

Operation Grapple – No. 49 Squadron, RAF

The Pacific programme of British thermonuclear tests began in 1957, following earlier atomic trials in Australia at Monte Bello and Maralinga.The tri-Service/civilian Task Force for Operation Grapple was commanded initially by AVM W. E. Oulton and latterly by AVM J. Grandy (later MRAF Sir John Grandy). Christmas Island, a coral atoll in the southwest Pacific, was selected as the base for the 'Grapple' series of tests.

No. 49 Squadron, based at RAF Wittering, was the Valiant unit chosen to participate in the trials, the squadron having been previously involved in the atomic weapon tests at Maralinga (Operation Buffalo) in 1956. The first bomb of the 'Grapple' series was dropped off Malden Island, some 400 miles south of Christmas Island, on 15 May 1957, from Valiant XD818 captained by Wg Cdr K.G. Hubbard, Officer Commanding No. 49 Squadron. Testing continued at Christmas Island until November 1958 ('Grapple X', 'Y' and 'Z'), during which time the squadron dropped a total of seven thermonuclear devices.

of cloud and I could see the runway lights ahead; I took over the control from Bob Beeson, called for full flap and settled the aircraft for the final approach and landing.

After clearing the active runway, we completed our after-landing checks, and as we slowly taxied to our dispersal, which was on the far side of the airfield, I turned to Bob Beeson and said 'If we had controllers of that calibre in the RAF they would be bloody well sacked'.

It had been a long day involving a total of 8.35 hours flying and another 4 hours of pre- and after-flight duty. I think we were all pleased to know that tomorrow was to be a rest day and that this evening we could enjoy a good meal and a bottle of wine. My initial impression of Travis AFB, however, left something to be desired.

When we climbed out, we were met by the Bomber Command Detachment Commander who was a Squadron Leader. I told him my opinion of the quality of the American GCA controllers but of course I realised there was nothing he could do about it. We were guests on the American base and therefore good manners prevented me from complaining. He handed me a signal from the Task Force Commander on Christmas Island, which requested me to pay my respects to the USAF Commanding General of the B-52 wing based at Travis, who was a Gen Arnold, and offer him a conducted tour of the Valiant. I asked the Detachment Commander to acknowledge and concur on my behalf, and made a mental note to contact the General next morning.

Having tidied up and made arrangements for refuelling, the Detachment Commander drove us all to the American single officer accommodation block, where we were all allocated rooms. I duly made sure that accommodation was arranged for Bill Caple the Crew Chief, and that he would be looked after in the American all ranks club, before arranging with Alan Washbrook, Ted Laraway and Eric Hood to meet them in the bar of the Officers' Club before dinner.

A quick shower restored my vitality and, since the time was now 19.30hrs, I lost no time in making my way to the Officers' Club. The American Air Force does not have Officers' Messes, but what is termed an Officers' Club which can be used by officers, their wives and children; thus the atmosphere is rather like a civilian night club rather than a mess, and often noisy.

I made my way to the bar which was extremely large and comfortably furnished, but the dim and subdued lighting made it difficult to pick out people until one's eyes became accustomed to the gloom. However, I spotted my crew by one side of the bar and joined them to find that Alan Washbrook had a well iced gin and tonic waiting for me.

The Americans are of course very friendly and hospitable people and it was not long before we were greeted by a USAF Major, who said 'Say, are you the guys who brought in that white bomber?' -I said 'Yes, please let us introduce ourselves'. Introductions complete, he bought us a drink and then enthused about the shape of the Valiant, for I must admit it does look a super aircraft compared to the rather ungainly B-52.

Our conversation was interrupted by a USAF Captain with an epaulette, which indicated he was in a personal appointment. He enquired if I was Wg Cdr Hubbard and introduced himself as the ADC to Gen Arnold, who sent his compliments and has asked if I would care to have coffee in his office the following morning. I accepted with pleasure.

The ADC left and I felt it was time we moved into the restaurant for dinner, for by this time we were more than ready to eat. The choices available were considerable – a massive display of various types of salad with fish or cold meat, or a hot meal. I opted for lobster and helped myself liberally to salad with french fried potatoes – the procedure was that one helped oneself and paid cash before leaving the restaurant. We selected a table, ordered two bottles of wine and settled down to a delightful dinner. It really felt good to be in California, and if time permitted the next day, I wanted to get in to see San Francisco where the tiny trams ran up and down the steep slopes within the city, and to see the famous fish harbour area.

After a very pleasant evening, I retired to bed just before midnight, feeling that it had been a tiring but satisfactory day. The following morning after breakfast I asked the Detachment Commander to provide transport so that we could get out to XD818, and also informed him that I needed to be driven to the USAF Bomber Wing base, in order to call on Gen Arnold. I arranged for my crew to remain at XD818 and departed to see the General. On arrival at the Wing HQ, the General's ADC was waiting and conducted me to the General's office. Gen Arnold rose from his desk as I came in, and I saluted; after shaking hands he invited me to sit down and we quickly and easily launched into a dialogue. He showed great interest in the Valiant as well as the Vulcan and Victor which were then coming into service. Since he had been with Strategic Air Command for a number of years he knew my own Commander-in-Chief well.

After coffee, he sent for his car and we drove out to XD818 where I introduced my crew and then showed him around the aircraft. Having completed his tour the General asked if we would care to see over a B-52; this of course was accepted without hesitation and we were duly whisked away to where the B-52s were parked. The General gave us a personal tour and I was much impressed with the flight deck layout at all crew positions; there was plenty of room to move around and crew comfort had not been overlooked.

The General drove us all back to XD818 where he had organised a photographer, and photographs were taken next to the aircraft. By that afternoon, copies were available and sent over to my room. Gen Arnold was a very charming and extremely knowledgeable man, with a tremendous personality, who I understand was a very popular and respected Commander. He was also a most considerate man, for realising this was our first visit to California, he arranged for a car to take us into San Francisco that afternoon, to enable us to sample the charm and unusual character of the city. Also of course, on the drive in, we were able to see the famous 'Golden Gate', although time did not permit a crossing over this famous bridge. Neither were we able to spend time in the well-known harbour fish bar area; perhaps we could fit this in on some other occasion.

On return from our pleasant trip into San Francisco, I quickly penned a note of thanks to Gen Arnold and said we looked forward to seeing him again on our return journey some five months hence. The next important duty was to visit the Meteorological office and make arrangements for a full Met briefing on weather and winds for our next stage to Honolulu, which was the longest leg – 2,130nm. For this leg to Honolulu we could only accept a headwind component not in excess of 30kt if we were to retain sufficient fuel for any unplanned diversion. (This limitation did not apply on later trips once the underwing fuel tanks were available.) The decision point to cater for this factor was at approximately 1,200nm, on track, which corresponded with the position of ocean weather ship 'November'.

That night we gathered in the Officers' Club for a quiet evening meal and a relatively early night in preparation for the next day's flight. Our scheduled time of take off was 10.00hrs local, so we had arranged for all meteorological route information to be available by 08.00hrs, which would give us ample time to have breakfast in the American transit buffet before completing the full pre-flight planning.

On arrival at the Met Office a quick glance at the upper air chart told us there was no problem of an unacceptable head wind component and the general synoptic situation showed a fairly heavy build-up of cloud roughly half way across, and we were warned of clear air turbulence at 40,000ft in this area. The weather in the Honolulu area looked good, and for the first time we should be experiencing some really warm weather, necessitating the change from blue to khaki drill. We were all looking forward very much to arriving at Honolulu, for the route programme allowed us a full day's rest before proceeding on the final stage of our 9,000nm miles journey to Christmas Island. I think we all had a very glamorous picture in mind of Honolulu and particularly the much publicised Waikiki beach, and we were soon to find out if our anticipated picture of this glamorous island was fact or fiction!

With all pre-flight procedures complete, the Travis Detachment Commander drove us out to Valiant XD818 where the ever reliable Crew Chief, Bill Caple, had everything under control. The Form 700 (RAF Technical Log of the Aircraft) was presented to me by Bill, and I signed it before getting down to the aircraft external checks with Bob Beeson. These complete, we climbed aboard, strapped ourselves in and quickly worked through the pre-start and start up drills. Control cleared us to taxi to the active runway and also confirmed we were cleared for a climb out after take-off, on the direct track for Honolulu. For this we were grateful, as having to proceed by a beacon holding and reporting pattern would have meant a great waste of precious fuel.

Take-off was uneventful, but it was surprising how many USAF personnel had turned out to watch this majestic white aircraft roar down the runway and rotate into an impressive rate of climb, so different from the B-52 which lumbered into the air, its initial rate of climb being very unimpressive.

Naturally, as I realised everybody was watching to compare the performance of the Valiant to that of the B-52, I made sure our initial climb was maintained at full power to produce an impressive sight.

Having completed the public relations exercise, we settled back into a cruise climb on track. This allowed us to see on our starboard side the magnificent Golden Gate suspension bridge. As this disappeared from view, every crew member concentrated on his own tasks and we were soon levelling at 40,000ft at a cruising speed of Mach 0.76 with the autopilot engaged. Our planned flight time for this leg was 6 hours; thus our estimated time of arrival would be 16.00hrs on Travis time but, as Honolulu time zone was 3 hours behind Travis, we should be arriving at 13.00hrs local time.

The flight progressed smoothly with the navigator using the powerful broadcasters in California for bearings during the first few hundred miles of the flight, then ultimately picking up the radar beacon from weather ship 'November' as we neared the half-way mark; and with no change in head wind component we were committed to the second stage of the flight. As we approached the half-way mark, we could see a large build-up of heavy cumulus cloud ahead, towering to great heights as can always be expected in the region with inter tropical fronts (or convergence zones, as they are commonly called) where two major air masses converge at vastly different temperatures and pressures, resulting in a violent build-up of heavy cumulus and cumulonimbus cloud.

By this time we were being subjected to fairly heavy clear-air turbulence and although the autopilot was coping well, I disengaged the system and flew the aircraft manually until we emerged from this unstable area. By this time it was apparent that at 40,000ft we should be just above the heavy cloud tops ahead and after about 1 hour we had flown over this large formation and the weather ahead was clear. Indeed, the visibility was excellent for the remainder of the flight and at approximately 600nm from Honolulu, the navigator reported he was able to obtain bearings from the powerful Honolulu Broadcaster, which enabled him to utilise this as a tracking indication until we came within range of the radio beacons on the Hawaiian islands.

The last compulsory reporting point was at North Hilo and here we commenced our descent to 25,000ft in order to comply with the requirement to be overhead Honolulu at this height.

As the Hawaiian islands came into view at a range of about 40 miles, they presented a picturesque setting, rather like a vision progressively emerging from the sea. Then as we came closer it was possible to see the beautifully green islands with majestic heights, and as overhead Honolulu was reached it was possible to see Pearl Harbor with the many American warships at anchor, and somehow my mind flashed back to those dark days in World War 2 when the American Fleet was surprised by the Japanese. The main island looked very attractive but by this time we were talking to Honolulu Approach Control, having confirmed our position as overhead at 25,000ft.

Since the weather was good, we were cleared for a visual descent on the standard pattern and control confirmed it had us identified on radar. Landing instructions were passed and we settled into our descent at 240kt, air brakes out, until levelling at 1,500ft on the airfield millibar setting. Approach control directed us on to the downwind leg of the runway and then on to the final approach heading, where we were handed to GCA.

With undercarriage down, 40° flap, we settled to a steady approach, selecting full flap at 400ft for a final landing. We touched down at precisely 13.00hrs local time, having completed the flight in exactly 6 hours.

We taxied in under instruction from control, for this too was a busy USAF airfield, with a considerable number of B-52s as well as their large transport and inflight refuelling tankers parked around the place. There were also a considerable number of fighter aircraft on the airfield.

On arrival at our dispersal, we were again greeted by the RAF Detachment Commander, who I should imagine was kept very busy with all the previous Canberra and RAF Shackletons that had phased through Honolulu *en route* to Christmas Island. Having completed all shut down engine drills, we descended from the aircraft to breathe the warm soft air of Honolulu, with a pleasant anticipation of a full day's relaxation in this much vaunted paradise island.

Whilst completing our post-flight arrival procedure, the Detachment Commander briefed us on the arrangements made for our stay. We would again be accommodated in the Single Officers' Quarters and take our meals in the Officers' Club. Having checked that similar arrangements had been made for the Crew Chief, we were transported to our quarters. Once on the ground in these climates the aircraft cockpit becomes very warm and you emerge from your aircraft in a flying suit soaked in perspiration. This was my condition when we climbed out of XD818, so first priority was a shower and a change into khaki drill, slacks and bush jacket.

Our accommodation was pleasant enough, but a reasonable walk from the Officers' Club. That afternoon we walked to the American PX, which is rather like a sophisticated NAAFI shop where American service personnel can purchase all manner of items at specially reduced prices. The Americans were kind enough to extend this privilege to the RAF and we all took advantage of this to purchase suitable lightweight civilian type shorts and Hawaiian type shirts which appeared to be the order of the day as off-duty dress. Air Cdre Ginger Weir had told me in a letter before departure from the UK to fit ourselves out at Honolulu; this type of attire was the standard dress in the evening at Christmas Island. We therefore accepted his advice and for a reasonable price set ourselves up with the approved local form of dress, although initially I felt this was taking informality too far; however, even I soon became accustomed and, much to the amusement of my crew, duly dressed accordingly that evening. Somehow I got the impression they considered me a little straight-laced regarding dress!

Having surveyed all the attractive goodies in the PX and made mental notes about presents to take home on our return in five months, it was time to walk back to our accommodation and change into lightweight slacks and our newly acquired Aloha shirts before going to the Officers' Club for pre-dinner drinks.

The Club was located near to the water's edge, and had a tropical Hawaiian atmosphere; even a small Hawaiian band was playing, with the Hawaiian men and girls all in the traditional grass skirts. The main bar was partly in the open and again, as is the custom with American clubs, the illumination very subdued.

Personally, I felt extremely relaxed as we sat at the bar drinking well-iced gin and tonics, and having seen the restaurant menu and the spread of really attractive salads, I was very much looking forward to a Lobster Thermidor to a background of Hawaiian music. When we did move into the restaurant and settle down at our table, everybody ordered to their choice; I think Alan Washbrook and Ted Laraway also ordered Lobster Thermidor like me. Perhaps the most amusing incident was that Eric Hood, our Nav Plotter had set his heart on roast duckling. At last the waiter brought our meals and the lobsters looked good; however, the plate presented to Eric Hood did not resemble roast duckling as we know it; the look on his face had to be seen to be believed for it turned out to be diced chunks of duck, obviously from a tin. He was so disappointed that I suggested he might wish to order something different, but no, he was determined to have duck even if in his opinion it left much to be desired – he never again ordered duck at Honolulu!

That evening after dinner we sat back in the soft warm tropical air to enjoy the cabaret put on by the local Hawaiian band, which apparently performed at the Officers' Club most evenings, with entertainment including local Hawaiian songs and dances, all of which was very pleasant and relaxing.

The following day saw us first of all out to Valiant XD818 where Bill Caple was busy with the refuelling team, and we busied ourselves cleaning up the aircraft ready for the next day's flight to Christmas Island. Although keen to get there, I was nevertheless extremely grateful that the Air Staff planners at HQBC had planned into our route a rest day at Honolulu, for the next five months on Christmas Island were to prove to be extremely tiring and at times exceptionally uncomfortable.

Once we had completed our tasks at the aircraft, I suggested to the crew that we might perhaps take a taxi into Honolulu to have a look round and certainly see the famous Waikiki beach and, as the American Officers' Rest Club was situated by the beach and we had been made honorary members, we would have lunch there. This agreed, we were soon *en route* to see the pleasures of this much publicised holiday area. Having arrived at the Officers' Club we dismissed the taxi and found our way on to the Waikiki beach.

The actual beach itself was not large and the sand a rather dirty brown; it was skirted by luxury hotels frequented by millionaires and retired American school teachers who had saved all their lives for this holiday of a lifetime. We wandered along the beach area surveying the shapes and sizes either enjoying the sun or sitting sedately under sun shade umbrellas. I recall saying as we strolled along the water's edge, 'Well, take a good look for I do not suppose any of us would have been able to afford to come here for a holiday, but from what I see it's highly overrated and certainly there is no sign of anything to set the adrenalin flowing'! However, we all decided to have a swim before going back to the Officers' Club for a shower and change back into slacks and shirt.

After a pleasant salad lunch (which was within our limited financial means), we decided to have a look round the town before returning to the airfield. Really there was little to see other than various types of bars and eating houses, and glancing at the menus displayed it was obvious that to eat out would be extremely expensive and well beyond our overseas allowances. I felt sure that the other side of the island, which was not so highly developed to satisfy the tourist trade, would be much more attractive and made a mental note to explore this side if ever an opportunity occurred to spend a few days leave at Honolulu.

That evening we again enjoyed a delightful meal at the Officers' Club, this time Eric Hook making no mistake about ordering roast duck. We all returned to our quarters by 22.00hrs having arranged transport to collect us at 08.00hrs the following morning, after breakfast at the Officers Club.

CHAPTER SIX

Christmas Island

The morning of 12 March dawned in the usual balmy tropical manner, with only wispy specks of cloud in the sky and the sun shimmering on the Pacific Ocean. By the time we had taken breakfast and completed pre-flight planning and meteorological briefing for the 1,160nm leg from Honolulu to Christmas Island, the temperature was rising fast, and even in our tropical lightweight flying overalls we were all hot and sticky on arrival at XD818. Bill Caple had everything in hand and the Technical Log Form 700 was duly signed.

The two navigators and AEO climbed into the aircraft whilst Bob Beeson and I carried out the external checks; with these completed we quickly got into XD818 and strapped ourselves into the ejection seats for the final leg of our 9,000nm flight to Christmas Island. With all engines running, the Crew Chief aboard and crew checks complete, we commenced our taxi to take-off position under the direction of the Controller. The planned flight time for this leg was 3hr 5min; as zone time on Christmas Island was 1 hour ahead of Honolulu and we were taking off at 10.00hrs local, the Christmas Island local arrival time would be 14.05hrs.

Once again there was considerable interest shown by USAF personnel in the Valiant as we taxied out for take-off, and it made one feel extremely proud to be at the controls of this superb aircraft. At the hold point for the active runway, we worked through all the pre-take-off drills and then declared ourselves ready for take-off.

Lined up on the active runway, we lost no time in obtaining take-off clearance for a direct climb on track. XD818 moved forward under the power of her four Rolls-Royce Avon engines, each rated at 10,000lb thrust, making an impressive noise, the initial climb after rotation from the runway being equally impressive. Naturally, as the Royal Air Force image was being demonstrated to an appreciative audience, I made sure the initial climb was maintained at maximum power until we turned on to our course for Christmas Island.

Navigation on this leg would not be difficult, initially working the Honolulu broadcaster for the first 600nm, enabling the navigator to monitor his Ground Position Indicator. Thereafter, we should be able to pick up the radio beacon located on Christmas Island. Once at 40,000ft we settled into a steady cruise pattern, but as there was no problem regarding fuel economy for this leg, we cruised at max cruising speed of Mach 0.82.

Some 300nm from Honolulu we could see a colossal cloud formation ahead which was obviously the inter-tropical front mentioned at met briefing, and it looked as if we should have to climb above 40,000ft to avoid the anvil shaped tops of the cumulonimbus cloud. To fly through this would entail severe turbulence; therefore we climbed to 46,000ft which kept us just above the tops of these clouds.

At a range of 250nm from Christmas Island this weather pattern was well behind us and the visibility ahead excellent, with patches of fair weather cumulus cloud, which did not restrict visibility. The navigator reported that at a range of 200nm he was picking up the radio beacon on Christmas Island and at 50nm we obtained our first sight of the island, by which time we were in contact with approach control. At this stage a maximum rate let down was commenced in order to approach Christmas Island at 1,500ft for a visual circuit and landing.

As we approached the island at this altitude, it was possible to see the Naval and Fleet Auxiliary supply ships in the harbour area, with the light fleet carrier HMS *Warrior* anchored offshore. I called control and said we would fly around the island for familiarisation with the area before joining the circuit for landing. He requested we give the airfield area a low fly over, to which I readily agreed. Indeed, I had dropped to 500ft above the airfield for the fly around the port area and the far side of the island.

We could see a very large tented camp area by the port, plus a few prefabricated type buildings; the island seemed to be dominated by palm trees and desert-type scrub. There was an inland lake and it was possible to see the coral reef just offshore. The actual airfield area provided one very good runway of tarmac finish approximately 3,000yd long, running parallel to the shore on an east/west direction. There was also an extensive concrete dispersal area on which could be seen the Coastal Command Shackleton aircraft, the Canberras of 76 and 100 Squadrons, also a Dakota and a Hastings aircraft. To one side of the airfield was a massive area of tents, obviously the domestic site.

Having surveyed the area, I called my crew on the intercom and said, 'Well, now we have seen it all, that's where we shall be for the next five months; so stand by, I am going to give them a really low fly over before coming in to land.' We made a high speed low run across the dispersal area at about 50ft pulling up for one further run at low level in the opposite direction, then returning to 1,000ft and positioning on the downwind leg of the runway. We were cleared for finals and a visual landing. With XD818 trimmed out, we turned onto finals at 600ft and settled into a steady approach. This new runway produced by the Royal Engineers looked good, and as we crossed the boundary and levelled out with power off, the main wheels gently touched the runway, the surface appearing very smooth; the nose wheel lowered and as speed dropped off we came to a standstill having used only just over half the runway.

Control cleared us to backtrack with instructions to follow the taxi track to the concrete dispersal; it also welcomed us to Christmas Island. We duly followed the instructions, and as we turned on to the concrete dispersal, the Controller said that the 49 Squadron parking area was by the tents we could see as we taxied in.

By this time I suddenly became aware of the fact that there was nobody in sight anywhere other than Flt Sgt Bill Asprey, my Senior NCO in charge of ground crew, complete with marshalling bats to position us on the dispersal. This I found rather strange, for at least I expected to see all of our ground crew plus Sgt W. Cressey to welcome us, and I felt far from pleased, making a mental note to sort this out once I got on the ground. As we slowly moved into position, I was even more astonished, for there was not a soul in sight. It was rather like coming to a deserted airfield with aircraft but no men.

I turned to Bob Beeson, my co-pilot: The bloody lot must have gone round the bend already; I'll soon sort this out when we get out of the aircraft.' We quickly shut down engines and climbed out. As I came down the steps a most unusual sight met my eyes; there was a tractor pulling a palm leaf-decorated bomb trolley, the tractor being driven by what appeared to be one of the local Gilbertese in straw skirt, with four others on the trolley holding large palm branches. They also had five chairs on the trolley.

As I stepped on to the concrete ready to demand from Flt Sgt Asprey what the hell was going on, the leader of these apparent Gilbertese came forward to greet and welcome me and offered a half coconut filled with some liquid concoction. By this time the crew had followed me from the aircraft and I politely refused, and turned to Flt Sgt Asprey demanding to know where the ground crew were. He saluted and smiling said he was sent direct to handle the marshalling by Air Cdre Weir.

I was hot and sticky but by this time thought we should humour things, for we were being persuaded to take seats on the bomb trolley, which we did and accepted the refreshment. With the entire crew on the trolley we moved towards a hut marked Operations Centre. By this time my sense of humour had returned, for I guessed that Ginger Weir was behind this in some way. As we neared the Operations Hut, a whistle blew and airmen appeared from all directions out of the palm trees, cheering. Then out of the Operations Hut came Air Cdre Ginger Weir, the Air Task Force Commander, with Gp Capt Freddie Milligan.

We were convulsed with laughter, for only Ginger could have gone to so much trouble to provide such a unique welcome. The Gilbertese turned out to be my own airmen, once the brown shoe polish was washed off. We descended from the trolley and went forward to salute the Air Commodore who had enjoyed the joke tremendously, particularly as he had watched my annoyance when I got out of my aircraft.

The other Squadron Commanders came forward to greet us and I could see Sgt Cressey with all of our ground crew who had obviously enjoyed the entire

Top: The tented accommodation of the Christmas Island
main camp.

Centre: Interior comforts.

Bottom: New quarters for Wg
Cdr Hubbard. *(Author)*

procedure. Knowing the type of things I expect, they must have been in stitches to see my face from a distance and probably guessed what I was saying!

With the arrival procedure complete and photographed, we returned to XD818 to unload the bomb bay panniers; by this time my ground crew were back at the aircraft. I asked them if all was well with their accommodation and then walked over to my office tent with Sgt Cressey, who gave me a briefing on how their journey out had gone. I congratulated him on the layout of the Squadron Office and crew room tent arrangements, having seen what we had to work with.

After sorting out a few domestic matters with Sgt Cressey, I walked over to XD818 where Bill Caple was busy with the ground crew removing the bomb bay panniers and the remainder of the airmen were already swarming over it cleaning the wing and fuselage area. I decided it was time for myself and my crew to take the Land Rover provided for my use, and drive to the domestic site and locate our own accommodation.

On the drive to the Officers' Mess tented area, a distance of about three miles, we found it pleasant through palm trees on either side of the access road (again cut by the Royal Engineers), for although it was very hot and humid, a slight breeze made things tolerable. We also had our first sight of the local land crabs which would appear in their hundreds during the periods of torrential rain. On arrival at the domestic site, we found the large marquee mess tent located by the shore and the 180lb accommodation tents neatly pitched adjacent to the Mess. We quickly found the two tents allocated for Alan Washbrook, Bob Beeson, Ted Laraway and Eric Hood; they were to be two to a tent, so they quicky paired off.

My own tent was pitched by the shore and furnished with a bed, table, chair and collapsible wash basin. With the humidity, I could foresee problems regarding clothes; however, we did not expect UK standards, and as every item had been transported over 9,000nm we could not expect to have anything but the bare essentials. This was amply demonstrated when I walked over to the ablution to inspect the showers and toilets, which reminded me of the primitive facilities we endured in Africa and Italy during the war. The toilets were merely wooden seat frames over buckets, each one screened at the back and sides by 5ft high canvas.

Having confirmed the fact that we were in for five months of basic living, I returned to my tent to sort out personal belongings; then, after sampling the showers, changed into slacks and Aloha shirt (which apparently was to be standard evening wear), and presented myself to the Task Force Commander's Mess where Air Cdre Ginger Weir had invited me for pre-dinner drinks.

The Officers' Mess lines were in fact divided into two separate messes; one for officers of the rank of Wing Commander and below, which, allowing for the scientists, Army Officers and RAF, numbered about 60. The Naval officers were accommodated in the port area mess or the lucky ones were aboard various ships. The second Officers' Mess was for Group Captains or equivalent rank and above, who numbered about 10, and this was termed the Task Force Commander's Mess.

Ginger Weir had asked me to meet him at his tent for a drink and since in that area the accommodation tents were few in number, it did not take me long to locate him. His tent was comfortably furnished and he produced a gin and tonic, even with ice. We chatted about the trip out and then I asked him about bombing facilities available on the island. I was delighted to learn that a bombing range had been sited at the southeast tip of Christmas Island for calibration and overshoot practice bombing. There was also a bombing range on Malden Island, where the live weapon was to be dropped. We should be able to utilise the Malden Island range for overshoot bombing in conjunction with the Scientific team based in the control ship HMS *Narvik*, which would be anchored off the island. In each case this target was triangular with 50yd sides and painted day-glow red.

After talking for about 20min we moved over to the Mess, which was a prefabricated timber building with a verandah which looked out on to the sea and coral reef. In the Mess was AVM Wilf Oulton, the Task Force Commander, Bill Cook the Scientific Director, Gp Capt Freddie Milligan, Air Cdre Dennis Wilson, the Principal Medical Officer, and Gp Capt John Mason (since deceased) whom I had not seen since my days in the Air Ministry. Also present was Brig Woolley, the Army Commander, and Capt Guy Weston, senior RN officer on the island. It was a distinguished gathering. After drinks I was pressed to stay for dinner and accepted with alacrity.

During the course of the evening I formed a very positive impression of Bill Cook the Scientific Director, at this our first meeting, and it was an opinion that never varied during the entire period we served on Christmas Island. His responsibilities in conjunction with the Task Force Commander would be heavy; and it was quite obvious during our conversation that here was a scientist with a charming personality, a sharp sense of humour and a ready wit.

In all subsequent meetings with Bill Cook, I found him to be relaxed no matter what the pressures were, invariably to be found smoking his favourite pipe and calmly capable of making a decision on any scientific aspect, once all the facts were made known to him. With such qualities it is not surprising that he was to work in complete harmony with both the Task Force Commander and Air Cdre Ginger Weir. This excellent team spirit was to spread throughout the entire 'Grapple' force.

It was arranged that I should come over to Task Force Headquarters the following day in order to discuss in some detail the training programme required for my crews and to be given details of the scientific requirement for the calibration drops of inert and HE weapons prior to the live round.

After a pleasant evening, I returned to my tent and turned in. On the following day, the first task after breakfast was to drive to the airfield with my crew to ensure that work was on hand with modifications to be fitted to XD818 before we could continue with our bombing training. Then, in company with

Top: Weapon telemetering equipment during assembly on Christmas Island.

Centre: The scientific team's control bunker.

Bottom: Painting the Malden Island target indicator.

Alan Washbrook, Ted Laraway and Eric Hood, I drove to Task Force Headquarters, enjoying the unusual experience of driving on rough roads lined with palm trees and dodging the land crabs that were determined to cross the road at all costs.

Once at Task Force HQ we got down to a detailed discussion of our own initial training requirements with Air Cdre Weir and Wg Cdr Butch Surtees, then on to details of the scientific work-up programme required with each weapon, followed by a general brief on the overall organisation of those forces to be deployed during a live drop. I was told that it was essential to have my squadron bombing training programme complete by 5 April, and thereafter flying was to be concentrated on the operational phase with scientific drops at Malden. The first live drop, dependent upon weather, was scheduled for about the middle of May; therefore I should be prepared for the fast Valiant courier flights (carrying the radioactive parts of the weapon) to be planned for the end of April.

The general briefing and discussions occupied most of the morning; by the time it was complete there was much to occupy my mind, for I now knew that all practice bombing training for my crews must be completed by 5 April. Thereafter, all flying was to be devoted to the requirements of the scientists in what was to be termed the operational phase, and every flight would be in the Malden area rehearsing the entire operational procedures. What did concern me was the warning that due to political implications we could find the present test series, planned for four live drops, reduced. However, there was no confirmation of this at the moment.

Should there be a curtailment of the present programme, this would mean that my own aircrews would be denied this invaluable experience of dropping a live nuclear weapon. I therefore made a mental note to study carefully the possibility of putting more than one Valiant in the air for every dress rehearsal and live drop and to submit my proposals to the Task Force Commander for approval.

That afternoon I held a meeting with Flt Sgt Asprey and my Technical Officer, Flg Off W. Budden, in order to find out if all ground equipment was adequate and to ensure they both understood the work load involved with all Valiants as they arrived, regarding the technical, navigational equipment and radio modifications which were necessary. Having cleared these matters, I then put them in the picture as to the anticipated training hours we should need to fly during the training phase up to 5 April, my plan being to ensure that all four Valiant operational crews – my own and those of Sqn Ldrs Dave Roberts, Arthur Steele and Barney Millett – had achieved the required consistency of accuracy in the overshoot (time delay) bombing technique for 45,000ft by this time. Thereafter, up to the live drop date, flying would be restricted to necessary air tests and scientific procedural drops in the target area. Finally, I highlighted the importance of having all four aircraft – XD818, XD822, XD823 and XD824 – fully serviceable on the day of the live operational drop.

With this complete, I called my own crew together to discuss in some detail the means of ensuring that each of the four drop crews obtained valuable operational airborne experience in the event of the number of live drops being reduced. We eventually came to the conclusion that if a second Valiant was flown for both the dress rehearsal and live drop, it would need to take off shortly after the dropping aircraft, making a rendezvous at a selected point on the bomb line 1½nm behind the dropping aircraft and 2,000ft below. Then, on the final bombing run, the second aircraft would commence its escape manoeuvre some 11 seconds before the dropping aircraft gave its 'Bomb gone' signal, to eliminate any chance of collision should either aircraft experience any difficulties in the post release escape manoeuvre. The second aircraft in the manoeuvre would then turn through a set number of degrees to ensure that at the time of bomb burst its tail was pointing to this point. Such a flight profile would not in any way conflict with the operational pattern of the dropping aircraft and would provide valuable operational crew training. Perhaps we could term this Valiant the 'Grandstand Aircraft'.

We agreed that this was a sound proposal, so that afternoon, I drafted it out in a memo to the Air Task Force Commander, and by the following day it had been approved; thus the provision of a grandstand aircraft became a reality.

By 15 March, some three days after our arrival, our second Valiant, XD822, captained by Sqn Ldr Dave Roberts, was expected to arrive. Signals coming through indicated it was at Honolulu and a check with Joint Operations Centre at Task Force HQ confirmed that he was estimating arrival at Christmas Island by 14.30hrs local time.

Valiant XD818 had now completed its first phase of modifications and I was keen to fly a practice bombing sortie that morning to assess the Christmas Island practice bombing range, and also to obtain our first use of the time delay system in the T4 (modified Mk 14A) bombsight and to see how accurate the quadrant sighting crews were in plotting the bomb bursts on the 1½nm overshoot technique.

Having checked that the range was manned, Valiant XD818 was bombed up and we planned a take-off for 10.00hrs, which would mean I should be back on the ground in ample time to welcome Valiant XD822.

Perhaps this is where it might be useful to explain in some detail the overshoot bombing technique, devised purely to meet a scientific requirement, and which was not in any way an operational procedure being used by crews in the V Force.

In order to ensure that there should be limited radioactive fallout from the live nuclear weapons being tested, they were to be set to detonate at 8,000ft above mean sea level when dropped from the Valiant at 45,000ft. Furthermore, for absolute safety, it was required to aim the weapon so that the point of detonation was 1½nm from the land aiming point on the southeast tip of Malden Island, on a pre-set geographical bomb line.

Thus on the island there was a triangular aiming point with 50ft sides painted in day-glow red. The geographical bombing line on which telemetering equipment was installed ran on a line parallel to the coast. In the bomb release mechanism in the Valiant, a time delay system had been fitted, which could be adjusted by the bomb aimer. On the run down the bomb line, the exact groundspeed of the dropping aircraft was calculated by the navigator; thus, in order to ensure a 1½nm delay, the appropriate time equivalent to this distance at the ground speed was set on the time delay clock in seconds. The point in space at which the weapon would be at 8,000ft after release was therefore known, and it was on this point that all ground cameras and other telemetering equipment would be focused. The important factor was that the turn on to the bomb line was made accurately from a set intercept point. Thereafter it was necessary for the bomb aimer, having assessed drift on the bomb line, to pass heading corrections to the captain, so that the ultimate heading of the aircraft would enable a perfect aiming point to be achieved by the bomb aimer with the graticule on his Mk T4 bombsight. At this point, although the bomb aimer would have pressed his release button as graticule coincidence was achieved, with the time delay in seconds fed in to the bombsight the weapon would not actually leave the aircraft until the time delay had elapsed. From that point the escape manoeuvre would be initiated.

The crucial factors for accuracy on this bomb run were that the height of the aircraft must be constant, the indicated airspeed maintained and a precise heading held. From the point where the bomb aimer pressed his release button, it was all important that during those 10 or 11 seconds of time delay, the aircraft heading, height and indicated airspeed did not vary in any way, otherwise large errors were immediately fed into the weapon burst point.

This then was the procedure to be practised on the bombing range at Christmas Island and, with 10 bombs on board, Valiant XD818 became airborne on 15 March at 10.00hrs local as planned. We climbed to 45,000ft and, having made contact by radio with the bombing range, checking that all was clear for practice bombing to start, we made our initial turn on to the bomb line.

A steady approach was quickly established with the navigator plotter confirming at an early stage of the run the groundspeed for the time delay mechanism. With one or two minor corrections from the bomb aimer, concluding with the words 'Steady, steady now', we had reached graticule coincidence at the aiming point and the time delay was now in operation. At this point my airspeed was Mach 0.76, height on the sensitive altimeter 45,000ft and aircraft heading 215°T. This must now be held without variation until the bomb aimer gave 'Bomb gone'. At this point we commenced the practice escape manoeuvre by rolling the aircraft to port into a 60° bank turn at the same time calling for full throttle by the co-pilot, and then maintaining the indicated airspeed of Mach 0.76 with a constant altitude of 45,000ft, and, by steady backward pressure on the control column, keeping the 'G' reading on the sensitive accelerometer at 1.7G, finally rolling out having turned through 135°.

On the ground, the crews in the two plotting quadrants would have plotted the splash of the 100lb practice bomb, and by the time we had flown into position for a second bombing run, the bombing error had been passed over the radio.

After 10 bombing runs, we cleared with the bombing range and commenced our let down from the Christmas Island radio beacon into the airfield circuit for a final landing. We had been airborne for 2hr 25min, landing at 12.25 local time. By the time we had taxied back to dispersal, it was obvious that the outside temperature had risen considerably and we were all feeling hot and sticky by the time engines had been shut down. On climbing out of the aircraft it was very noticeable that the temperatures were high, as was humidity, although there was a gentle breeze blowing.

The exercise had been a good one and we were well satisfied with the bombing run results and the standard of instrument flying both during the time delay phase and throughout each escape manoeuvre; in this final steep turn, the aircraft was being flown close to its high speed stall configuration and any rough handling could result in a rather unpleasant high speed stall. Now on the ground there would be a careful analysis of each bombing run result, for every error had to be pin-pointed and diagnosed. This was always a self-critical exercise, for every fault had to be eliminated in order to achieve consistent accuracy.

By the time this had been completed, a check with Joint Operations Control confirmed that XD822 was on schedule and should be joining the circuit for a landing in 10min time. Sure enough, I was delighted to see XD822 dead on time make a smooth landing and taxi into dispersal to be met by its own ground crew, eager to get their hands on it, and by myself to welcome Dave Roberts and his crew. They had been delayed *en route* with technical problems but had arrived fully serviceable; thus we now boasted two Valiants at Christmas Island. XD823 was expected on the 18th and XD824 the following day.

Once Dave Roberts and his crew had unloaded their belongings, I drove them over to the Officers' Mess lines to settle in to their tented accommodation, leaving the XD822 Crew Chief, Chief Tech Sam Small, to clear all technical matters with Flt Sgt Asprey. That night, over dinner, I briefed Dave Roberts on the current plans, including the intention to fly a grandstand Valiant on all dress rehearsal and live drops.

Our third aircraft *en route* was Valiant XD823, captained by Sqn Ldr Arthur Steele, and latest information indicated an expected arrival at Christmas Island on 18 March. The fourth aircraft was Valiant XD824 under command of Sqn Ldr Barney Millett (since deceased), scheduled to arrive the day after XD823. With the arrival of Arthur Steele, the Squadron Training Officer, I was able to brief him fully on the detailed task ahead of us, both in training and operational phase.

We then drew up a specific flying training programme for each crew. Although I had already decided on the order of crew participation for the four planned live drops, my requirement was that in this pre-operational training phase all four crews must achieve, over an intensive practice bombing

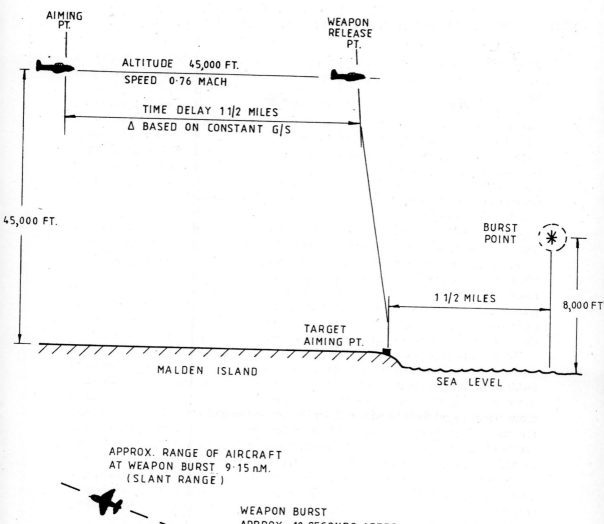

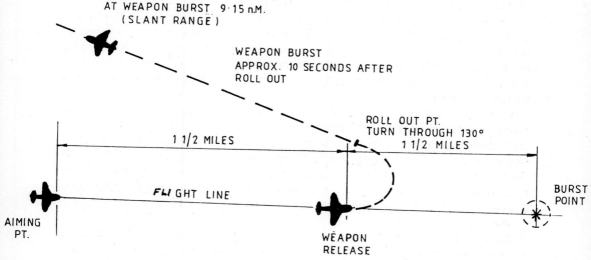

The escape manoeuvre employed by the Valiant captains after the release of a thermonuclear weapon. (*Author*)

programme, a proven consistency of accuracy with the time delay technique, by 5 April. From this point we should have moved into the operational phase, and flying would be strictly limited to the scientific requirement of special drops over the range at Malden Island. This was to be in co-operation with HMS *Warrior to* exercise her radar, and working under the control of HMS *Narvik*, which was the forward control centre specially equipped with linked telemetering equipment to the dropping aircraft. Thus from the date of 5 April I must be convinced that all my aircrew had achieved the standards demanded and could then confirm to the Task Force Commander that all four crews were at operational readiness.

The pattern of flying training was set, and after every bombing sortie there was held a post flight assessment and analysis of results, followed by a weekly review of these; all were carefully examined by the training officer and myself.

During those first three weeks there were many problems to contend with; firstly, although Christmas Island could sometimes go without rain for 12 months, we experienced torrential rain from the inter-tropical front, making life extremely unpleasant when coupled with the very high humidity and the effect of damp on sensitive equipment in our aircraft. Indeed, the rain at times was so severe that it ran through my office tent like a small river.

In spite of these conditions the ground crew, by working extremely long hours, maintained a high serviceability rate with our aircraft, and still managed to keep the equipment modification programme on schedule. Owing to the non-availability of Decca navigator equipment in the UK, all this had to be fitted at Christmas Island, which in itself was a considerable task. However, with all special aircraft equipment modifications we were well served by the special engineering team sent out by Vickers-Armstrong, and the specialist representative of Decca. Both my own ground crews, led by the four Crew Chiefs – Bill Caple, Sam Small, Roy Quinlan and Colin Mathers – under the co-ordination of my Technical Officer, Flg Off W. Budden, and Flt Sgt Bill Asprey, worked in complete harmony with the specialist representatives who could always be found at the aircraft whenever help was required.

It is always of interest to note that whenever a team of men are involved in a task of special interest, with a common aim, albeit under unpleasant conditions, they produce the most prodigious efforts with great cheerfulness and within this team the real characters emerge.

Because our initial work load on the airfield was so heavy and men were working incredibly long hours, it was an absolute blessing that the 'Grapple' planners had arranged to site a tented airfield buffet conveniently near to the aircraft dispersal area. Thus I was able to arrange for late night meals for my ground crew and my requests were always met with great cheerfulness by the catering staff.

Although to a great extent we were expected to be self-sufficient within our own technical means, I always found that the assistance and support of the Task Force Technical Officer, Wg Cdr Ron Boardman, was ever on hand and no task or problem was too much trouble for him. If the ground crews were working late at night to rectify some particularly tedious fault, I would always find Ron Boardman there when I drove to the airfield to see how work was progressing. I think it true to say that this standard of interest and practical help epitomised the relationship that existed throughout the 'Grapple' organisation.

In spite of the many difficulties experienced, our training programme was completed in the allotted time scale. Although each aircraft had the Decca Navigator system fitted during the training phase, regrettably due to a lack of Decca inflight log charts and initial teething problems in the ground Decca chain, we were unable to utilise this valuable navigational aid until well into the operational phase. This aid was to enable the navigator to position the aircraft accurately over the geographical bomb line should difficult cloud cover be experienced.

By 5 April I was able to report to the Task Force Commander that 49 Squadron had completed its training programme and all four crews had achieved the consistency of accuracy required and were therefore at operational readiness to meet the scientific requirement. Whilst confirming that from this time our flying would be restricted to necessary air tests and scientific programme drops at Malden Island in conjunction with HMS *Narvik,* I pointed out that due to the non-availability of the Decca chain, we should need one or two training exercises once this became operational. Other than this requirement, all flying hours would be conserved for the operational tasks.

With the training phase behind us, Valiant XD818 now required the final airframe modifications designed to protect control seals from the over-pressure wave which would be experienced after the explosion of the live megaton weapon.

No time was lost in beginning the operational phase, because on 6 April, in response to the scientific programme, I flew XD823 (XD818 was being modified) on the first scientific training sortie, bombed up with a full scale weapon fitted with telemetering equipment, for what we termed an Inert Drop on the range at Malden Island. The entire flight was to be in accordance with the full operation procedures, under control from HMS *Narvik,* with HMS *Warrior* in position to exercise its ground radar. A full scale pre-flight briefing was carried out and take-off scheduled for 09.00 local time.

Fortunately, we were not troubled at this time by the inter-tropical front and it was a lovely morning, the slight breeze reducing humidity. The temperature had not really built up by this time and only intermittent patches of cloud appeared in a clear blue sky.

At exactly 09.00hrs we were rolling down the runway for take-off and were quickly on course for Malden Island, climbing to our bombing level of 45,000ft. The 400nm to Malden was completed in just under 50min during which time the co-pilot and myself fitted all the metal anti-flash screens, leaving only the front panel free for outside visibility. The bomb aimer also fitted his screens leaving the shutter open for forward visibility on the bomb line.

As we neared Malden, two-way contact was made with HMS *Narvik* and with HMS *Warrior*, which confirmed they had identified us on their radar screen.

The operational procedure was that initial rendezvous would be made at a point on the extended geographical bomb line 75nm from the target indicator at an altitude of 45,000ft. At 50nm from the target, on a bomb line running nearly south on a track of 200°T, was the intercept point, and from here to the target the navigator would assess his drift and pass this to the bomb aimer who, on this first run, could align the aircraft to the set geographical bomb line as the island coast line and ground features came into his bomb sights. However, once the Decca navigational chain was operating, the positioning would be done by the navigator using this equipment.

The first run down the bomb line was called a navigational run, to allow the crew to clarify exact drift, calculate an accurate ground speed and feed in the appropriate time delay to achieve the 1½nm overshoot, calculated from ground speed. After this run was complete a 30° bank turn was made to port on to a reciprocal heading on what we termed a race track pattern, the aircraft being required to report position on this leg at five set points to HMS *Narvik*, which was recording the flight path by means of telemetering equipment in the aircraft.

At the final reporting point, known as Echo, the aircraft would turn to port in a rate one 30° bank turn, thus returning to the intercept point on the bomb line 50nm from the target.

The second run was termed an 'Initial Run' which was to enable the Scientific Weapon Team on board HMS *Narvik* to test correct functioning of all telemetering recording equipment in the aircraft and the arming circuit in the weapon. This related to a strict weapon equipment drill carried out by the Air Electronic Operator at precise points on the bomb run. Only when the weapon team was satisfied that all equipment was operating correctly could the Valiant be authorised to carry out a weapon release run.

Since this was the first time a full procedural drop had been carried out with all telemetering and recording equipment operating both in the aircraft, on the ground and on board HMS *Narvik*, I did not expect it to be without problems and was therefore not surprised when on completion of this run, John Challons, the Scientific Controller on board HMS *Narvik*, requested a second 'Initial Run'. Having completed my turn on to the 'race track', I duly acknowledged that we would fly a further initial run and settled down to relaxed instrument flying, having now fitted all metal anti-flash screens in the cockpit.

The crew drills on these two runs had been smooth; all transmissions were made as planned and the bomb aimer had on each occasion lined the aircraft upon the bomb line at an early stage, thereby keeping heading corrections to a minimum. My own instrument flying had been accurate although I had allowed a slight variaton in altitude to creep in, which was not acceptable. Having turned on to intercept point, I reported this position to the controller and settled back in my seat, relaxed and determined to fly with no variation in height, speed and course.

Eric Hood, the Navigator, confirmed no change in ground speed or drift, the Air Electronic Operator, Ted Laraway, reported all switching circuits operational, and the bomb run began with the bomb aimer, Alan Washbrook, giving me the initial corrections to align the aircraft on to the bomb line. From this point, each crew member had a set duty to perform and the only comments on the intercom would be the bomb aimer correction, and the navigator calling distance from target, to which was associated a switching drill by the AEO on the weapons telemetering panel.

With the bombing run to aiming point complete, I again turned port in a rate one turn on to the race track, reporting completion of the Initial Run to the controller. I was very satisfied with this run from a crew point of view and hoped all telemetering signals had been positive, but knew that clearance for a weapon release would not be given until these had been carefully evaluated.

By point 'C' on the race track, the controller reported all satisfactory on the Initial Run and clearance was given for the 'Inert Drop'. I duly acknowledged and told the crew that this would be the weapon release full drill, complete with the approved escape manoeuvre immediately on weapon release.

Having turned through point Echo on the race track to intercept point, the subsequent bombing run went smoothly, the navigator initially giving me a course to maintain the bombing line, followed by corrections from the bomb aimer as he aligned the aircraft on the geographical line.

There were few corrections on this run, for we had assessed drift carefully, and as we progressed along the bomb line the various switching sequences by the Air Electronics Operator were called and transmitted to control. I felt very relaxed as attention was concentrated on the blind flying instrument panel; speed steady at Mach 0.76, height 45,000ft and compass heading held at 202°T with the bomb aimer calling 'Steady, steady'. As he achieved graticule coincidence, he called 'Steady, steady now'. This meant he had pressed the bomb release button and now came the time delay in seconds (approximately 11) for the 1½nm position from the target aiming point to actual release of the weapon from the aircraft. During those 11 seconds there must be no variation in heading, height and airspeed, all of which would be accurately recorded on the automatic observer installed in the aircraft to monitor height, speed and airspeed.

Throughout the bomb run, all crew drills and switching procedures were being transmitted to the controller aboard HMS *Narvik* who, in case of some major malfunction, had the facility to break through our transmission in order to cancel the drop. From the point of weapon release the captain was required to maintain on transmit a running commentary throughout the escape manoeuvre.

Thus immediately the bomb aimer called 'Bomb gone', I announced the start of the escape manoeuvre and rolled the aircraft into a 60° bank turn to the left, simultaneously calling for full power from the co-pilot, and at the same time applying backward pressure on the control column in order to achieve a reading on the sensitive accelerometer of 1.7G. Speed was held at Mach 0.76 and height 45,000ft until we had turned through 135°, then the aircraft was rolled back to level flight.

The turn took 40 seconds, which meant that there would be some 10 seconds before the weapon passed through 8,000ft, which was to be burst point. In theory, at this particular point, the slant range distance between the aircraft and weapon burst point would be approximately 9nm with the tail cone of the aircraft pointing directly to burst point.

Having completed this first full scale exercise over the operational target area, with all metal anti-flash screens fitted, we requested clearance to return to Christmas Island, thanked the controller and set course for base. On route all the screens were removed and we were soon homing to the radio beacon for a planned let down to arrive at 1,500ft over the beacon.

The weather was perfect, so we went into a visual circuit and landing, having been airborne for 4 hours. Since we were returning around 13.00hrs, it was really hot on the ground, and although a light wind was blowing, the humidity was high. We all soon became soaked with perspiration as we taxied into dispersal; however, we were well satisfied with the outcome of this first exercise in the operational phase.

Having shut down engines and handed XD823 over to Bill Caple, we headed for my office tent to check with Joint Operation Control the actual bombing error plotted. We were delighted to learn that it was 245 yd, which was well within the operational requirement. After a full crew debriefing, we drove over to the airfield crew buffet for a light lunch and discussed details of the trip from each crew member's point of view.

From this moment onwards the operational phase programme moved into top gear and all four dropping crews carried out planned drops in the operational target area so as to exercise fully every aspect of the forthcoming live drop. The 49 Squadron flying programme was now dictated by the requirement of the Scientific Team and I had regular meetings with the Scientific Director and his Weapon Teams.

For the Shackletons of 240 Squadron, this was to become progressively a very active phase as their responsibility was to police a vast maritime area already declared a prohibited zone to all shipping. No. 76 Canberra Squadron, detailed to take radioactive samples from the mushroom cloud following weapon burst, was now busy rehearsing its procedures, and the Canberra PR of No. 100 Squadron was committed on a daily basis to flying high-level sorties through a regional pattern to provide meteorological information on the upper airto the Meteorological Team.

Thus the entire pre-operational plan was slowly but surely being exercised and made ready to be put into effect when both the Scientific Director and Task Force Commander considered that the team was at operational pitch and the scientists were satisfied that their plans were complete and that the weather factors were favourable.

Linked with this plan was the requirement for 49 Squadron to provide two Valiants from 'B' flight left at RAF Wittering, to fly the special components for the atomic device from the UK to Christmas Island, on a non-stop basis, by positioning slip crews at Goose Bay, Namao, Travis and Honolulu. This was scheduled for the first week of May, by which time the operational training phase should have been completed.

Security on the island was extremely strict and even though my own crew was to drop the first live weapon, it was considered that our knowledge of the details of this should be restricted to the appropriate switching drills on the aircraft weapons panel. Our know-how was concentrated on the aircraft, its capabilities and various emergency procedures to be adopted in the event of weapon malfunction or fault in release mechanism.

In the UK, although the Prime Minister had made an announcement in Parliament confirming that Britain was to undertake a series of thermonuclear weapon tests in the South Pacific, there was little reaction in the national press at the time. No indication had been given regarding dates and there was no intention of having either press or diplomatic observers on the island for the first live drop; that was to come later.

This was the time of CND marches to AWRE at Aldermaston and there had been threats that certain CND protestors were planning to sail into our maritime area, which had been declared a prohibited zone, in order to stop or delay the tests. Thus all round there was to be strict secrecy and the Shackleton aircraft of 240 Squadron were combing the vast expanse of ocean to ensure that no unwelcome visitors came into the area.

Although there was a great deal to do at all times on the squadron, the most difficult task fell upon the ground crew in maintaining these very complex aircraft under such difficult weather conditions, varying from torrential tropical rain to extreme humidity; the latter could create problems with the high technology electronics in the Valiants' systems.

Flying for all crews was severely restricted until the end of April; during these weeks each crew carried out trial drops over the Malden Island target area, which enabled the Scientific Team to test out every aspect of the forthcoming live drop. In addition, it enabled us to demonstrate that each of the four selected operational crews was maintaining the accuracy required.

All was set for the big day and one could sense a certain atmosphere of excitement on the island, although no-one knew of the precise date. All would depend on the weather and general pattern of the upper winds.

No-one would have guessed, had they arrived at Christmas Island on a Saturday evening, that we were all shortly to be involved in a very historic occasion, for Saturday night in the Officers' Mess was always something special. Dress was always slacks and Aloha shirts, and after dinner we could usually expect the Task Force Commander, AVM Wilf Oulton, plus Air Cdre Ginger

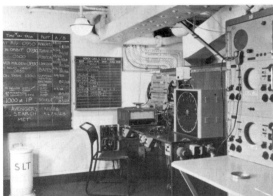

Top: Blast gauges on Malden Island, with HMS *Warrior* passing in the background.

Centre: The forward control room in HMS *Narvik*.

Bottom: Zero minus 30 seconds aboard HMS *Narvik*.

Weir and Bill Cook, the Scientific Director, accompanied by Capt Guy Weston RN and Gp Capt Milligan, to arrive from the TFC Mess. It had become a custom for AVM Wilf Oulton to sit down at the piano and play a selection of popular tunes, suitable for all to sing. It even got to the stage of some enterprising officers producing song sheets to ensure that we all enjoyed a pleasant sing-song evening.

My own social life varied between the Saturday sing-song to being invited for dinner on one or other of HM ships where one tasted again the delights of sitting down to a really good dinner with splendid silver. On these occasions, of course, the hospitality was such that going ashore often presented problems when climbing down the ladder into the cutter that was to return one to shore. My crew and I always appreciated these invitations, for our own mess conditions were primitive. We could only return Naval hospitality in a limited way, but whenever we had air tests to carry out I always ensured that either a sailor or soldier got the chance to fly in a Valiant.

The Royal Engineers had built a delightful little church for the garrison, shared by all denominations. Our own C of E Padre was a Rev Eric Allsop whom I knew well because he was ex-Bomber Command. Every Sunday I made it a duty to attend morning service. The Church was normally filled to capacity, for the padre was a man who loved to come and talk to airmen as they were working on their aircraft, and I told Eric Allsop that he was welcome at any time. His genuine interest paid off. It was always pleasant to see a sprinkling of my own airmen in Church on Sunday.

We were now at the third week of April 1957, and at a special meeting with the Air Task Force Commander, Air Cdre Ginger Weir, he told me that Bomber Command had been requested to set in motion the positioning of 49 Squadron crews for the two fast courier Valiants detailed to carry the vital nuclear components from the Atomic Weapon Research Establishment. Therefore I should arrange to position two crews from the Christmas Island detachment to Travis AFB, California, to be in position by 5 May. The joint operation staff would provide air transport once I named the crews.

He then gave me an approximate date for the first live drop, but stressed that the actual date would depend on the weather conditions prevailing, and would be jointly agreed by the Task Force Commander and Scientific Director; he pointed out that I should now decide which crew was to be selected for the operation, plus naming the crew for the grandstand aircraft and which captain I intended to make available on HMS *Narvik* as adviser to the Task Force Commander in the event of some emergency to the Valiant carrying the live megaton weapon.

All of these were matters to which I had given very careful thought, although there was never any doubt in my mind that as Squadron Commander it would be my duty to carry out the first live drop in Valiant XD818 with my crew.

There were many aspects of this first live air drop in which problems could develop, and as it had always been my way to lead by example I had no hesitation in telling Air Cdre Ginger Weir that my crew would be carrying out the first live weapon test and that the aircraft would be XD818. Sqn Ldr Barney Millet and crew would fly 'Grandstand' in XD824, and Sqn Ldr Dave Roberts, my deputy, would be adviser to the Task Force Commander on any matter relating to the Valiant. He agreed with my decisions and I left the meeting feeling a sense of satisfaction and elation to think that we were at long last all set for the major task.

We were now in mid-April, some four weeks away from the possible date for a live drop, to be designated 'D' Day. All flying now on the Valiants must be strictly limited to that required by the Scientific Team, in order to conserve flying hours. However, within this restriction I had to ensure that all of the four operational crews each participated in the scientific flying programme so that any one of them was capable and at operational readiness to undertake the first live drop.

Over the next three weeks a number of full procedure inert weapons and high explosive weapons were dropped in the operational area, in order to test out various weapon electronics, including the device to ensure it exploded at 8,000ft above mean sea level. In all of these sorties consistent bombing accuracy was maintained, and from the ground radar traces on board HMS *Warrior* it was possible to confirm that the escape manoeuvre turn was being enacted within the time scale of 40 seconds, with a roll out on the correct heading to put aircraft tail cone cameras on to burst point.

My planned programme for the first and subsequent live weapon drops was to be as follows:

First Drop
'Short Granite' – Valiant XD818, Wg Cdr K. Hubbard and crew.
Grandstand Aircraft – Valiant XD824, Sqn Ldr B. Millett and crew.

Second Drop
'Orange Herald' – Valiant XD822, Sqn Ldr D. Roberts and crew.
Grandstand Aircraft – Valiant XD823, Sqn Ldr A. Steele and crew.

Third Drop
'Purple Granite' – Valiant XD823, Sqn Ldr A. Steele and crew.
Grandstand Aircraft – Valiant XD824, Sqn Ldr B. Millett and crew.

There was doubt as to whether a fourth live drop would be included in this series, therefore, no allocation of crew or aircraft was included at this stage; however, should plans change, the fourth live drop would be undertaken by Sqn Ldr Millett and crew. All crews were extremely keen to be able to undertake a live megaton weapon drop; it will therefore be appreciated how disappointed Barney Millett and his crew were to learn that there was doubt about a fourth one, but as professional airmen they accepted the situation without allowing their enthusiasm to diminish. As will be seen at a later stage in this account, Barney Millett and crew did carry out a live drop on our second detachment to Christmas Island.

During the final phase, having ensured that all crews had an equal share of the pre-live drop sorties in the operational area of Malden Island, the final scientific trials drops with HE weapon corresponding to the live megaton weapon code names 'Short Granite' were carried out by my own crew, with the grandstand aircraft flying on each occasion.

There were three major drops of this calibre, following the full operational procedure carried out by my own crew in Valiant XD818, during which not only was the Scientific Weapons Team on board HMS *Narvik* able to test every aspect of the weapon and telemetering equipment, but we were also able to undertake a completely blind drop using Decca navigational equipment.

The first courier operation commenced on 5 May, using Valiants XD825 and XD827, and within 24 hours they landed at Christmas Island and were immediately handed over to the Scientific Weapons Team. The entire operation had gone without a hitch and with the arrival of their very sensitive loads in the bomb bay panniers, we all knew that everything was now available to mount the big 'D' Day live drop operation.

The next 10 days were to be extremely busy ones for the Shackleton squadrons, which shouldered the responsibility for searching and policing the extensive ocean area prohibited to shipping, which had at all costs to be kept clear. On the day prior to the drop, the Task Force Commander had to be assured that there was no shipping in the area before he could authorise the operation to proceed.

The Canberra photographic reconnaissance squadron was also heavily tasked during this period, for it was essential that the meteorological team had daily reports on all upper winds to enable them to produce current high level fall-out patterns; again, only if the pattern cleared Christmas Island could the operation proceed. Finally, by regular sorties by the Canberras of 100 Squadron, providing medium level meteorological data, a full weather situation could be recorded and a forecast outlook given by the Meteorological Team.

The full scale dress rehearsal was scheduled for 11 May, in 10 days time. Prior to this date I would give Valiant XD818 an intensive air test to satisfy myself that everything was fully serviceable; then after this flight the aircraft would be handed over to the Scientific Weapons Team for loading the dress rehearsal weapon, armed with a high explosive warhead rather than an atomic device.

Also at this stage, all personnel on the island were made aware of an elaborate personnel safety plan, devised by the staff of Task Force Headquarters. Although personnel on Christmas Island would be 400nm from the test site at Malden Island, arrangements had to be carefully planned for the dispersal of all non-essential personnel from the airfield area in the event of Valiant XD818 crashing on take-off with the live nuclear weapon in the bomb bay, or in the event of an accident on landing, should the drop be cancelled after take-off and the aircraft required to land back with the weapon aboard.

Should such an accident occur, there would be a possibility of the weapon exploding with the impact of the aircraft, which could result in a significant level of radioactive fall-out. To allow for such a possibility the plan necessitated all personnel being assembled in designated areas and every man being accounted for. Transport would be allocated to each area so that in the event of such an accident resulting in radioactive fall-out, the instructions would be passed by radio to proceed to a certain area of the island away from the fall-out pattern.

The airfield crash crews had been specially trained to handle any accident and were equipped with special protective clothing and equipment to cut the aircraft crew free if possible, and they would be augmented on the day with a qualified scientific weapon adviser.

For the crew of HMS *Warrior*, the light aircraft carrier, and HMS *Narvik*, the control ship, which would be within 20nm of the airbursts, special instructions had been issued and here again all non-essential personnel would be below decks. Those on deck were to be issued with anti-flash clothing, and gloves and hoods to cover the head and arms. With this clothing only a small circle of the face was exposed and this was to be turned away from bomb burst point and covered by the hands. Those assembled on deck would be seated on the side facing away from the bomb with their knees drawn up to their faces. Just prior to the explosion, when the bomb aimer's voice came over the broadcast system, saying 'Bomb gone', the order 'Close eyes' would be given.

With a nuclear weapon explosion at the instant of detonation, a very bright flash of light of some seconds duration would occur, of a brilliance that would damage the retina of the eye and cause blindness if exposed to the direct flash, up to a distance of 20nm. This brilliance produces intense heat within the resulting fireball, and would cause mild burns to bare skin, which is why everyone was protected by the special anti-flash clothing.

Those personnel in the forward area would remain in the assembled position until the blast wave had passed. This in itself – with a high airburst at a range of 20nm – would be quite harmless to personnel and could only cause damage to light objects or structures where the surface area was large in comparison with the mass.

When a nuclear weapon explodes, the atmosphere in its immediate vicinity is violently compressed, and this pressure wave then travels outwards at approximately the speed of sound in the same way as the waves move out from a stone dropped in a pond. Thus personnel on board HMS *Warrior* would feel the blast wave approximately 1 min after weapon detonation, accompanied by a very loud bang.

While the immediate effects of heat, flash, blast and radiation of a nuclear weapon explosion represent the most dramatic and obvious hazard, radioactive fallout is also potentially harmful. This consists of fine particles of bomb debris or of dust or water particles from the surface of the earth which have been contaminated by being in contact with the fireball. These particles are drawn into the upper air in the hot column of gases and carried to heights exceeding 50,000ft. From the upper air strata they are carried on the upper air pattern and progressively fall back to earth at different rates, depending on their size, and may be distributed over a very large area. The radioactivity in this fallout comprises all three forms of ionising radiation – alpha, beta or gamma – which because of their differing penetration and physical properties can cause harm to humans in various ways.

However, since in all 'Grapple' tests the weapon was detonated 8,000ft above sea level, the fireball never touched the sea or the earth. Thus the amount of fall-out was reduced to that given from the actual material from which the bomb was made. These particles are extremely small and therefore take a very long time to return to the earth or the ocean from the upper atmosphere. When they do so, they are so widely scattered that their effect on the general background level of radiation is negligible, and all radioactivity decays with time. This decay rate can be estimated by dividing the dose rate in Roentgens per hour by 10 and multiplying the time after burst by 7. Thus, if the time of weapon burst is H hour, and the dose rate measured one hour after burst is R Roentgen per hour, then:-

At H + 1 hour dose rate is	R	rph
At H + 7 hours dose rate is	$\dfrac{R}{10}$	rph
At H + 2 days dose rate is	$\dfrac{R}{100}$	rph

From what I have described above it will be seen that the most elaborate precautions were taken to safeguard personnel under all situations.

With all personnel on the island aware that 'D' Day was rapidly approaching, a general atmosphere of excitement prevailed in the camp. We were moving to that crucial point for which so much time, careful planning and intense work had been undertaken by all three services and the Scientific Team.

Ultimately, the responsibility would rest with 49 Squadron to ensure that this effort and the hopes of so many had not been in vain. It has been said that pride of place in this operation fell to 49 Squadron which had the responsibility of delivering Britain's first live megaton weapon, to a pre-set point in space with an accuracy that would enable full scientific data and recording to be completely achieved.

The full scale dress rehearsal was now set for 11 May, and this would involve all Shackletons on their search duties as well as being used for airborne observation of the test, the Canberra aircraft of 76 Squadron detailed for cloud sampling after the development of the subsequent mushroom cloud following weapon detonation, and PR Canberra of 100 Squadron for high-level upper-wind recording.

Every aspect of the operation would be tested fully on this rehearsal, and all timing to be as for 'D' Day. Thus, I knew take-off of the Valiant would be at 09.00hrs local with full meteorological briefing and operational briefing by the Air Task Force Commander at 07.00hrs local.

For this dress rehearsal, the Task Force Commander and Scientific Director, accompanied by Sqn Ldr Roberts as Valiant adviser, would be on board HMS *Warrior*. The Air Task Force Commander would remain at Joint Operations Control on Christmas Island.

Although the Christmas Island personnel would be 400nm from the scene of operations, they would all be able to listen in to the Valiant on the bomb run, and hear the commentary during the escape manoeuvre. Thus, having contributed so much to the operation, they could all feel fully involved, thanks to good planning and sound communications.

On the day before the dress rehearsal, Valiant XD818, its full daily technical pre-flight servicing completed, was handed over to the Scientific Weapons Team in the weapon bombing area, for loading of the dress rehearsal weapon fitted with a high explosive warhead. We handed over control of the aircraft and departed, for only the weapons team was allowed to remain for the weapon final checks and bombing up. The area was enclosed by screens and a 24hr guard mounted.

That afternoon I held a final detailed briefing with my own crew and that of Sqn Ldr Barney Millett who was to fly the grandstand aircraft. The next day the only squadron airmen on the tarmac would be the ground crew of Valiant XD818 and Valiant XD824. All otherground and aircrew would be assembled at their designated places in the Personnel Safety area.

Fortunately the weather over the past few days had been good and the meteorological forecast for the next day looked encouraging, with no sign of any tropical rain from the inter-tropical front. We returned in my Land Rover to the Officers' Mess lines, feeling that at last we had reached the penultimate sortie that would exercise every aspect of the live weapon drop, and I felt complete confidence that my crew could produce the result required.

After a quiet evening in the mess and a pleasant meal, we all returned to our tents for an early night in order to be completely fresh for the following day's flying. Before turning in, I strolled along the shore; the moonlight was shimmering on the clear blue waters of the Pacific, with waves breaking over the coral reef. I often found such a walk at night completely relaxed me and enabled me to reflect upon the past day's work or problems. After about 20 minutes, I returned to my tent and was soon asleep.

By 06.00hrs the following day, 11 May, I was up and about; after a quick shower I joined my crew for an early breakfast, before we drove over to Joint Operations Control for the operational briefing. Whilst we had slept the entire Joint Operations Control had been busy going through the full pre-test sequences. The Shackletons had flown their final search sorties and the area had now been declared 'clear'. The Meteorological Team had worked through the night to produce up-to-date weather situation reports and a forecast for the Malden area over the schedule dress rehearsal time.

The Air Task Force Commander and the Scientific Director had been in the Joint Operations Control for most of the night, checking and re-checking, as they would be on the night prior to 'D' Day. All then was ready for the dress rehearsal to proceed.

All briefing complete, we drove to the airfield and changed into flying kit, Sqn Ldr Barney Millett and crew arriving about the same time. Bill Caple, my own Crew Chief in XD818, reported that the aircraft was fully serviceable and all weapon checks complete. Colin Mathers, the Crew Chief on Valiant XD824, confirmed that the grandstand aircraft was serviceable; we were then ready for our part.

Most of the Shackletons were already airborne; only those destined to position for observation duty in the test area were on the tarmac. The Canberras which were to undertake the cloud sampling stood ready for take-off at their appointed time after we had become airborne. The only airmen to be seen on the dispersal area were those responsible for the two Valiants, the Shackletons and the Canberras; everybody else would be at their various assembly points.

Sgt Wally Cressey – with his usual uncanny ability – brought a mug of tea into my office tent and wished us good luck. He then disappeared to be at his own assembly point, and before I could finish drinking tea, Flt Sgt Bill Asprey came in to say he hoped everything would go well, and he too then disappeared to his assembly point.

Sqn Ldr Dave Roberts had already departed with the Task Force Commander, in an aircraft of HMS *Warrior,* to fly to the Malden Island area where she was on station. They would then transfer to HMS *Narvik,* the control ship, by helicopter.

By this time my crew were all in their flying kit and ready to walk over to Valiant XD818 in the weapon area. The time was now just after 08.00hrs and take-off was scheduled for 09.00hrs. Having checked that all was well with Barney Millett and his crew, we strolled over to XD818, still hidden by the canvas screens; these were removed as we arrived to accept the aircraft and weapon assembly. The RAF Form 700 Technical Log duly signed, Bob Beeson and I started our external checks, having a good look at the 10,000lb monster in the bomb bay, which today would only contain a high explosive warhead. By the time we had completed our checks, Air Cdre Ginger Weir and Wg Cdr Ron Boardman arrived to check if all was well and confirmed that so far everything was going according to plan.

Alan Washbrook, Eric Hood and Ted Laraway were already in position on the flight deck checking their equipment, so Bob Beeson and I climbed in and strapped ourselves into the ejector seats. With all engines running, I cleared with control to taxi, waved away chocks and moved out towards the runway.

We already had some of the metal anti-flash screens fitted and the remainder would go into position during the climb to altitude.

Dead on 09.00hrs local time we commenced our take-off run and were quickly airborne and settled into the climb to 45,000ft heading for Malden Island and the RV point, which was reached by 09.50hrs. By this time we were in contact with the controller on HMS *Narvik* and could hear the Shackleton and Canberra aircraft reporting that they had arrived at their designated orbit points.

We now had all the metal anti-flash shutters in position, with only the bomb aimer's sliding shutter open. Alan Washbrook reported that visibility was good with only one-eighth cloud coverof fairweather cumulus, which seemed to be normal in the Pacific. Eric Hood reported that the sea was very calm, presenting difficulties in getting Green Satin to lock on, but Decca was satisfactory. Ted Laraway confirmed all electronic and signals equipment working.

Control cleared us to carry out the first run down the bomb line in order to assess drift, and obtain an accurate ground speed at an indicated airspeed of Mach 0.76 in order to set the correct time delay into the bomb release mechanism. All proceeded smoothly, with Alan Washbrook giving a good steady run with few corrections, and Bob Beeson and I relaxed and flying accurately in our enclosed cockpit, with our attention concentrated on the blind flying instrument panel. With the navigational run completed, we were cleared for the initial run on which every switching sequence would be tested with the exception of the final arming of the weapon.

On board HMS *Narvik* all telemetering signals from special equipment on board the aircraft and in the actual weapon were being checked, including the aircraft cameras in the bomb bay, wing trailing edge and tail cones. Additionally, the Scientific Team would be checking correct signal response from all recording and camera equipment located in the target area. Only if every aspect was correct, and the Task Force Commander was certain that his entire force was correctly positioned, would clearance be given for a 'Live Run' to drop the weapon.

Obviously all was not correct for, having turned on to the race track after completing the initial run, we were instructed to carry out a second initial run. This did not surprise me on a dress rehearsal, for now was the time to rectify any last minute problems, not on 'D' Day. I heard Valiant XD824 report his position on the race track, confirming that it was correctly 2,000ft below and approximately 1nm behind.

We therefore settled down for a further run up the bomb line, transmitting the full switching sequence. Once again the navigator used his Decca to position us well for the turn on to the bomb line, and Alan Washbrook, in his usual very experienced manner, passed corrections to keep us well aligned up to the point where the target was set centrally into his graticule sights. We turned again on to the race track, hoping a clearance to bomb would be given; by the time we reached point Charlie I was relieved to hear the controller's voice confirming we were cleared for a live drop. This clearance was then broadcast to all aircraft in the area informing them that the dropping Valiant was approaching intercept point on the bomb line and instructing all to remain listening to its transmissions.

Once again we quickly settled down to a steady run on the bomb line: speed Mach 0.76, height 45,000ft, heading settling to 203° after initial correction from the bomb aimer, who confirmed that the time delay based on ground speed was set.

As the run progressed, I settled back in my ejector seat to retain a comfortable posture for relaxed instrument flying; any over tension tends to produce errors in over correcting instrument indications; so, a relaxed attitude, coupled with smooth alterations, was essential.

The AEO, Ted Laraway, called his weapon and telemetering switching sequence calmly, interspersed with small corrections to heading from Alan Washbrook, until the point where the final switch to arm the weapon was called; at this point the bomb aimer was giving 'Steady, steady', meaning we were dead on course and I must maintain that heading with no deviations.

Finally, Alan gave 'Steady, steady – Now'. This meant that he had graticule coincidence with the target indicator and that we were now in the period of approximately 11 sec before the weapon was released. At this point the grandstand aircraft would be starting its escape manoeuvre. Bob Beeson placed his left hand on the throttles ready for my order and I concentrated on maintaining the aircraft heading, precise indicated height and accurate airspeed. Those 11 seconds to me always seemed an eternity but were so crucial to the success of the drop.

I was relieved to hear the bomb aimer's voice say 'Bomb gone' and be able to roll into the escape manoeuvre giving the order for 'Full Power' from the co-pilot.

With 60° of bank on the artificial horizon and steady backward pressure on the controls, the sensitive accelerometer reading was held at 1.7G, height kept to 45,000ft, airspeed at Mach 0.76; the aircraft felt steady in the turn and all could feel the effect of positive gravity as it progressed. During this period I maintained a steady commentary so that everybody in the area knew exactly what was happening. As a turn through 135° was completed, we rolled back to level flight, calling for the co-pilot to reduce power to cruise conditions. The turn had to be completed in 40 seconds, which left 10 seconds before the weapon released passed through its detonation point of 8,000ft.

Sure enough at the 50 seconds point the controller came through on a break through in our transmission to say 'Weapon Exploded'. We were now required to continue a broadcast until, on the real live weapon drop day, the over pressure wave had passed the aircraft. Today, purely with a high explosive detonation, there would be no pressure wave.

After some 3 minutes we were cleared to return to Christmas Island, for now it was the turn of the sampling Canberra aircraft to carry out their rehearsal plan, the Shackletons to follow their low level search routine and the scientists on board HMS *Narvik* to assess all results from their telemetering and camera equipment. Meantime, Valiants XD818 and XD824 returned to Christmas Island, their task completed.

On taxiing back to dispersal, the Scientific Team was waiting to remove cameras, automatic observer and other telemetering equipment for examination and evaluation of all aspects of the weapon and aircraft performance. We had been airborne for 3hr 20min and were more than ready for the mug of tea produced by the ever attentive Sgt Cressey.

The aircraft had performed perfectly and as far as we were concerned all equipment was fully serviceable. As soon as I had removed my flying overalls, for by this time of the day it was extremely hot and humid, I rang Joint Operation Control and spoke to Air Cdre Ginger Weir, who confirmed that all had gone well and the bombing accuracy was excellent. This of course gave us all great satisfaction, for one was extremely conscious of the efforts of all concerned to bring this operation to a point of full dress rehearsal.

That afternoon, with the Task Force Commander back from the forward area, a meeting was called by the Air Task Force Commander, for all senior personnel and the Valiant, Shackleton and Canberra Squadron Commanders, to discuss all aspects of the dress rehearsal. This lasted until nearly 18.00hrs, but it was fascinating to hear reports showing how the entire operation had linked together, and (with one or two minor exceptions) it looked as if the months of planning by the Task Force Commander and the Scientific Director had paid off.

In conclusion, the Task Force Commander announced that provided all weather factors were favourable, the date for the live drop would be 15 May.

I drove back to the Officers' Mess lines, satisfied that all had gone well, for it had marked the penultimate operation of a long period of training by all concerned in the squadron, and I could not have had under my command a more loyal and dedicated team. Every man had played his part, whether at RAF Wittering or on Christmas Island.

That night in the Mess, Dave Roberts put me in the picture regarding the action on board HMS *Narvik* and we both agreed that as far as we were concerned, the squadron was at peak efficiency for the full live drop. After dinner we were joined by my own crew and Arthur Steele, Wilf Jenkins (his bomb aimer), Barney Millett and Wg Cdr Ron Boardman; we sat enjoying canned beer, looking out over the gentle Pacific waters lapping languidly across the coral reef barrier with, as usual, the reflection of the moon on the clear water – all very peaceful and so much in contrast with the task ahead.

On the following day, Air Cdre Ginger Weir invited me to the Task Force Commander's Mess for dinner, which was always a pleasure, as the food was invariably of a higher standard than we received in our Mess, purely because to cater for a total number of 12 or 14 is more personal than for some 100 or more officers.

At around 19.00hrs I presented myself at his tent for drinks and, as was always the case, most of the TFC Mess members called in – Ginger always seemed to have 'open house'. Certainly over all the years that we had known each other, his hospitality and that of his wife Muriel was generous in the extreme.

After a very pleasant dinner in company with the Task Force Commander and Gp Capt Freddie Milligan, Ginger and I took a stroll along the beach area and he talked seriously about the forthcoming live drop. He explained that there would be no observers coming to witness this first test, and every effort was being made in all quarters in the UK from the Prime Minister downwards, to maintain a low profile until the test had been completed. Britain would then announce to the world that it had exploded its first live megaton H-bomb, being the first country ever to drop one in a test series from an aircraft for an air burst. All the American tests had either been ground bursts in the Nevada desert or under water.

He further explained that Air Ministry public relations had current photographs of myself and my crew, which would be released to the national press, complete with a description of the drop. Thus I could expect a great deal of publicity in the UK on the day following the drop. This information was strictly for my ears and not to be communicated to any other member of my crew. Needless to say, he stressed the exceptional importance of a successful drop on 'D' Day, highlighting the great responsibility of 49 Squadron in its participation. He complimented me on the high standards displayed by the squadron and was most impressed by the professional attitude and high morale of both ground and air crews.

Our conversation then turned to the possibility of a serious malfunction of the weapon release on the final bomb run. The procedure to be adopted by the Valiant crew had been carefully laid down and we had all rehearsed the drill for final abandonment of the aircraft. Although the possibility of an electrical fault resulting in the weapon not falling from the aircraft was remote in the extreme, it had to be catered for.

Should such a situation occur, we could not risk landing the aircraft back at Christmas Island where 3,000 men were in camp, with a live weapon likely to fall from its housing on to the bomb doors as the aircraft touched down. The risk of a nuclear explosion with resultant fall-out was far too great. In these circumstances, I was well aware that the rear crew members would be instructed to bale out near to HMS *Warrior*. The co-pilot and myself would then set course at 5,000ft downwind of Malden Island, setting into our automatic time and distance system a set time in minutes plus the appropriate miles.

We would fly the aircraft to a distance of 50nm away, then with 200nm and a time of 30 minutes set into the automatic system, the automatic pilot would be engaged, the co-pilot would be ordered to eject, followed by myself. The aircraft would then fly on at 5,000ft for a further 200nm or 30min, whichever were the sooner. At this point, the system was designed to close the throttles, shut off fuel and put the Valiant into a nose-down attitude so that it crashed into the sea under control. The resultant explosion would cause a low-yield nuclear reaction with limited radioactive fall-out, but well away from any inhabited area. HMS *Warrior*, having picked up the the rear crew members, would then steam towards the point where the captain and co-pilot had ejected, although a Shackleton would have been despatched to mark our position and stay with us until picked up by one of *Warrior's* helicopters.

I assured Ginger Weir that this aspect was understood in every detail, and it was my intention to have one final run through this procedure with my crew, on the day prior to the live drop.

Finally, he informed me that for the second live drop, the Government had authorised the presence of representatives of all national newspapers, plus a party of diplomatic observers. With the first live drop behind us we should be certain that the weapon mechanism performed perfectly, so we could afford to allow official observers for No. 2. In this respect I confirmed that Sqn Ldr Dave Roberts and his crew would carry out this drop.

Having covered all those points it was time for me to take my leave after thanking him for a pleasant evening.

The next day was Sunday and the squadron had organised a cricket match for the afternoon: officers versus airmen, with myself as one of the umpires. However, before this I attended morning service in the little garrison church and Padre Eric Allsop came over to me and asked if I would read a lesson, to which I agreed. As usual Eric selected lively hymns, and his sermons were always worth listening to; he had the ability to connect day-to-day life with the broader religious message, and he could relate to life on Christmas Island.

On this day he dwelt on the task we were all on the island to undertake. As I sat there listening, I could not help but compare the entire operation to one huge jigsaw. So many units and people had been responsible for various parts, all equally important if the final pieces were to be carefully put into place on 'D' Day. One of these final pieces would be the responsibility of 49 Squadron. I suppose that as Eric surveyed his congregation from the pulpit, he must have noticed the serious expression on my face. His sermon concluded, as usual with several bangs on the side of the pulpit to highlight his final words of wisdom, we sang the last hymn. On leaving the Church, Eric took me to one side and said, 'Ken, you looked very serious during my sermon and I am sure it was not because you were digesting my words'. I replied, 'Yes Eric, I regret that my thoughts had wandered. I was reflecting on the size of this operation and the vital parts played by so many units and people'. He then said 'Well good luck Ken, for I know you are undertaking the first drop; I have said a little prayer for you.' I thanked him and drove to the Mess for lunch. After lunch I acted as umpire for the squadron cricket match in which Alan Washbrook gave a very good account of himself both as a batsman and in the field, but then he was related to Cyril Washbrook the England cricketer! I believe the officers won but the result was not important, for there were so many amusing incidents – I forgot to call 'over' on several occasions! Needless

Top: Time to relax. From left to right: Wg Cdr Ken Hubbard, Air Cdre Ginger Weir (Air Task Commander) and Wg Cdr Ron Boardman. *(Author)*

Centre: The weapon assembly area on Christmas Island.

Bottom: Preparing the high-speed cameras on Malden Island.

to say, Sgt Cressey managed to organise refreshments for all and it was not orange juice!

The following day being a Monday, I was on the airfield early, for with 'D' Day two days away I wanted four aircraft fully serviceable. XD818 was scheduled to be taxied to the weapon area and handed over to the Scientific Weapons Team to test and load the live nuclear H-bomb, code named 'Short Granite'. After a session at the aircraft with Bill Caple and my ground crew, I spent time with each Crew Chief and their ground crews, satisfying myself that all was well.

I told my crew that after lunch we would have a detailed crew briefing in my office tent, in order to run over the entire flight profile for a live drop and spell out actions in the event of various emergencies. So on return to the airfield after lunch, we settled into my small office and I ran over the entire flight profile from take-off to weapon drop. I pointed out that on 'D' Day there would be no variation to that of the dress rehearsal, the only difference being that this time we were dropping a live Hydrogen bomb in the megaton range; therefore, on weapon burst, we should experience flash on the aircraft surface and after roll-out from the escape manoeuvre the aircraft would be subjected to the over pressure wave. There was no reason to believe the effect of this to be anything more than hitting severe turbulence: We could expect this some 2½ minutes after weapon burst, by which time our slant range from aircraft to burst point would be approximately 12nm. At weapon burst our range would be approximately 9nm. I stressed the importance of achieving a very good bombing accuracy, and told Alan that if in any doubt on the final run regarding accuracy, he was not to hesitate to call 'Dummy Run' and control would be told that we required a second one.

The entire success of this operation depended on our bombing accuracy; therefore everything from our point of view must be perfect before the weapon was released. This point in the operation represented the culmination of months of hard work by a vast number of people and units. No. 49 Squadron was privileged to be given the responsibility of 'delivering the goods' and the prestige of the squadron and of Bomber Command would be in our hands on this day.

I then turned to the rather delicate subject of a possible weapon release malfunction, which would not permit us to land the Valiant back on Christmas Island, due to the risk of a radioactive incident should the weapon release itself and explode during the landing run. This was a most unlikely possibility but had to be faced; therefore it was important that they all understood exactly the drill I should follow. I then explained that rear crew members would bale out from 5,000ft near to HMS *Warrior* and the co-pilot and myself fly the aircraft away from the area downwind, ejecting at a range of 50nm, leaving the aircraft with the automatic time and distance set for 200nm or 30min for a controlled crash into the sea. We would be pinpointed by a Shackleton and then picked up by helicopter from HMS *Warrior*.

This concluded the briefing and then our task was to taxi XD818 to the weapons area, carrying out all aircraft equipment tests prior to handing over. From this point we would not be allowed near the aircraft until the morning of 'D' Day with 'Short Granite' loaded and ready for the first full scale test.

We were now one full day away from 'D' Day and the airfield was busy with the Shackletons and PR Canberras carrying out their pre-test sorties and providing information on which the Task Force Commander would base his final decision. Already there was a quiet air of expectancy around the airfield and one could sense the tension prevailing as every unit with a major part to play checked and double checked to ensure that their arrangements were complete.

At dinner that night in the Mess, I thought my own crew was a little more serious than usual; no doubt their thoughts were 9,000nm away. With any test such as this, we were all aware that certain risks existed with an untried nuclear weapon system. I was confident that in the operational training phase the Scientific Weapons Team had tested every possible mechanical and electronic device within the weapon system, its arming mechanism and altitude detonation device. They could not have been more thorough, cautious and professional; often to the point when flying over the Malden area for practice drops, they made me fly so many race tracks that I was known to have exploded on one occasion to tell them 'For – sake, let's get on with it; I'm fed up with going round and round!'.

The next day was a busy one for the Shackleton and high level Canberras detailed for weather reporting. By the end of the day the Task Force Commander had to be certain that the entire maritime ocean area was clear of shipping. The Meteorological Team had sufficient weather data to give an accurate forecast for 'D' Day, plus a high level wind pattern to predict possible radioactive fall-out areas.

'Blue Danube' – Britain's first atomic bomb. This type of casing was also used to house the thermonuclear devices that were detonated off Malden and Christmas Islands.

In the afternoon my own crew plus Sqn Ldr Millett and crew attended the major briefing by the Task Force Commander, the Scientifiic Director, Air Task Force Commander and Chief Meteorological Forecaster. All looked set for the live operation to go ahead tomorrow.

The evening was to be a quiet one with early bed, for I wanted to be absolutely fresh for the next day's flying task. Before turning in I allowed myself a leisurely walk along the shore watching the magical colours visible in the coral reef as the clear blue waters of the South Pacific rolled over its undulating and picturesque contours. Not that I needed to relax myself, for my attitude to the drop was completely clinical; to me it was a routine exercise but one which demanded from myself a very high standard of instrument flying under severely enclosed conditions. My only real concern was that I could keep myself relaxed on each bomb run to ensure that no tension crept in to affect the accuracy and smoothness of my flying. Fortunately I enjoyed instrument flying.

After a refreshing stroll, I returned to my tent and was soon fast asleep.

CHAPTER SEVEN

'Grapple'

awoke early, to the usual sounds of the sea gulls and the gentle lapping of the waves on the shore and the noise as they cascaded over the coral reef barrier. I quickly got out of bed and stood outside the rear of my tent which looked out over the Pacific and the coral reef, and pensively surveyed the scene, for this was to be a very special day. The air at this early hour felt good; fresh and clean although warm. There was no cloud, although I realised that as the morning temperature rose, fair weather cumulus would form. The sun was still at a low angle, producing a glittering effect on the clear blue Pacific.

Nothing could be more tranquil and peaceful at this hour. I absorbed the scene with pleasure, although by contrast, in some 4 hours time, 400nm away, the clear air over an uninhabited island would be shattered by man's scientific and technological ability, in the shape of a nuclear device to release fantastic energy into the atmosphere. Tomorrow the world would know that Britain had a Hydrogen bomb in her armoury, with the means of delivery by one of the most advanced bombers in the Royal Air Force V Force. This force would now have additional nuclear teeth heralding the commencement of Britain's role as an independent nuclear deterrent power and her effective contribution to the maintenance of peace over the next 25 years.

Having enjoyed my morning reflections, I hurried over for a quick shower and returned to change into khaki drill uniform; thence to join my crew for breakfast. They all looked fit, well and alert, so I was sure they had slept soundly.

There was already considerable activity in the mess, because both Shackleton and Canberra crews would be attending early briefing. I greeted Wg Cdr Alexander, OC of the Shackleton squadron, who was also in for early breakfast.

Our first task of the day was to hear, at Joint Operations Control, a full-scale briefing of the current situation by the Task Force Commander. Whilst we had slept there had been great activity at Joint Operations Control and both the Air Task Force Commander and the Scientific Director had been on duty all night checking and rechecking the search reports from the Shackletons, assessing with the meteorological staff the upper wind structure for fall-out pattern. The Scientific Director had been in constant touch with his weapons team working at XD818 who, after loading, were required to work through a very comprehensive test schedule, the weapon being constantly monitored for radioactivity.

It was not surprising therefore that both Air Cdre Ginger Weir and Bill Cook looked a little tired, but very cheerful. For the Task Force Commander, the Scientific Director and the Air Task Force Commander, today was the culmination of all their endeavours over the past 12 months. For the Scientific Director, it signified the final proof of the success of the work at the AWRE over the past three years.

The hopes of so many that day were pinned on the success of this operation. We all had a vital part to play and it was equally important that every man involved should carry out his allotted task to as near perfection as humanly possible.

As the briefing proceeded, it was clear that everything was suitable for the live drop to take place – the weather forecast was excellent, with about one eighth cloud cover of fair weather cumulus by about 10.00hrs local, visibility was unrestricted but surface wind was light and variable, which would give a smooth sea surface making it difficult for the Green Satin equipment to lock on; however, this we could overcome.

Bombing height was to be 45,000ft, therefore the grandstand aircraft would operate at 43,000ft and one mile behind XD818.

Take-off time for Valiant XD818 to be 09.00hrs local; therefore, all watches were at this point synchronised. The Air Task Force Commander quickly confirmed the emergency services that would be on hand for the Valiant take-off and reaffirmed that initial control would be exercised from Joint Operations Control until I transferred to the Controller on HMS *Narvik,* where control then passed to the Task Force Commander, by that time on board. Details of the personnel safety plan were briefly outlined and it was confirmed that the transmission by the Valiant dropping aircraft would be broadcast by tannoy to points throughout the island, so that all would be able to follow the final operation. The Task Force Commander wished us good luck and we climbed into my Land Rover to drive to the airfield, followed by Sqn Ldr Barney Millett and his crew in a second Land Rover.

Already personnel were assembling and one could sense the excitement prevailing, for as everybody had to be accounted for, every man knew he was involved. We arrived at the airfield which was strangely empty *of* personnel, except for airmen belonging to the Canberras of 76 Squadron due to carry out the cloud sampling, and the two Shackletons that were to position for medium level observations. The only 49 Squadron airmen on dispersal were my own ground crew of Valiant XD818 and those of XD824 under control of their Crew Chief. Of course, as NCO in charge, Flt Sgt Asprey was present and I was not surprised to find Sgt Cressey at the office tent.

The time was now 08.00hrs so we quickly changed into flying kit and walked over to where XD818 was parked; she looked absolutely splendid in her brilliant white anti-flash finish, spotlessly clean – the ground crew had done a marvellous job; they were very proud of their aircraft, and their enthusiasm was directly due to the attitude and interest of their Crew Chief, Bill Caple.

As we walked round XD818, checking everything against the check list, Bob Beeson and I paused to inspect our vital bomb load – all 10,000lb of bomb containing the equivalent of a million tons of high explosive energy. Just as we were completing our checks, Air Cdre Ginger Weir and Wg Cdr Ron Boardman drove up in a Land Rover, to wish us good luck and to confirm that all was ready at the Malden Island end. Final connection of the bomb batteries was then completed by the Weapon Team.

The rear crew members were already on board, so having thanked the Crew Chief both Bob Beeson and I climbed in, closed the fuselage door, settled into our seats and commenced the start engines drill. Having then checked with each crew member that his equipment was serviceable, I gave the order to the Crew Chief to clear chocks, obtained taxi clearance from air traffic control and Valiant XD818 was moving on the most historic flight of its service life.

As we taxied out, the sense of the occasion must have penetrated every crew member, although any crew conversation, as was always the drill, was kept to essentials. For myself I was conscious, more than anything else, that my every word transmitted on that bomb line, and the image of our professionalism, would be witnessed by the 3,000 personnel on Christmas Island. This must be a perfect operation as regards our performance, for every ear would be tuned for those final vital seconds to bomb release and listening to the entire escape manoeuvre commentary. Every man would feel he was present on that bomb run; and indeed my own airmen confirmed this afterwards.

We lined up on the runway ready for take-off and, at precisely 09.00hrs, control gave permission. I ordered the crew to stand by, and opened the throttles for take-off. We were airborne by one minute past the hour. Once into our climb, every crew member was busy with his normal duties and the flight immediately settled into a routine sortie. Our fuel load on take-off was 5,500gal allowing for the flight time to Malden Island, with a navigational, initial and final bomb run, the aircraft all-up weight after release of the bomb would be 102,000lb for the escape manoeuvre, which was ideal.

During our climb towards the rendezvous point 75nm from the target indicator, all metal anti-flash screens were securely fitted and the bomb aimer confirmed that only his sliding shutter was open. The flight deck was completely blacked out and we were flying in strict instrument conditions; it always took a few minutes to become completely acclimatised to the fully enclosed situation.

The climb proceeded smoothly, and during it the AEO maintained contact by both high-frequency and VHF radio with joint operations control and HMS *Narvik*, the operation control ship in the target area. We could hear the other aircraft reporting in on their assigned positions and Valiant XD824 confirmed it was one mile astern, 2,000ft below. As bombing altitude was reached the aircraft was trimmed out, power adjusted to settle at Mach 0.76. Some 50 minutes after

Top: The Joint Operations Control Room.
(*Royal Engineers*)

Centre: The mushroom cloud as viewed from
HMS *Narvik*.

Bottom: Scientific recovery personnel leave
HMS *Narvik* by helicopter to collect records
from Malden Island.

take-off we reported that Valiant XD818 was at RV point. This transmission, plus all others, would now go out on High Frequency to be re-transmitted at Christmas Island.

As expected with such a calm sea, the navigator, Eric Hood, reported that the Green Satin equipment would not lock on to the sea surface; thus we would be denied this vital equipment to obtain an accurate ground speed. Fortunately the Decca navigational equipment was operating. Therefore, he would need to utilise this to obtain ground speed times and distances on the bomb run, which was of considerable importance to the bomb aimer for the 1½nm delay factor. The bomb aimer now confirmed that visibility was excellent and the one-eighth cloud cover was not sufficient to obscure the forward view.

At the intercept point of the bomb line, Control from HMS *Narvik* gave clearance for the navigational run to enable us to assess ground speed and drift and establish a bombing heading to maintain the bomb line.

With this complete, we turned on to the race track, reporting the navigational run complete. Control came back stating it was ready for the initial run, during which every switching sequence was followed and all telemetering equipment in the aircraft and on the ground checked by the Scientific Weapon Team. Only if every piece of equipment was operating correctly would final live weapon drop clearance be given by the Task Force Commander and Scientific Director.

Having flown down the race track we turned again on to intercept point, being positioned by the navigator using Decca, and commenced the Initial Run. The only words spoken on this run would be confirmation of ground speed and distance by the navigator, the weapons telemetering switching drill by the AEO seated at the weapons panel, and from the bomb aimer, passing correction of headings to me as we flew down the bomb line.

The bomb aimer quickly aligned the aircraft to the bomb line allowing for drift so that our final heading settled at 202°T, with few corrections. I concentrated completely on my blind flying instruments, maintaining heading and an accurate 45,000ft on the sensitive altimeter, with air speed at Mach 0.76 indicated. To achieve this the major flight instrument is the artificial horizon which provides a presentation of the aircraft's attitude in flight. Flying was smooth and I felt relaxed; Bob Beeson monitored my flying, ready to adjust power should this be necessary, the entire procedure being a well-exercised and disciplined team exercise.

When the bomb aimer called 'Now' it indicated graticule coincidence on his Mk T4 bombsight; I therefore called 'Initial Run complete; turning on to the race track'-this was acknowledged. I did not expect any immediate clearance to proceed with the live weapon drop, for on board HMS *Narvik* every aspect of the results of the equipment checks would have to be evaluated. In addition, the Task Force Commander would be checking that all aircraft were in position. Only when both the Scientific Director and Task Force Commander were satisfied that all was operationally ready would we be given clearance to bomb.

It is awe-inspiring, when looked at in retrospect, to consider the vast power five airmen had in their possession at that time. Somehow we were all too absorbed with the task in hand, to allow such thoughts to enter our heads.

By the time we had reached point Charlie on the race track, the major decision had been made. The controller's voice came through to clear Valiant XD818 for a live drop. This I acknowledged, and then the controller's voice could be heard warning all aircraft that the Valiant had been cleared to bomb. I now called 'Captain to crew, we are now cleared for the live weapon drop, so let's make it a good one'. The navigator gave me a turn on to the intercept point, from which we settled on to a heading of 203°T, the bomb aimer continuing with visual corrections. I called 'Valiant now at intercept point, commencing live bombing run'.

The run up to weapon release was steady, and thanks to good initial positioning on the bomb line by the bomb aimer, I only had very minor corrections to make to aircraft heading, which contributed greatly to smooth and accurate instrument flying, and at no stage therefore did I get tense in holding corrections given. A precise altitude of 45,000ft was maintained, with airspeed Mach 0.76 and heading steady at 203°T. The time delay and distance had been set and I knew that from the point of bombsight gracticule coincidence with the target indicator, there would be 11 seconds delay before the weapon left the aircraft. The bomb aimer's voice was giving 'Steady, steady' and the AEO called 'Weapon Master Switch ON' which meant that the arming mechanism was now switched to its batteries and therefore fully armed.

Next came 'Steady, steady, NOW' and here I knew that over the next 11 seconds I must maintain my complete instrument flying accuracy; height, airspeed and heading must not vary. The co-pilot's left hand was in position on the throttles and when the voice of the bomb aimer came over with 'Bomb gone, shutter closed' I heaved a sigh of relief as I called 'Full throttle, rolling into escape manoeuvre'. With 60° bank to the left, on the artificial horizon, I applied backward pressure on the control column bringing the sensitive accelerometer to a reading of 1.7G, height of 45,000ft, speed Mach 0.76. This I continually broadcast, giving progress through the turn to the point of having turned through 135°, our heading now 073°T. I called 'Rolling out, on heading of 073°T, time elapsed 40sec'. The commentary was continued, stating that after 50 seconds, no flash effect had been experienced in the aircraft. At 2½ minutes after estimated weapon burst, I reported that the aircraft experienced shock waves, but not violent ones. After a further 5 minutes, control gave clearance for all anti-flash screens to be removed and Valiant XD818 could turn to observe the development of the fire ball and mushroom cloud effect.

We removed all anti-flash screens and I turned the aircraft through 90° to port; as we turned, the sight which met our eyes was truly breathtaking. There, towering above us (remember we were at 45,000ft), was a huge mushroom shaped cloud, with the stem a cauldron mass of orange as the fireball had developed and the hot gases risen into the atmosphere, progressively fanning out and forming a foaming white canopy which can only be compared with the top of a mushroom. This top must have reached an altitude of approximately 60,000ft, with ice caps forming.

It really was a sight of such majesty and grostesque beauty that it defies adequate description.

The rear crew members could only see from a porthole on either side of the fuselage, so I allowed each in turn to climb up to the flight deck, so that they could see this fantastic development. Their exclamations of incredulity were many and varied but I think it true to say that for all of us, it was something we would remember for the rest of our lives.

Having fully observed the results, I cleared with control for a return to Christmas Island, for it was now busy with the Canberras which would be commencing their task of taking high level samples for evaluation by the Scientific Team.

The return flight to Christmas Island was uneventful; the aircraft performed normally, and therefore there was no reason to believe that the over-pressure wave had caused any damage or that flash had affected our electronic equipment. We carried out a normal let down from 45,000ft, homing to the radio beacon and joined the circuit for a visual landing.

After landing we taxied in to dispersal to be met by Flt Sgt Asprey, Chief Technician Bill Caple, Sqn Ldr Arthur Steele and Air Cdre Ginger Weir.

With engines shut down, we climbed out into the hot, humid atmosphere. Ginger Weir congratulated us on a first-class drop, for all indications were that the accuracy was good and so far the Scientific Team was well satisfied with the results. Eveybody on the island had felt involved, being able to listen in to the bombing run and the escape manoeuvre commentary.

Whilst we were talking, Bill Caple and the ground crew were busy examining XD818 in detail to see if there was any visible damage from blast, but she appeared in perfect shape.

By this time members of the Scientific Weapon Evaluation Team had arrived to remove telemetry recording equipment and the automatic observer that would tell them every move I made on each bombing run. They also removed all tail cone, wing and bomb bay cameras – masses of evidence to assess the full test evaluation.

Both my crew and I felt relieved that the flight was over and that it had all gone so well. No. 49 Squadron had maintained its proud record of achievement and today we had added yet another chapter to its history.

I walked over to my office tent with Air Cdre Weir, feeling very hot and sticky in the heat, but extremely satisfied with the sortie. I would not be completely happy until the forward weapon team produced the accurate bombing result. In the event I received this later in the evening, which was extremely good.

The invaluable Sgt Cressey produced mugs of tea for Ginger Weir, myself and my crew, which was much appreciated. Ginger then said the entire operation had gone well so far and he hoped the samples being obtained by the

Canberras would be satisfactory, as these, once landed and secured by the Scientific Team in lead containers, would be flown back by a Canberra to the Weapon Research Establishment at Aldermaston.

Before leaving, he invited all of my crew for a special celebration at the TFC Mess at 18.30hrs. We accepted with pleasure, for after all the months of preparation, now was the time to relax as our task had been successful. However, I was not to realise at this stage that my entire squadron in their various messes had decided to celebrate the occasion, and over the evening my crew and I would be required to join in at each mess!

Since it was now lunch time, my immediate requirement was a can of cold beer and something to eat. We therefore climbed into my Land Rover and disappeared to the Officers Mess Tent, perhaps to fortify ourselves for the evening ahead of us. First of all though, there was work to be completed on the airfield.

After the euphoria of the success of the first live drop had evaporated, it was necessary to turn once again to preparing aircraft for the second stage of the scientific programme leading to live drop No. 2, planned roughly for the end of May.

The next crew selected for the task was to be Sqn Ldr Dave Roberts, bomb aimer Flt Lt Ken Lewis, navigational plotter Flt Lt Ted Dunn, the AEO Flt Lt Ted Beattie, and co-pilot Flg Off Alan Pringle. This was an extremely experienced crew which had contributed so much to the entire 'Grapple' programme, ever since it was decided that a Valiant was to be used as the dropping aircraft. Flying the grandstand aircraft would be Sqn Ldr Arthur Steel, in order to provide him and his crew with experience for live drop No. 3.

Whilst we were turning our attention to preparing for this stage of the scientific programme, the scientists themselves were busy evaluating the results and recordings of the first live drop. Depending upon their findings, the scientific training programme would be amended or revised accordingly.

During the seven days following the first live drop, indications of the press coverage given to the event in the UK were reaching us, and many friends sent cuttings from all the national papers. I received a great number of congratulatory letters and signals from service friends, as well as a considerable amount of mail from people who opposed our nuclear test programme, on both moral and religious grounds. Indeed, many of these were abusive in the extreme, including threats of violence. All of these letters I handed over to our security staff for them to deal with as they thought best. Personally, I had no intention of answering or even reading them fully.

Once the next stage of our programme was resolved, I thought it would be an excellent idea to let my own crew enjoy a few days leave in Honolulu, for they had worked extremely hard ever since we arrived on the island and a few days to enjoy normal civilised living would do them a power of good. The Air Task Force Commander agreed with me and authorised their flight to Honolulu in the Hastings aircraft which faithfully plied between Christmas Island and Honolulu carrying mail and fresh vegetables. Alan Washbrook tried hard to persuade me to join them but this was not possible with the next live drop due within 14 days. They therefore departed without me.

For this next phase of the scientific programme, the actual test was to be witnessed by various prominent members of the national press, including Chapman Pincher, Defence Correspondent of the *Sunday Express,* and by diplomatic observers invited by the Government. To accommodate this party which was flown out in a chartered aircraft, additional tents were being erected in the area by the Task Force Commander's Mess. The plan was that these observers on 'D' Day would be flown out to Malden Island, then transferred to HMS *Warrior* from where they would watch the entire test and listen to the commentary from the dropping Valiant.

Dave Roberts' crew in Valiant XD822 completed the pre-drop scientific training programme with excellent results and once again we found ourselves fully committed to the dress rehearsal.

By this time, my crew had returned from their seven days' leave in Honolulu where they stayed at the American Officers' Club. They looked extremely fit and well and had obviously thoroughly enjoyed their stay. Indeed, on hearing some of their experiences over a glass of beer, I came to the conclusion that it had been a most successful leave.

Alan Washbrook, who was extremely short of hair on the top of his head, had certainly been burnt by the sun, his cranium being well tanned. Indeed, he told me that on one evening at the American Officers' Club, after a few drinks in the bar, he had gone to the toilet and a very tall Texan came and stood beside him. Looking down at Alan he remarked 'Say skinhead, you sure have caught the sun today!' Since the Texan was much larger, Alan decided it was wise not to take offence!

Two days before the planned second live drop, now scheduled for 31 May, the official observers arrived on the Island to be met by the Task Force Commander and Air Task Force Commander. Amongst our visitors was Air Cdre John Grandy (later MRAF Sir John Grandy) who was designated to succeed AVM Wilf Oulton as Task Force Commander on completion of the present 'Grapple' programme.

Our distinguished visitors were entertained that night at the Task Force Commander's Mess and on the following day they were to be given a tour of the airfield and port facilities. I was briefed very thoroughly that under no circumstances should I be drawn into discussing any details of the first live drop with the various defence correspondents. Thus, when our distinguished visitors came to see the squadron on the airfield, I was careful to stay clear of the subject and concentrated on showing them round a Valiant and introducing various squadron members.

Since they would all be on the island on the night of this next live drop, I thought it a good idea for the squadron officers to give a party in the Officers'

Mess that night to celebrate the occasion. This was quickly and easily arranged by the excellent cooperation of Wg Cdr (now AVM) Douglas Bower, the island Wing Commander Admin. All the members of the Task Force Commanders' Mess were invited with all our distinguished visitors, all Squadron Commanders, and each officer inviting his own guest. We would make this a 49 Squadron party to celebrate this second drop, and one for our visitors to remember for a long time.

Once again, the night before 'D' Day arrived and Valiant XD822 had been handed over to the Scientific Weapons Team for the loading and monitoring of the weapon – code named 'Orange Herald'. Dave Roberts and his crew were all fit and looking forward to their task. That evening I drove to the airfield to check with Flt Sgt Bill Asprey and Chief Technician Sam Small that there were four Valiants fully serviceable. All was once again ready for tomorrow's big day. Sqn Ldr Barney Millett would go forward as Valiant aircraft adviser to the Task Force Commander and I was to remain at Joint Operations Centre with the Air Task Force Commander.

The morning of 31 May dawned and by 07.00hrs there was intense activity as all units prepared for their allotted task and personnel began moving to their dispersal positions. The weather was again excellent so all looked well for a visual drop. The morning briefing proceeded smoothly and it was soon apparent that the maritime area was clear, meteorological reports good and serviceability of all aircraft participating satisfactory. The Scientific Director reported all weapon loading tests completed; therefore the operation was declared on.

We proceeded to the airfield and Sqn Ldr Dave Roberts and his crew changed into flying kit and made their way to Valiant XD822 in the weapon area, and Sqn Ldr Arthur Steele and his crew to Valiant XD823, which was again to act as grandstand.

Before Dave Roberts and Alan Pringle had completed their external checks of Valiant XD822, the Air Task Force Commander arrived to wish them luck, and having done so myself, left them to get on with starting engines. I walked over to check that all was well with Valiant XD823 and then waited by my office tent in my Land Rover to watch the take-off of both aircraft.

The airfield was deserted except for those airmen working on the Canberra sampling aircraft and the Shackletons.

I watched Valiant XD822 taxi slowly out to the runway carrying its important load, and I could imagine the feelings of all aboard the aircraft as they moved forward on this historic occasion. They knew that success on the bomb run depended upon their performance as a team and the high standard of accurate instrument flying of Dave Roberts, particularly during the vital last 10 to 11 seconds.

Valiant XD822 moved majestically on to the runway and commenced its take-off run, becoming airborne at 09.07hrs local time. With undercarriage retracted she quickly settled into a climb heading towards Malden Island. As the mighty full-throated roar of its four jet engines receded, Valiant XD823 positioned itself ready for take-off.

Once Valiant XD823 was airborne, I left the airfield and joined Air Cdre Weir at Joint Operations Centre, to listen to the commentary as Valiant XD822 executed its task.

Whilst waiting for Valiant XD822 to arrive in the Malden target area, Air Cdre Weir told me that the Task Force Commander had agreed to both myself and Dave Roberts giving a recorded interview to the BBC representative in the official party, but warned we must be extremely careful not to divulge any detail of operational technique or height. I could see this would be a difficult one to handle, but agreed to be interviewed.

However, our conversation was cut short as transmissions were now coming through from the dropping aircraft and it had been cleared to carry out the 'Navigational Run'. The Operations Centre was a hive of activity as the Canberra and Shackleton aircraft reported they were on station.

The master sampling Canberra for this test was being flown by Wg Cdr Geoffrey Dhenin, the RAF's most experienced Flying Medical Officer and an expert on radiation. Geoffrey Dhenin later became Air Marshal Sir Geoffrey Dhenin, having risen to the top medical appointment in the Royal Air Force, as Director General Medical Services. Geoff Dhenin and I were old friends, having served at the Royal Air Force Flying College together. At this present time, he was on the staff of HQ Bomber Command as the specialist in aviation medicine.

All was then set; I could feel more excitement being virtually a spectator than I experienced as the pilot of the dropping aircraft on 15 May. There was plenty of activity in the Joint Operations Centre but I was able to sit back and listen carefully to the comments from Valiant XD822 as the aircraft flew on the bomb line for the initial run.

Ken Lewis, the bomb aimer, could be heard giving calm and steady corrections to Dave Roberts, until such time as the run was complete and Dave Roberts called 'Initial Run complete, turning on to the race track'. All attention in the Operations Centre was now concentrated on listening for the controller's voice giving the 'all clear' for the live run. At last this clearance was given to Valiant XD822 and all aircraft warned that the dropping aircraft was authorised to proceed with the live drop.

As the voice of the navigator, Ted Dunn, confirmed they were at intercept point, tension heightened as we then listened to the bomb aimer's steady corrections; for to me it sounded like a good bomb run. Finally the bomb aimer said 'Steady, steady, NOW' – this meant the grandstand aircraft would be commencing its escape manoeuvre; the dropping aircraft holding the course, height and airspeed for those vital 11 seconds set within the time delay system in the bombsight. I checked these vital seconds on my watch, and then clearly came through 'Weapon gone, shutter closed'. At the same time Dave Roberts' calm voice called 'Full power, rolling into escape manoeuvre'. He then continued a steady commentary concluding with 'Rolling out on to heading of

030°'. This turn was completed in approximately 45 seconds and then some 5 seconds later the controller's voice came over the tannoy announcing that we had achieved 'weapon detonation'. The dropping Valiant reported they had experienced the blast wave and following this the crew was cleared to remove screens and observe the effects of the mushroom cloud development.

To me, on the ground, it sounded as if everything had gone extremely well with XD822 and I felt sure the bombing accuracy result would be good.

Knowing that Dave Roberts would now be heading Valiant XD822 back towards Christmas Island, I left the Operations centre and drove back to the airfield in order to welcome the crew and congratulate them on a very professional sortie. As I left the initial instructions were being passed by the controller to the Canberra sampling aircraft.

What I did not know, until Dave Roberts had landed and he was giving me his initial verbal report, was that during the escape manoeuvre he had experienced an electrical fault in his accelerometer, which was vital in order to hold the accurate gravity pressure needed in the escape steep turn. This sensitive instrument failed to operate, and thus in applying backward pressure on the control column in the turn, the aircraft suddenly reached a high speed stall point. To find oneself in a high speed stall in this configuration is an unpleasant experience, and it is to Dave Roberts' credit that he was able to recover attitude and resume the escape manoeuvre utilising the mechanical accelerometer which was not placed in a position in the instrument panel layout to facilitate easy reference whilst flying to the full blind flying instrument panel.

To have recovered from this situation in a 60° banked steep turn, under full instrument conditions, was a supreme feat of airmanship, for there were only seconds in hand before the weapon would explode when it reached 8,000ft. Even more credit to Dave Roberts was the fact that although experiencing the rather unpleasant incident during the escape manoeuvre, his voice never wavered during the commentary; certainly those of us listening on the ground did not realise the difficulties this crew was experiencing at a very critical period after weapon release.

The second live thermonuclear weapon had been dropped on 31 May 1957 at 10.44hrs local time. Thus we had completed the second phase of our operational programme.

That afternoon, the official observers were scheduled to visit 49 Squadron and be allowed to see round a Valiant. With all ground crew back on duty from their dispersal points, we lined up the Valiants ready for our visitors, including Valiant XD822 which had just completed its historic flight. The official observers had obviously been impressed by all they had witnessed in the forward area from HMS *Warrior*, and were extremely keen to see round a Valiant, but although questions were fast and furious, the answers had to be very guarded.

At last we were clear of visitors and attention could be turned to the squadron party planned for that evening, to which all the official guests had been invited, including all members of the Task Force Commander's Mess. By the time I got back to the Officers' Mess, the official bombing result was given to me by the Scientific Director. It was a good one, and the news was quickly passed to Dave Roberts and his crew.

The squadron party later that evening was a great success and I think everybody enjoyed themselves. Both the Task Force Commander and Scientific Director were in good form as all results coming in indicated that the test had been successful.

On the following day both Dave Roberts and myself were scheduled to record interviews for the BBC and this was something to which I was not looking forward. However, in the event we both managed to keep this very undramatic and the interviewer seemed disappointed that our general reaction was as to a routine sortie, for which we had undertaken special training.

With the departure of the official observers, we resumed normal preparation for live drop No. 3, tentatively scheduled to take place on 19 June, provided the weather patterns were acceptable. Sqn Ldr Arthur Steele and crew were earmarked for this operation with Sqn Ldr Barney Millett and crew flying grandstand.

We had now been on the island for 10 weeks, under very uncomfortable domestic and climatic conditions. Every effort was made to keep squadron personnel occupied in off duty hours, with sports competitions, but I could sense there was a general longing to be getting back to more civilised conditions.

Many personnel had brought with them hobbies to pass the time and I was surprised at the number of men who by the aid of 'painting with numbers' kits produced some really good oil paintings. One airman, namely Colin Jeffries, was in absolute heaven with the various insect species he collected. He was a member of the ground crew on XD818 and normally had some peculiar specimen to display whenever I came near the aircraft.

Boredom in the evenings, after a while, was the problem; therefore, to have a hobby or interest to follow was an asset. Indeed, I brought out with me one of the painting by numbers sets, hoping this might enable me to discover some hidden talent. However, it was not to be, for although following the instructions carefully, I never could achieve any recognisable results on canvas. Indeed, I found the task far too demanding on my limited store of patience, and on one particularly frustrating evening, when oil painting and myself decided we had nothing in common, the entire box of tricks was consigned to the other side of the reef and permanent residence in the South Pacific!

During the third pre-drop scientific training programme, we saw quite a lot of Air Cdre John Grandy who had remained after the official observers returned. He was designated to take over from the Task Force Commander on completion of this present test series. John Grandy had a distinguished fighter background, but was extremely keen to learn more about the Valiant. A man of great charm and tremendous personality, he was soon to be a great favourite with all personnel.

Once again 'D' Day approached and it looked as if all would be well for the live drop to take place on 19 June.

Sqn Ldr Arthur Steele, with his bomb aimer Flt Lt Wilf Jenkins (since deceased) were at operational readiness; the dress rehearsal had gone off without a hitch and the bombing result excellent. This was, without a doubt, one of the best crews in the entire V Force. Arthur Steele himself was a perfectionist, who drove himself hard and consistently maintained the highest possible standard both in the air and on the ground. His attention to detail in formulating and controlling our squadron training programme had been the vital factor in achieving the high standards of consistent bombing accuracy we had produced to date.

On 19 June all was set for the third live megaton weapon test to take place and the usual programme of aircraft preparation, weapon loading and crew briefing proceeded in the now well established pattern. For this drop Valiant XD823 would be used, the regular aircraft flown by Arthur Steel and his crew.

After the morning briefing Air Cdre Ginger Weir handed me a memo, which announced that the planned fourth drop, for which Sqn Ldr Barney Millett and crew were standing by, would not now take place. Officer Commanding 49 Squadron was instructed to prepare all Valiant aircraft for a planned departure to UK in accordance with the flight schedule issued by HQ Bomber Command two days after completion of this third live weapon drop.

Whilst being pleased at the thought of returning to RAF Wittering, I was extremely disappointed for Sqn Ldr Barney Millett and his crew, who had now endured all the hard training and would unfortunately be denied a live weapon drop experience. It would also be a bitter disappointment to the ground crew of Valiant XD824 which had worked such long hours in extremely uncomfortable conditions to maintain this aircraft at a high standard of serviceability.

I decided I had to talk to Barney Millett, his crew and ground crew as soon as the day's live weapon drop was concluded. My full attention had first to be concentrated on the task ahead of us, for this was Arthur Steele's big day and his crew was looking forward to the experience of putting all of its training into a realistic operation.

With Arthur Steele and crew at Valiant XD823 in the weapons loading area, I walked over to wish them good luck, and in doing so was joined by Air Cdre Ginger Weir and John Grandy, who had also come to see the dropping aircraft take off.

Having given our best wishes to Arthur Steele and his bomb aimer, Wilf Jenkins, we walked back to my office tent. Ginger Weir then explained to me that the tests to date had been so successful that it had been decided to forgo the fourth planned test. There was a possibility that 49 Squadron would be required to participate in a further test series later in the year, but for political reasons this was still only in the planning stages. Thus we would be returning to our conventional bomber role once back in the UK. This would entail a demodification programme on all of the Valiants in order to refit the radar navigational bombing system. From this information I realised that a very lengthy retraining and re-equipping programme lay ahead.

Strangely, although pleased to know we would shortly be leaving Christmas Island, I hoped the next test series would be agreed, for I knew every squadron crew was keen to gain the operational experience of releasing a live nuclear weapon. In the meantime, my attention must be concentrated on today's live drop, so, having seen Valiant XD823 and the grandstand aircraft safely airborne, I headed for Joint Operations Control. Once there, I listened to the now familiar operations pattern developing, allowing my mind to dwell on the planned withdrawal phase that had already been drawn up some time ago.

As I heard the controller's voice clear Valiant XD823 for the Initial Run, my attention came back sharply to the day's task and my concentration centred on the actions of Arthur Steele and his crew. The initial run was completed without any problems and obviously all was well in the forward area, for clearance was given at an early stage of the race track for Valiant XD823 to carry out a live weapon drop.

The usual atmosphere of excitement and anticipation was present as we heard the intercept point called, and all knew that the Valiant was now tracking the bomb line at 45,000ft with all four jet engines emitting those distinctive vapour trails. Bomb aimer Wilf Jenkins was giving heading corrections and all sounded calm. Finally, the call 'Steady, steady, NOW' indicated the button had been pressed for the time delay for weapon release to operate – I sat tense as the 11 seconds delay ticked by, then 'Weapon released, shutters closed' came over the tannoy, immediately followed by Arthur Steele's voice 'Full power, rolling into the escape manoeuvre'. His commentary continued calmly and clearly to 'Rolling out'. I glanced at my watch; yes, he had completed his turn in 40 seconds, therefore, 10 seconds to bomb burst. As I glanced up, the controller's voice announced weapon burst. Some 2½ minutes later Arthur Steele announced they had experienced the blast wave and requested permission to remove the metal shutters and view the mushroom cloud development; this was given by the controller. After a brief chat with Air Cdre Ginger Weir, I left the Operations Centre and headed for the airfield to meet Arthur Steele and crew on landing.

Once Valiant XD823 had landed and taxied in to dispersal, I listened to Arthur Steele's verbal report and congratulated the entire crew on a first-class operation. I quickly informed Arthur that this drop was now to be the last in the present programme and that we should be putting the withdrawal phase into operation during the next two days. First though, I must talk to Barney Millett and his crew as well as his ground crew. Naturally, they were disappointed but as professional airmen they accepted this as a fact of life. I explained that if it were decided to carry out a further test series later in the year, they would be given the first live drop.

A meeting was next, with the Squadron Engineering Officer, Flt Sgt Bill Asprey and Crew Chiefs, to finalise the withdrawal phase, because with underwing tanks now available, the route back would be Honolulu–Travis–Goose Bay–RAF Wittering. Therefore all aircraft were now to have underwing tanks fitted and serviced to the departure plans. I spoke to all aircrew regarding return, which was met with general approval, and told them to liaise with their captains on departure briefing. The ground crews would clear up the dispersal site on departure of our Valiants, prepare all Valiant ground equipment for storage, and they would then return to the UK by civil charter aircraft. The withdrawal phase was now scheduled to begin on 21 June, with my crew leading the way.

Having completed all this, I was pleased to receive the bombing result for the third live drop. It was excellent, being the best to date.

With all the scientific tests completed and my thoughts concentrated on preparation for the Squadron's return to the UK, perhaps it was time to look back over the past 10 months and assess the achievement to date, for on my return to RAF Wittering one of the first tasks confronting me would be the requirement to produce a detailed operations report covering all aspects of the 'Grapple' task to date. I felt satisfied that 49 Squadron had acquitted itself well, and had accomplished, with distinction, the task which it had been assigned.

Looking to the long term from a V Force point of view, the results of these tests would no doubt influence the size and yield of future warheads destined to play an important role in Britain's deterrent force. Furthermore, 49 Squadron, by participating in these tests, had demonstrated to the world that the Royal Air Force had the capability to deliver nuclear weapons with precision to any target within V bomber range.

From a technical point of view we had been able to prove that even sophisticated aircraft such as the Valiant could be operated to a high state of serviceabilty in hot, humid and extremely wet conditions, with only basic technical servicing support. This had been achieved by highly professional technical Crew Chiefs and ground crews who possessed a pride in their aircraft and refused at any time to be discouraged by unpleasant climatic conditions.

Perhaps finally, on a more personal note, the 3½ months detachment to Christmas Island had provided me with a realistic opportunity to assess the true capability of both air and ground crew, under conditions which demanded personal initiative and a true ability to work as a well-trained team. The result was that the men of 49 Squadron had maintained and demonstrated a uniquely high standard of morale and pride in their unit that was the envy of other units on the island.

Yes, I was satisfied with the manner in which the operation had been completed, and proud to have commanded 49 Squadron. It had been a pleasure and a privilege to have worked within the 'Grapple' Task Force organisation. Somehow I sincerely hoped that we should be called upon to take part in an extension of the present test programme, although well aware that due to political considerations there were, at this stage, no firm plans for further tests. Thus, unless the politicians had a change of heart, 49 Squadron would be reverting to its normal V Force role once settled back at Wittering.

Over recent months there have been many comments in the national press regarding radiation hazards; this had also been a matter on which many people wrote to me, following the release of our identity in the national press. This was a subject to which I had never particularly addressed my thoughts during the three live drops, for the simple reason that with such a high air burst as was employed, there was no radiation hazard to the dropping Valiant.

When a nuclear weapon is detonated at an altitude of 8,000ft as was standard in these tests, the weapon itself is vapourised completely and these minute vapourised particles are carried up into the stratosphere, taking many months to return to the earth's surface, by which time the bulk of radioactivity has decayed and these particles are spread literally all over the whole surface of the globe. With this type of air burst the fireball does not come into contact with the surface of the sea or land at the target area; therefore, other than except for a very low level of induced radioactivity near the target there was no contamination off Malden Island, and certainly none at Christmas Island, 400nm away. In spite of this, the most elaborate plans were rigorously enforced for personnel safety throughout the entire test programme. Every man was accounted for and included in this very realistic safety plan. These were my thoughts in retrospect, as I spent this final evening on Christmas Island, for tomorrow would be a busy day checking that all departure arrangements were complete, including the follow-up departure of the ground crew, once all Valiants had returned to the UK.

CHAPTER EIGHT

Return to Wittering

On 21 June we commenced the withdrawal phase, and leaving Sqn Ldr Ted Flavell in charge of the 49 Squadron detachment, Sqn Ldr Dave Roberts and I plus crews took off in our Valiants from Christmas Island on the first stage of our 9,000nm flight back to RAF Wittering. We stayed at Honolulu, Travis AFB in California and Goose Bay in Newfoundland, and had been scheduled to arrive on 26 June at 10.00hrs local time; exactly on time, I landed at Wittering and taxied into our old familiar dispersal, having been welcomed back by Air Traffic Control who on initial contact said 'Welcome home 49!' As I shut down engines, I heard Dave Roberts call control giving his estimated time of arrival, which was exactly as planned.

We climbed out of the Valiant and were delighted to see that the Air Officer Commanding No. 3 Group, AVM K. Cross, and the Station Commander, Gp Capt John Woodroffe, had come to welcome us back and in doing so congratulated the squadron on results achieved. As I chatted to the AOC, I could see Mr Dolby, my batman, with Crusty, waiting to let him come forward. The AOC said 'Well Ken, there is somebody else waiting to see you' and beckoned to let Crusty loose. He came bounding forward and as I bent down to make a fuss of him, he got hold of my service dress cap and proudly marched around with it in his mouth, to the amusement of all concerned. Whilst all this was taking place, Dave Roberts and his crew had landed and taxied in to dispersal, so I walked over with the AOC and the Station Commander to greet them.

My 'B' Flight ground crew also all seemed in great shape – they had remained at RAF Wittering to handle the courier task; should we be requested to return to Christmas Island for any further nuclear tests, then it would be their turn to have a spell on the island. Wives and families had been allowed to come out to dispersal in order to welcome us home, so after the official welcome, the two crews were reunited with wives and families. I told them all they were free until Monday, when we would complete all remaining arrival details. In the meantime my Squadron Adjutant, Flg Off Denis Belcher, had kindly brought out my service car, so with Crusty aboard we drove back to the office in order to bring me up to date with anything that had occurred during my absence.

With this complete, as it was Friday, and my next aircraft were not due back until the following Tuesday, I also decided that a weekend in Norwich would be pleasant. Therefore, back to the Officers' Mess where Mr Dolby had anticipated my intentions, and then with Crusty aboard my own car, we drove to see my parents and hear about their surprise when invaded by the Press on the morning after the first live drop had been made public. Since I had never told them anything of our task on Christmas Island, the news came as a shock and, bless their hearts, they were not ready for any press interviews.

After a restful weekend Crusty and I returned to RAF Wittering on the Sunday evening, ready to get on with normal squadron duties and concentrate on the operational report I was required to produce.

After a refreshing weekend in the unspoiled surroundings of East Anglia, my energies were now directed towards preparation of detailed plans for transforming the squadron into its normal strategic bomber role. This meant that every crew must be put through the Bomber Command Crew operational classification scheme and aircraft progressively modified back to the standard V Force specification.

However, before turning one's attention to these rather tricky problems, some very encouraging news came through as the Queen's Birthday Honours List was announced. My entire crew, plus Sqn Ldrs Dave Roberts and Arthur Steele, had been awarded the Air Force Cross. At a later date the efforts of Flt Lt Ken Lewis and Wilf Jenkins were rewarded by a Commander in Chief's Commendation, and Flt Lt Ted Dunne, the Navigation Plotter in Dave Robert's crew, received the Queen's Commendation. Naturally we were all delighted to have been so honoured but, in reality, these awards belonged to the entire squadron and we were merely those privileged to be entrusted with the medals on their behalf.

After so long working on a specialised task, with top priority being accorded to our every requirement, it was not easy to adjust to the hard fact that we were now set to become a standard V Force squadron, committed to the less exciting outlook of regular participation in defence and dispersal exercises as well as routine training to achieve crew classification. This was to be accepted as the future pattern unless a change in political thinking dictated the continuation of nuclear weapon trials in an extension of the programme at Christmas Island.

Whilst turning my full attention to the immediate re-training programme, I retained a secret belief that we should soon be returning to a 'Grapple' task.

In the meantime, the 'A' Flight ground crews had returned from Christmas Island and the Air Officer Commanding agreed that I could give the entire squadron seven days leave before we settled to our new role. Everybody was more than ready for a break and with this behind us it would be easy to get the new training programme and aircraft modification programme underway.

The next two months passed quickly, during which time the squadron gave a major cocktail party in the Officers Mess to celebrate the completion of our involvement with Operation 'Grapple', and our guests of honour included Air Cdre Ginger Weir, Air Cdre Dennis Wilson, Jock Bryce (the Chief Test Pilot of

Vickers), also Brian Trubshaw who was Deputy Chief Test Pilot and an old friend from our RAF Manby days. It was a good party attended of course by the Station Commander, John Woodroffe, and I think everybody enjoyed themselves; 49 Squadron had a reputation for giving good parties!

I suppose it is true to say that most of my brother officers envied us the privilege of gaining first hand experience of dropping a live nuclear megaton weapon; for ultimately, should the deterrrent philosophy fail, the entire V Force crews would be required to deliver live nuclear weapons. Whenever we had Squadron Commander meetings on a group level, I was usually quizzed by my fellow Squadron Commanders regarding the operational hazards or otherwise regarding these weapons.

There were other pleasant side-effects of being involved in Operation 'Grapple'. I received an invitation from the Commandant of the Royal Air Force Flying College to lecture the current course. This was a considerable honour and although I accepted with pleasure, it was not without a certain amount of trepidation, for I should be addressing a potentially very distinguished gathering of officers, many of them possibly earmarked for Air Rank. However, this was to be later in the year, so there was plenty of time for me to prepare myself for this appointment.

Because there had been great publicity over the dropping of Britain's first live thermonuclear megaton weapon, and my name had been well and truly divulged, I could not avoid, on being introduced to new acquaintances, being ultimately subjected to the usual range of questions regarding the moral aspects of nuclear weapons.

Such questions on this subject neither embarrassed or presented any difficulties to me as a regular serving officer. The entire V Force aircrew was hand-picked for its ability, experience and genuine belief in the philosophy of our nuclear deterrent policy. We were all well aware that firstly Britain would never use this force in an act of aggression against another country, and the V Force would only be responding to any threat or premeditated strike against this country.

We firmly believed if the Eastern Bloc possessed a strategic nuclear strike capability this could only be contained provided Britain possessed an effective independent nuclear deterrent force capable of inflicting unacceptable damage to any aggressive major power. Not only did we have the formidable means of delivery, but the world knew that this force now had thermonuclear teeth.

Only if such a force was a realistic fact of life could we preserve our own democratic freedom by the simple means of demonstrating that this was a quality of life that we were prepared to protect. The V Force therefore was designated to protect and maintain peace; should the day have come when this force had been required to strike in retaliation against any nuclear attack on this country, then the deterrent policy would have failed.

Every V Force crew member understood this entire philosophy and although targeted for primary and secondary targets in the USSR, they knew that was

Personnel undergoing statutory radiation monitoring checks on their return to HMS *Narvik*.

part of an insurance policy for peace. Let there be no mistake about the determination and dedication of this force; had the day come when it was required to attack its pre-planned targets, there would have been no hesitation in undertaking the daunting task ahead of it, even though under such circumstances the attrition rate would have been high and, in such an interchange of high-yield nuclear weapons, there may have been no bases for aircraft to return to. Had we been committed to this course of action, no doubt survival of the vast majority of our people would have been doubtful in the extreme.

Regarding the moral issue of nuclear weapons, of course I agree as to the devastation they can create if used in anger. All weapons of war through the ages had been seen to be horrific at the time, but if one country is so equipped in its fighting forces, then any other country that does not wish to be overcome or occupied by force must have at least an equal military capability in order to deter an aggressor. This is history and until we reach a state of utopia, then a major country must be prepared to protect itself.

Today, with the advance of technology, those weapons are thermonuclear, and even if multilateral disarmament were achieved, the knowledge of how to produce nuclear weapons is still held in some under-developed countries of the world; therefore a nuclear threat would always exist from terrorist and extreme political groups, even though they might not possess an effective means of delivery.

Therefore, if we are living in a nuclear age, this must be accepted and our armed forces be capable of operating effectively in this age of technology. To shut one's eyes to this is foolishness, and those who cling to the unrealistic aims of the Campaign for Nuclear Disarmament organisations should first of all take their views and disruptive activities to Russia and observe the response. I am sure many would return home sadly disillusioned with the realisation that very wise heads had provided them with the V Bomber Force protection.

Some readers will remember that at the 1957/58 period we were constantly being treated to CND marches, under the leadership of politically suspect individuals who, in my opinion, were no more than reluctant travellers in the beliefs of democracy. Regrettably, this organisation is still with us today in perhaps a more sinister role, and on this matter I shall comment in later chapters.

CHAPTER NINE

'Grapple X'

In September 1957 instructions arrived from Headquarters Bomber Command informing me that 49 Squadron was detailed to participate in the next phase of nuclear weapon trials at Christmas Island under the code name of Operation Grapple X. With the arrival of the command training directive and operation order, it was apparent that the next detachment would be departing for the Pacific in the first half of October. Thus the period now available to revert to the 'Grapple' training task and prepare aircraft was again short.

The squadron was delighted at the news, for now the 'B' Flight ground crew would have the experience of a spell on Christmas Island, and Sqn Ldr Barnet Millett plus his bomb aimer, Flt Lt Wilf Jenkins, would gain a live megaton nuclear weapon drop experience. At a special meeting at RAF Wittering, with Air Cdre John Grandy (Task Force Commander Designate) and Air Cdre Ginger Weir, we were informed that it had been decided to move the operational area from Malden Island to the southeast tip of Christmas Island. Target indicators were being built and the bomb line would be on a heading of 164°T. This would be marked by northern and southern markers, to provide a visual geographical line for the bomb aimer, the main scientific instrument telemetering equipment being carefully sited well forward near the target indicator. Thus ground zero, indicating, weapon burst point, would be some 20nm from the main Christmas Island airfield. For this test, a revised Personnel Safety Plan would be issued as this would be the first occasion that a live nuclear weapon in the megaton range would be released from an aircraft to be detonated at 8,000ft, but over a target area only 20nm from the airfield, where some 3,000 men were based.

On the day of the live weapon drop, all airfield personnel would be assembled on the airfield tarmac area, once the two Valiant aircraft had taken off. Prior to this, they would be assembled in designated areas complete with transport, to facilitate a rapid evacuation to other parts of the island in the event of the Valiant carrying the live nuclear weapon crashing on take-off. Once the Valiants were airborne, the assembly on the main concrete dispersal area would begin. Roll calls would be taken and all personnel then given instructions over the tannoy system.

Each man would be required to sit on the ground with his back to the target area; he would be able to listen to the radio calls being passed by the dropping Valiant to Ground Control and would be able to hear the replies from Ground Control. For those sitting on the ground it would be fascinating to be able to look up to the sky and observe both Valiants flying at 45,000ft with vapour trails coming from their four jet engines. They would be free to observe in this way until such time as the Valiant was cleared to make the live drop; then, as the aircraft flew the final phase of its live bombing run, every man would be instructed to close his eyes and cover them with his hands in order to shield them from flash after weapon detonation. When this occurred, most people would feel a little heat on the back of the neck, though once this has passed, hands would be removed from eyes and personnel warned to expect a blast of air as the weapon detonation bang was heard, followed immediately by the over-pressure wave. All aircraft not flying and parked on the dispersal would be placed tail to the target area, so none of them would suffer from the pressure wave. Once this phase has passed, all personnel would be cleared to observe the development of the fireball and the progressive build up of the mushroom-shaped cloud.

Thus, throughout the entire island at the airfield and port area, every man would be accounted for before the operation. They were to be assembled in designated areas both before and during the actual drop; they would be protected from flash and blast and would be able to hear and feel involved with every aspect of the bombing operation as the flight progressed. Finally, they would be able to observe from relatively close quarters the result of the operation as the post weapon detonation phase developed. This is how all those based at Christmas Island who were not flying on 'D' Day would be able to experience the atmosphere of the operation.

Since results of all previous live weapon drops in the Malden area had shown conclusively that with an air burst at 8,000ft the residual radiation in the target area had been of such a low count as to be ignored for personnel safety, and that 49 Squadron had proved conclusively that it could guarantee an accuracy from 45,000ft of 245yd, there was obviously no reason why the next tests should not be conducted off the southeast tip of Christmas Island.

Without a doubt this decision was a major vote of confidence in the squadron's ability to deliver a weapon with great accuracy in the right place. It also showed that the scientists could be relied upon to ensure that the weapon exploded at the correct height, so that full scientific measurements were obtained. I briefly outlined my immediate training plans and named the crews which would form the detachment for 'Grapple X'. This to include my own crew plus those of Sqn Ldrs B. Millett and Arthur Steele, Flt Lts R. Bates and T. O'Connor.

In view of the extremely limited time available to complete the intensive practice bombing programme specified by HQ Bomber Command for the above crews, I suggested that to eliminate the unpredictability of UK weather, where visual bombing from 45,000ft could not be guaranteed, a detachment of

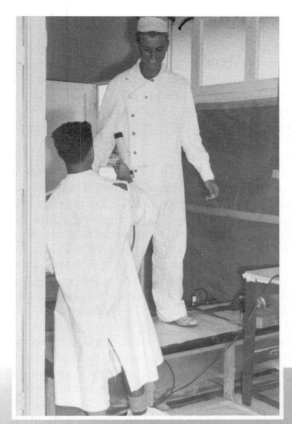

Top: Personnel were also monitored at a centre on Christmas Island.

Bottom: A Valiant B1 at dispersal on Christmas Island – note the long-range fuel tanks fitted under each wing. *(RAF Museum)*

four aircraft and crews under Sqn Ldr Arthur Steele should fly out to RAF El Adem in Libya, where we enjoyed the use of an excellent bombing range and weather conditions at this time of the year would be perfect. A 10-day period at El Adem would enable a concentrated bombing programme to be undertaken in order to ensure that these crews achieved the bombing accuracy conditions necessary before committing them to the overshoot technique bombing once we reached Christmas Island. My suggestion was accepted and in a matter of days authorisation arrived from Group HQ for this detachment to RAF El Adem to proceed.

Since returning from our first detachment on Christmas Island, I had made one change in appointments within the squadron. For some time I had felt that 'B' Flight needed a change in command, for it never seemed to match the efficiency of 'A' Flight under Dave Roberts. I therefore decided to make Sqn Ldr Arthur Steele Officer Commanding 'B' Flight, for he had completed a difficult and demanding task as Training Officer for the first 'Grapple' with distinction. Sqn Ldr Ted Flavell, the present OC 'B' Flight, had tremendous background experience of training for Operation Buffalo in Australia and had dropped the first live nuclear weapon in the kiloton range; therefore, he should be the ideal man now to have a crack at the task of Training Officer. So the change was made and it was one I never regretted on either side, for they both responded to their changed appointments with zeal and enthusiasm.

Whilst the detachment was away at RAF El Adem, my attention turned to planning details of the courier phase for fast transit of the radioactive weapon devices, and to producing the squadron operations order covering all aspects of our preparation and transit to Christmas Island for both ground and aircrew.

For this detachment I would have our Squadron Engineering Officer, Flg Off W. Budden, available, and the disciplinary SNCO, Sgt Wally Cressey, must come out at all costs, because of his versatility to cope under the primitive conditions of Christmas Island. Also on this detachment I should include my squadron adjutant, Flg Off Dennis Belcher who had been posted in whilst I was on Christmas Island. Dennis Belcher had already proved himself to be a very efficient and pleasant young officer who had gained the respect of the squadron, so his inclusion would relieve me of many administrative tasks.

Although all our Valiants were now fitted with underwing tanks, which gave us a considerable increase in range, the route out to Christmas Island was only slightly changed. Thus we would fly by way of RAF Aldergrove, Northern Ireland to Goose Bay in Newfoundland, then on to Offutt AFB, Nebraska, USA, and to Travis AFB in California, USA; thence to Honolulu with the final stage to Christmas Island: in all a total distance of 9,000nm. I was pleased to note that once again we could enjoy a two-night stop at Honolulu, which made a pleasant break on the rather long journey. The ground crew would be travelling by civil airline, departing from London Airport and routeing through New York, San Francisco and Honolulu.

With the return of our detachment from RAF El Adem, having completed a very intensive and satisfactory bombing training programme, we were once again ready to launch ourselves into another 'Grapple' test programme.

The complicated and detailed courier programme outlining movement of crews and aircraft I handed over to Sqn Ldr Dave Roberts, who would be in charge of the elements of 49 Squadron remaining at RAF Wittering during my absence for the second detachment to Christmas Island. Once again we packed our bags; Crusty was entrusted to the care of my parents until my return. Mr Dolby my batman had offered to look after him for me, which was greatly appreciated, but on balance I thought it more practical for Crusty to stay in Norwich.

Thus on 6 October 1957 XD818 with my crew on board, once again roared down the runway at RAF Wittering and headed for Goose Bay in Newfoundland. XD824 with Sqn Ldr Millett followed on 8 October, XD823 with Sqn Ldr Arthur Steele on 10 October and XD825 with Flt Lt R. Bates on 12 October.

We duly arrived at Christmas Island on 11 October to be met by Air Cdre Ginger Weir and our own ground crew who had preceded us in departure from the UK in order to have everything ready on Christmas Island for the arrival of our Valiant aircraft. All Valiants arrived on schedule and with our full complement in position no time was lost in commencing the all important pre-drop practice bombing phase. My briefing after arrival was that there would only be one operational weapon tested; therefore, our detachment on this occasion would be a short one. I had already nominated Sqn Ldr B. Millett and crews for this live drop and intended to fly Flt Lt R. Bates and crew in the grandstand aircraft.

There had been few changes in the camp domestic arrangements on the island, so my pre-departure briefing to the squadron personnel, warning them of the somewhat primitive conditions to be expected, was well founded. However, the 'B' Flight ground crews included a number of characters who were very capable of adjusting themselves to any situation; lack of modern facilities was no deterrent to them. In this respect I must mention Cpl Fred Vening, an air radio fitter; and I know Sgt Wally Cressey must have been delighted to have Senior Aircraftsman Bennington in the squad, for somehow this lad had a natural knack of getting things wrong!

By the end of October I was well satisfied with the consistent bombing results from 45,000ft and the weather had been perfect; there had been no signs of the inter-tropical front which meant we were spared those violent tropical downpours which left tents a soggy mess and electrical ground equipment saturated with all the consequential serviceability problems.

We therefore completed our arrival training phase within the time scale laid down by Task Force 'Grapple', and having reported to the Task Force Commander on the operational state of readiness of the squadron, he authorised the commencement of the scientific pre-operational phase and indicated that the most likely live drop date would be 7, 8 or 9 November, depending on the weather.

During that first week of November, Sqn Ldr Barney Millett and his crew flew all the scientific practice drops over the target area, culminating with the dress rehearsal completed to the satisfaction of everybody. The Task Force Commander and Scientific Director decided that provided weather conditions were satisfactory, 'D' Day for the live drop would be 8 November.

On 7 November Valiant XD824 was handed over to the Atomic Weapons Team for loading of another weapon in the megaton range code named 'Round C'. Sqn Ldr Barney Millett with his crew of Alan Pringle as co-pilot, Frank Corduroy as bomb aimer, Derek Tuthill as navigator and John Tuck the AEO had a final crew briefing.

Once again we had arrived at the eve of another live drop day. For the ground crew of 'B' flight this was very exciting and everybody hoped there would be no weather snags to delay the next day's operation.

That evening I dined with Barney Millett and his crew, for it is always rather a tense period before such an operation. You are well aware that tomorrow all eyes and ears will be focused upon the dropping aircraft and every crew member must be on top of his job to ensure that there is a perfect weapon delivery, essential for the scientific test to be a success.

I wanted this crew to be relaxed and not using unnecessary mental resources worrying about their task. They would find that on the day it all reverted to a fairly routine flight once airborne, thanks to the intensive training programme to which they had been subjected.

The weather on 8 November 1957 was good, and everything looked set for a visual bombing live drop. At morning briefing the Task Force Commander confirmed that the maritime area was clear, the upper winds satisfactory, and therefore the day's operation would proceed. Sqn Ldr Millett and crew proceeded to the airfield from the Joint Operations Centre to prepare for their important flight and begin external aircraft checks. I remained behind at JOC talking with Air Cdre Ginger Weir and the Scientific Director, Bill Cook. I was told that although there would only be one live drop in 'Grapple X', the next series was to proceed and would make greater use of the ground radar system for complete blind drops, with the Valiant being directed on to the target by ground directors from the Radar Plotting Teams.

The Task Force Commander designate, Air Cdre John Grandy, was keen to evaluate this method in order to eliminate any visual weather restrictions. I was not overjoyed at the prospect for it did not appear to have any operational value to the Valiant crews, and I could not see from our recent trials with this equipment that bombing accuracy would be improved.

By the time I arrived at the airfield, Barney Millett and his crew had completed all external checks and were ready to climb into the aircraft. I wished them good luck and walked over to ensure all was well with Flt Lt Bob Bates and his crew, who were to fly the grandstand aircraft.

After watching both aircraft take off, I returned to Joint Operations Control in order to listen to the dropping crew calling their drills once clearance had been given to carry out a live drop. By now this routine was becoming a habit, but as always I could sense the excitement around me as reports came in, indicating that the vast organisation was taking up its designated operational position.

At last I heard the Valiant cleared for an Initial Run, which was completed without any problems, and we all waited for the controller to give clearance for the live drop. This was duly given and I sat back listening carefully to every transmission from Valiant XD824 as it flew down the bomb line, until the bomb aimer called 'Weapon gone' and I then heard the captain call for full power and commence his escape manoeuvre commentary. When he called 'Rolling out, steady on escape heading' I heaved a sigh of relief and glancing at my watch noted the time taken.

The controller's voice at this time came through stating 'Weapon detonated' and I knew we had completed yet another successful delivery. The exact bombing error would be available later. With the next phase of the operation commencing I left JOC and returned to the airfield in order to see both aircraft and crews on their return. Some 30 minutes later they landed and Barney Millett's very satisfied crew climbed out of Valiant XD824.

No. 49 Squadron had now successfully dropped four live thermonuclear weapons, all in the megaton range, and very soon we should once again be flying eastwards on that 9,000nm return journey to the UK; then after a brief rest, restarting another intensive training programme.

Instructions for the squadron to return home arrived and on 13 November 1957 my crew and I in Valiant XD818 once again set course for RAF Wittering, followed by all other squadron aircraft at one day intervals. We arrived back at Wittering on 18 November, one day late, having been forced to return to Travis AFB in California in the face of appalling weather experienced on the leg from there to Offutt AFB.

Once all aircraft were back home and each crew had been allowed a few days with their families, we returned to the task of bringing the next batch of crews to operational readiness; this time I had been instructed to perfect in conjunction with a Ground Radar Team, a precise and accurate blind drop technique.

During this last spell on Christmas Island we received very sad news; on 9 October, Gp Capt J. Woodroffe, our Station Commander at RAF Wittering, who had been on detachment to Pinecastle in America as Detachment Commander for the Bomber Command teams competing in the Strategic Air Command Bombing Competition, was killed in an American B-47 on a familiarisation flight. His death was a sad loss, for he was a most popular Commander, who enjoyed the respect of all ranks. Our return therefore, to RAF Wittering, was tinged with sadness at this tragedy.

His successor was Gp Capt Alan Boxer, another old friend, but a man of very different type of personality, who would find the task of following John Woodroffe difficult initially. Indeed, this was to prove to be the situation.

The Squadron having settled, once again, back at base and the 'B' Flight ground crew returned from Christmas Island, it was time for me to give considerable thought to a new requirement stipulated by Headquarters 'Grapple'. This was to concentrate with the Mk 7 Gun-Laying Radar Team, now positioned at the Orfordness bombing range in Suffolk, to perfect a drill whereby, with the use of its electromagnetic indicator plotting table, set up on a predetermined bomb line, accurate feed-through information could be transmitted to the Valiant and portrayed on the pilot's instrument landing system indicator needles.

Provided the Mk 7 gun laying radar equipment was correctly positioned on a geographical bomb line, correctly aligned on the EMI plotting table, then with the pilot following the ILS localiser needles, this aircraft, in theory, should be flying on the bomb line with drift eliminated and with ground speed calculated and the exact bomb release point could be given to the aircraft bomb aimer verbally, by high-frequency radio control.

Whilst appreciating that by this system we could eliminate the need for the weapon test to be dependent upon visual conditions suitable for the bomb aimer to see the target indicator, this, to a great extent for a scientific trial, complicated the entire bombing procedure drill by introducing an additional team on the ground on whom the aircraft captain became completely dependent. Thus, if ground radar alignment was not correct, the signals being sent to the aircraft would be inaccurate resulting in the captain releasing a weapon well wide of the target, and with the cockpit completely shuttered against flash, he would have no means of identifying the error.

These were views I pressed home at meetings with Task Force 'Grapple' staff for having trained crews to this exceptional standard of visual bombing accuracy, I could see major morale problems with bomb aimers if they were required to sit through a live bombing sortie feeling completely redundant.

We arrived at a compromise; since the bombing results for all tests had been excellent to date, nobody wanted to take risks. Therefore, it was agreed that the Mk 7 radar system, once perfected, would only be used if weather conditions at the time of a live weapon drop precluded a visual release by the bomb aimer. This I accepted, and said that to ensure every aspect of safety, I would make available a Valiant captain to advise the Ground Radar Team on every sortie where blind bombing was undertaken with this method.

Thus by December 1957 the squadron was once again fully committed to yet another intensive training period, and with the weather prevailing at the time I was grateful to be able to utilise the Mk 7 radar system under realistic visual contact from 45,000ft.

We now had a number of changes to accept, for firstly, following the death of John Woodroffe, Gp Capt Alan Boxer had taken over command of RAF Wittering. Since he was not in any way familiar with the role of 49 Squadron in Operation Grapple, I spent a considerable amount of time putting him fully in the picture. Alan Boxer had been a member of the directing staff at the RAF Staff College during my year there a student; we therefore knew each other well. He had a difficult job to follow John Woodroffe and to do so successfully would need the full support of his Wing Commanders. I assured him that he could count on my support in all aspects of station life.

Next of course, there were changes at Task Force 'Grapple'. John Grandy had taken over from AVM W. Oulton with the rank of Air Vice Marshal, and Ginger Weir had handed over to Air Cdre Jack Roulston as Air Task Force Commander.

AVM Wilf Oulton had been appointed to command Task Force 'Grapple' when the political decision had been taken for Britain to embark upon the nuclear weapons trials programme. He had been responsible for the formidable task of planning the largest joint service operation ever mounted in peacetime and thanks to superb qualities of leadership and meticulous planning, the operation in conjunction with the Scientific Director (now Sir William Cook) had been an unqualified success. This success, to a very great degree, must be linked with the close and experienced support of his Air Task Force Commander, Air Cdre Ginger Weir, who had taken up his appointment at the same time as the Task Force Commander. At all times they, as a team, had provided balanced judgement and neither hesitated to make decisions.

We were sorry to see them depart, but fortunate to have somebody of the calibre of AVM John Grandy take over. Here again, we would be working with a commander of vast experience and a personality that had the ability to obtain the best results from all ranks by positive qualities of leadership. His number two was to be Air Cdre Jack Roulston who, although an unknown entity initially, soon proved himself to be a worthy successor to Ginger Weir.

A Canberra being cleaned after a cloud sampling sortie.

Christmas was fast approaching and for 49 Squadron 1957 had been a memorable and successful year; I felt the entire squadron, plus wives, should enjoy a party before everyone stood down for the Christmas break. In our usual manner, 49 Squadron hired the Assembly Rooms at Stamford and all concerned had a thoroughly good evening. I took the opportunity to congratulate everybody on what had been achieved over the past year, thanked the wives for their support and told all concerned to be ready for a really hectic 1958.

CHAPTER TEN

'Grapple Y'

Having received my directive covering the next planned test series at Christmas Island, I lost no time in getting a new training programme under way once the squadron had returned from the Christmas break.

Firstly, to overcome UK weather conditions, we resumed a full scale detachment of crews to RAF El Adem in Libya to carry out visual high-level bombing. Secondly, with the Mk 7 Radar Gunlaying Team, plus its EMI equipment established at Orfordness bombing range, every opportunity was taken to fly blind radar high level sorties to perfect this system. By making a Valiant captain available to the Mk7 Radar Team, a greater appreciation of exactly what was happening in the aircraft when flying on the bomb line was obtained and the net result of this was that the bombing errors were progressively reduced. Although it was costly and often inconvenient to provide a Valiant captain for the Ground Radar Team on every sortie, the improved results indicated that this was an acceptable price to pay.

Early in February I was summoned to attend a meeting at HQ Task Force 'Grapple', in company with Sqn Ldr Ted Flavell, my Squadron Training Officer, to discuss with AVM John Grandy (later MRAF Sir John Grandy) and Air Cdre Jack Roulston certain amendments to the drills required to be followed on the bomb line for this next series of weapons.

This was my first meeting with Jack Roulston and I was interested to note his reaction to the 'Grapple' task and see if he had new ideas to put forward. In the event, I found him amenable to accepting the advice we gave from past experience and willing to assist in any way that would contribute to improving bombing results, even though to date they had been well within the limits set by the Weapon Scientific Team.

The Task Force Commander stressed the importance of having the ability to revert to a blind live-weapon drop utilising the ground Mk 7 radar should weather conditions on the day preclude a visual drop. In this respect I pointed out that to date the average bombing error by use of ground radar had been double that achieved by crews making a visual drop. Until the Ground Radar Team achieved more experience and we were at least seeing a bombing accuracy consistency comparable to that being obtained by crews dropping visually, I recommended that radar should only be used as a last resort.

Whilst appreciating the Task Force Commander's requirement to retain this option, so that the date for a live drop could be set with certainty irrespective of cloud cover, I did not wish to see radar accepted until there was more proof of its ability to guarantee results.

Having argued on these lines, I was well aware that my own requirement was to retain a visual drop where the entire crew was utilised; for we had trained hard to this end and if on the day the bomb aimer's job was virtually handed over to a Ground Radar Team, it was a trifle demoralising. However, I had a duty to provide every assistance to the Ground Radar Teams and this I would do.

Before departing, I extended an invitation to both the Task Force Commander and Air Task Force Commander to attend a sherry party given by the squadron officers on 12 February, which they both accepted. This presented an ideal opportunity for me to introduce both men to the crew but, in particular, to Sqn Ldr Bob Bates' crew, which was scheduled to carry out the next live drop; also to Sqn Ldr Bill Bailey and crew who were selected to fly the grandstand aircraft in preparation for the subsequent live weapon test.

February passed quickly and training progressed with detachments to RAF El Adem for visual bombing and maximum sorties being flown over Orfordness bombing range, utilising the blind radar drop technique. With March upon us, the Operation Order from HQ Bomber Command had been received and our own squadron operations order issued, covering all details of the next detachment for 'Grapple Y', including the revised route for all Valiant aircraft and a detailed schedule covering the courier task.

'A' Flight ground crews once again departed via Heathrow for Christmas Island to prepare for the arrival of our aircraft under the control of Flg Off Dennis Belcher my adjutant, Flg Off Bill Budden, Squadron Engineering Officer, and of course the indispensible Sgt Wally Cressey. All Valiants had now been fitted with underwing fuel tanks, thus providing a much increased range, eliminating the need to proceed via Aldergrove in Northern Ireland or to call at Namao. The new route would be direct from RAF Wittering to Goose Bay in Newfoundland to Travis AFB in California, then to Honolulu and finally on to Christmas Island.

Thus, with all pre-departure arrangements complete, including once again depositing Crusty back home, the squadron aircraft were ready, and with Sqn Ldr Dave Roberts left in charge of 'B' Flight, on 19 March I took off from Wittering in Valiant XD818 on the first stage of my journey back to Christmas Island for a third stay. On 22 March Sqn Ldr Bob Bates in Valiant XD825 and Sqn Ldr W. Bailey in Valiant XD822 left Wittering, followed on 24 March by Sqn Ldr Ted Flavell in XD827. The journey out in all cases was relatively uneventful, although on the leg from Goose Bay to Travis I was forced to divert into McCelland AFB in California because of bad weather. This diversion meant an increase in flight time making the airborne time from Goose Bay 7hr 10min, rather a lengthy time in an ejector seat.

On the following day we proceeded to Travis AFB and after refuelling took off for Honolulu in order to regain schedule. We arrived back on Christmas Island on 23 March and by the 28th all four Valiants were once more standing in the dispersal area, majestic and gleaming white, ready for the next phase.

The ground crew had been busy recovering all the aircraft ground equipment having arrived well ahead of the Valiants; so once the squadron had arrived, no time was lost in starting the pre-operational training phase.

My first task was to check that the Mk 7 Ground Radar Team was correctly positioned on the bomb line, as obviously it would require one or two calibration flights to ensure alignment and positioning for the overshoot technique. To make sure we obtained maximum utilisation of aircraft and practice bombing facilities, it was decided that on every training bombing sortie, each aircraft would carry out an equal number of visual drops with blind radar drops, the radar team monitoring every run and assessing the bombing result. In order to improve the team's operational capability, a Valiant captain was made available to it on each occasion.

The pre-scientific test period was brief as the two nominated crews plus my own were well experienced in the time delay overshoot technique and the crew bombing average of results was extremely gratifying. During the practice bombing period, followed by the scientific high explosive weapon drops the average bombing error using the visual technique was 275yd from 45,000ft and on the blind radar technique the average was 320yd. The results being achieved by use of the radar technique had improved considerably since a Valiant captain had been made available to work alongside the radar tracking and directing team. However, 320yd was still not good enough, but I was sure that this could be improved upon as the radar team gained more experience.

In spite of difficult and uncomfortable weather conditions which made life unpleasant for all concerned, the pre-live drop work-up programme was completed as planned, and once more we found ourselves moving into the final period of aircraft preparation prior to handing over Valiant XD825 to the scientific team for live weapon (code named 'Grapple Y') loading. The first courier Valiant carrying the weapon radioactive parts had departed from RAF Wittering as planned and, with crews prepositioned at Goose Bay, Travis AFB and Honolulu, had arrived at Christmas Island as scheduled, by mid-April.

With the squadron once again established in its old quarters on the airfield, an intensive pre-drop training programme was undertaken. With this completed to the satisfaction of the Task Force Commander, a tentative live drop date was decided upon.

We had now come to 28 April and on this occasion the Task Force Commander was host to the Deputy Chief of the Air Staff, Air Marshal Sir Geoffrey Tuttle KBE, CB, DFC plus an official party of British, Australian and American observers. This latter party was under the guidance of Gp Capt Alan Boxer.

On 'D' Day all the official observers remained on the airfield to observe the test, but the Deputy Chief of the Air Staff went forward with the Task Force Commander and Scientific Director. It was particularly appropriate that Sir Geoffrey Tuttle should be with us at this time, for he had been actively involved with all the initial planning for Operations Buffalo and Grapple. We were therefore delighted to have him with us on this day.

Sqn Ldr Bob Bates and crew flying Valiant XD825, although scheduled for a take-off at 08.00hrs local, were delayed due to an unacceptable degree of cloud cover on the day – not unexpected, as the previous two days had produced heavy showers from the intertropical front. However, after a wait of 1½ hours, the cloud cover decreased considerably and the Task Force Commander gave the order for the operation to proceed. Bob Bates and his crew were briefed to the effect that if conditions, once airborne, were not ideal for a visual weapon release, the Task Force Commander would authorise a ground radar control weapon drop in view of the recent blind-radar drop bombing results.

Once airborne, Valiant XD825 was quickly followed by Valiant XD822 being flown by Sqn Ldr Bill Bailey and crew. By now the weather was improving rapidly and I was optimistic that a visual release would be possible. Therefore, when some 20 minutes after take-off Sqn Ldr Bob Bates reported at 45,000ft that conditions were suitable for a visual drop, although the bombing line was obscured in places, I was undoubtedly relieved for there were still reservations regarding radar accuracy.

By this time I had gone with the Task Force Commander to the Forward Control Point, which was some eight miles from the target area. Here, the Mk 7 radar gun laying equipment was located, so we could observe the trace of the dropping aircraft along the bomb line as it followed its flight path.

It was an interesting experience to observe how all reports came in to both the Task Force Commander and Scientific Director, confirming the position of all participating aircraft and correct responses from all scientific telemetering equipment as the Valiant flew along the bomb line. With the initial run completed without incident, and all scientific reports satisfactory, the Task Force Commander gave the order to clear the Valiant for a live drop.

I observed the plot as the Valiant turned on to the bomb line. The voice of the bomb aimer, Flt Lt Tiny Finnis, was clear and calm as he gave corrections to the pilot as the aircraft was established on the bomb line; this was interspersed by the AEO calling weapon and telemetering switching drills as certain points were reached as the Valiant headed for the target indicator.

Before settling myself behind the sand bag blast protection, I watched Valiant XD825, followed by XD822, beautifully silhouetted against the clear blue Pacific sky as they streaked along the bomb line with pronounced and persistent white vapour trails emitting from each of their four jet engines, indicating a perfectly straight course. As I watched, the bomb aimer's voice called 'Steady, steady, NOW and the grandstand aircraft flying behind Valiant XD825 began its escape manoeuvre, presenting a really eye-catching sight. I now had to get myself behind the sand bags and cover my eyes to protect them from the flash as the weapon detonated. The voice of the bomb aimer announced 'Bomb gone' and Sqn Ldr Bob Bates commenced his commentary as he rolled the Valiant into its escape manoeuvre.

The weapon detonated as planned some 53 seconds after release, which meant at an altitude of 8,000ft above sea level. Through fingers over one's eyes a bright flash of light could be detected and the heat was apparent; with this past, we all awaited the over-pressure wave accompanied by a massive bang. At that range the outward movement of air from the area of detonation was extremely impressive and had we been standing without protection, there is no doubt we should all have been blown off our feet. With this safely past, we moved from our sheltered positions to observe the fire ball and the majestic build-up of the mushroom-shaped cloud, already towering to a great height.

The fire ball appeared as a huge red and orange cauldron of fantastic energy, which gave the impression of revolving. As it did so, it emerged at its apex into a stream of orange-coloured cloud mass moving upwards all the time, and as it ascended the colour changed to white. Then somewhere in the region of 50,000ft it curved and fanned outwards from its centre making a cap similar to the top of a mushroom. All the time this fantastic formation moved upwards, progressively increasing the spread at the top until it stabilised, then the edges of the actual mushroom shape partially drifted from the main structure as upper winds began to carry these white whiffs downwind.

Although this was the fifth megaton weapon detonation I had witnessed, it was surely the most impressive due to my own close proximity. By the time I had finished observing this result of man's creation in the atmosphere, the Valiant had been cleared to remove anti-flash shutters and observe the cloud. The ground controller was already talking to the Canberra sampling aircraft and it was time for me to get into my Land Rover and drive back to the airfield in order to be on dispersal when both Valiants landed. Before departing I checked with the radar plot which showed an excellent trace, indicating that the bombing result should be good.

The subsequent scientific report after all telemetering recordings had been analysed and camera film developed, showed an excellent result of 245yd. Thus the weapon had been delivered to the point required by the scientists.

Having congratulated Bob Bates and his crew on a first class operation, I told them all to remain on the airfield as the Task Force Commander and Deputy Chief of the Air Staff would be visiting the squadron on their return from the forward area. Indeed, they arrived about an hour later and were introduced to every member of Bob Bates' crew, and the DCAS asked many questions about bombing technique and the escape manoeuvre. After a lengthy chat with Bob Bates, I introduced Bill Bailey and his crew, who were scheduled to undertake the next test.

That evening, I was invited to have dinner in the TFC Mess with Sir Geoffrey Tuttle, whom I had met many times before during my tour as PSO to the Air Member for Personnel. On the following day I was officially informed that in view of the excellent scientific results, there would be no further live weapon tests in the present series and 49 Squadron was to make preparations to start return flights to the UK from 4 May. My return operation order was already prepared and only dates had to be inserted, so that was quickly produced and I gave instructions to fit all Valiants with underwing tanks ready for the journey.

However, before much of this work got under way, we had a visit in the morning by the entire official observer party. Squadron members were detailed to show small parties around the Valiant and I was requested to give them a short talk covering the operation from the squadron's point of view. Needless to say the questions were numerous, but I was cleared to answer freely.

Following their visit to all squadrons on the airfield, the Task Force Commander gave an official lunch to which all Squadron Commanders were invited. Not to be outclassed, and in order to maintain the squadron record, we gave a cocktail party in the Officers' Mess to which all the official observers were invited; indeed, on this occasion we entertained 100 guests.

The official observers were scheduled to depart from Christmas Island on the following day after lunch. Therefore, being aware that I had three Valiants to be air tested, having had the underwing tanks fitted, I asked the Task Force Commander if we could provide a low level formation display before his guests departed and that perhaps he would allow one observer to fly on the flight deck of each Valiant. He agreed without any hesitation, and said he would fly with me in XD818. We planned an 11.00hrs take-off, the aircraft being Valiant XD818 flown by myself, XD822 by Sqn Ldr Bill Bailey and XD825 by Sqn Ldr Bob Bates.

On the following day all aircraft were ready as planned and, with AVM John Grandy as my co-pilot and one volunteer observer aboard the other aircraft, we taxied out to the end of the runway ready for take-off, XD818 leading the way. We were quickly airborne, followed by XD822 and XD825 at sufficient intervals to avoid the preceding Valiant's jet wake.

Once airborne, we climbed to 1,000ft and headed for the harbour area of the island to the north; this allowed time for XD822 and XD825 to form up, one to either side of XD818 in 'Vic' formation. Our intention was not only to give a good and impressive display to the official observers, but also to all the sailors, soldiers and airmen on the island, who had contributed so much to the success of this and previous tests. 49 Squadron had pride of place and the 'glamour' but, although we were the leading actors, I was very aware that without the un-glamorous work of so many personnel on the ground, our task would have been impossible. Thus this formation was a salute of thanks to everyone on the island.

With both Valiants tightly tucked into position, I turned XD818 out to sea over the harbour and descended to 100ft, then headed back on southerly heading flying directly over the harbour, the Navy ships and Fleet Supply vessels. As we passed over, one could see the sailors on deck waving to us as we flew now at mast height. Then on to the airfield, over the main domestic camp; it was a marvellous feeling to be flying so low, with the shadow of all three aircraft following us as we flew low over the palm trees and on across the airfield turning so that we were flying directly in front of the Airfield Operations Centre, where the official observers were standing.

Once past this point, we continued on a westerly heading for a turn back towards the airfield for a second low pass heading east; then turning port on to north in order to return to the harbour area for a second visit to the ships. With this completed we flew round the west side of the island, clearing with Air Traffic Control for a final low pass over the airfield and a high pull up break-from formation, to peel off for a visual landing. For those of us flying the Valiants it was an exhilarating experience and I understand it was thoroughly appreciated by all on the ground.

With this pleasant interlude behind us, all efforts were now concentrated on final preparation for departure, and on 4 May 1958 Valiant XD818 once again took off from Christmas Island on the first stage of another 9,000nm journey to RAF Wittering. At one day intervals the remaining squadron Valiants followed, with yet another successful test operation completed.

On 9 May 1958 we landed in XD818 at RAF Wittering exactly to the minute as planned in the flight schedule drawn up at Christmas Island. By 16 May all Valiants were back at base; the ground crews, with all aircraft departed, carefully serviced all ground equipment before placing it into store ready for our next detachment to the island. By 2 June they too were back at RAF Wittering and once again the entire squadron was to be given block leave, but not before we participated in the annual Air Officer Commanding's inspection parade on 5 June.

After one week's leave, which gave me time to collect Crusty from home, the squadron was busy turning its attention to the training requirements of the next detachment to Christmas Island, under the code name 'Grapple Z'. For this we planned to depart on 23 July, and again my crew would be required to accompany me flying Valiant XD818. This would make the fourth detachment on the island for us and I appreciated that at times they must have felt that the distinction of being a member of the Squadron Commander's crew had a number of disadvantages.

This initial training phase contained a very pleasant interlude, for I was pleased to see that my recommendation for Flt Sgt Bill Asprey to be awarded the British Empire Medal had met with success, as his name appeared in the Birthday Honours List. His contribution to the technical organisation, both at RAF Wittering and at Christmas Island, had been of the highest order and far in excess of what could normally be expected. Seldom has a decoration been so well deserved and welcomed by all ranks in the squadron. On 18 June at a station parade, the Commander-in-Chief, ACM Sir Harry Broadhurst KCB, KBE, DSO, DFC, AFC, honoured us by flying to RAF Wittering and presenting the BEM to Flt Sgt Bill Asprey. It was an occasion I shall remember with great pleasure and satisfaction.

Following the presentation, the C-in-C inspected the squadron facilities and talked to me in great length about the experience we had gained to date during these nuclear trials. I was gratified to learn of the high regard he had for 49 Squadron and he expressed his complete satisfaction with the results and the impression we had given to all units participating in Operation Grapple. Turning to the future, he indicated that the next test series might be the last for some time and I must expect some of my more senior and experienced crews to be posted into other squadrons in order to spread the operational experience. Before he left he told me that it was his intention to visit Christmas Island to observe the next live drop, which was something I welcomed very much indeed.

For the next few weeks priority of training was accorded to the crews earmarked for the next Christmas Island detachment. These included the following captains and their crews: Sqn Ldr Bill Bailey, Flt Lt Tiff O'Connor and Sqn Ldr Tony Caillard. The allocation of bombing sorties was again divided between visual and blind radar technique over the Orfordness bombing range.

Although the time available for training prior to departure for Christmas Island was short, we were blessed with reasonable weather enabling crews to carry visual practice drops from 45,000ft. By the time we were required to undertake the final pre-departure preparations and despatch of the ground contingent, the training task had been completed and results justified my faith in the crews selected for the next test series.

However, before that time, I was required to honour a promise given to the Commandant of the Royal Air Force Flying College, to lecture the present course on Operation Grapple and its demands and problems from a V bomber point of view. Since our return from Christmas Island on the conclusion of 'Grapple Y', I had given considerable thought as to the best way of presenting this lecture. All students were of Wing Commander or Group Captain rank, either pilots or navigators and security cleared to all levels, so that my talk could be completely uninhibited and I must be prepared for some extremely intelligent and searching questions. In order to cover the subject thoroughly I decided that part of my lecture should include a talk by my bomb aimer, Alan Washbrook, to explain the theory of the overshoot technique and outline the visual and radar error factors. We discussed this in some detail during our last period on Christmas Island and the draft of our lecture had been written so that once back in the UK a short period preparing diagrams for display was all that was necessary.

We travelled to RAF Manby by road on the evening before our lecture, having been invited as guests by the Commandant, Air Cdre Teddy Donaldson CBE, DSO, DFC, a famous fighter pilot who at one time held the world's speed record; he was a great character known and respected throughout the Royal Air Force. For myself it was a great pleasure to be back once again at RAF Manby and I was more than delighted to find that they had given me my old room in the Mess with Mr Godbold, my original batman, to look after me. For Alan Washbrook it was a unique experience and I know he was greatly impressed by the friendly atmosphere.

Left: Working on the weapon assembly equipment.

Bottom: High-speed cameras. These were activated by telemetry signals.

On the following morning we made our way over to Tedder Block, which was the main lecture and tutorial assembly, and into the cinema where we were to present our lecture. Having set everything up we retired to have coffee with the Commandant, before returning with him to the cinema where all students had assembled.

We were duly introduced and from that moment the ball was in our court. As I looked around at that very distinguished audience, I felt for a few brief seconds much more apprehensive than at any time during the final phase of dropping a live nuclear weapon. This nervousness soon disappeared as I launched myself into the lecture, for the simple reason that I was talking about a subject on which I was not only well versed but regarded within the RAF as an authority. It is this personal knowledge of a subject which always provides a lecturer with confidence.

It was not long before I was completely relaxed and enjoying the presentation, for it was a pleasure to be able to outline the 'Grapple' organisation, the details of the task given to 49 Squadron, our initial problems and progressive results leading to the operation of the actual live drop. Having set the overall scene and covered the experience of dropping such a weapon, I handed over to Alan Washbrook who then very expertly outlined the theory of our visual bombing technique and discussed the problems experienced with radar bombing using information fed to the pilot by means of the ILS alignment needles, In conclusion, I left the audience with some ideas of possible means of utilising the navigational radar bombing system for any future weapon tests, provided a geographical ground zero could be established which would eliminate the overshoot function. For this to be acceptable, weapon detonation would need to be at a greater height than 8,000ft to eliminate the fireball drawing ground debris into the atmosphere resulting in radiation fallout problems.

After a lengthy and interesting question period, the Commandant thanked us both for such an interesting talk and we all retired for lunch, after which Alan and I drove back to RAF Wittering. It is pleasant to reflect that we were again invited to lecture at the Flying College in the following years, which indicated that our performance had reached acceptable standards.

CHAPTER ELEVEN

'Grapple Z'

By 20 July the 'B' Flight ground crew under Flt Lt Dennis Belcher was ready to depart for Christmas Island by civil airline, via New York; it duly arrived on the island on 23 July. This was the day when Valiant XD818 with my crew on board set off on that now familiar route to Goose Bay, Travis AFB, Honolulu and Christmas Island, and on 27 July we once again landed smoothly down on the runway after a pleasant and uneventful journey. We were followed by XD822, XD824 and XD827, the last aircraft arriving on 31 July, two days late, having been delayed by a fuel tank leak.

From the start of this detachment we experienced considerable cloud cover over the island, for the inter-tropical front was active, and indeed on the leg from Honolulu to Christmas Island it was necessary to climb to 50,000ft in order to avoid any turbulent cloud tops in the frontal area. The Task Force Commander therefore stressed to me the importance of concentrating on perfecting the ground radar technique, for he did not wish to delay the next two weapon tests because of weather, for political reasons. Our training programme therefore got into full swing giving priority to radar bombing, but balanced with visual bombing sorties as and when cloud cover permitted.

On Friday 8 August the Air Task Force Commander, Air Cdre Jack Roulston, asked if I would care to fly over to Honolulu and pick up AVM John Grandy who had been attending a conference. Valiant XD818 was serviceable, so I agreed at once and we were soon airborne, arriving at Honolulu in time for lunch.

Operation Control gave us the time AVM John Grandy would arrive at our aircraft, so we were there all ready for take-off. Once airborne Bob Beeson gave up his co-pilot's seat and John Grandy climbed up from the flight deck and flew XD818 all the way back to Christmas Island. Bob Beeson took over again as co-pilot for the final landing, purely because John Grandy was not familiar with the fuel switch panel on the co-pilot's side console. The flight time to Honolulu had been 2hr 55 min and the return flight 2hr 50min, a trip thoroughly enjoyed by the Task Force Commander, who was an extremely accomplished pilot.

Saturday, 9 August was to be a rest day from the flying point of view, although there were a considerable number of technical tasks to be undertaken.

However, it was to prove a very sad day all round; for as I walked over to breakfast, I saw Sgt Wally Cressey coming towards me. He certainly was the carrier of distressing news; Sgt Phil Phillips, a very popular and experienced engine fitter, had suffered a heart attack during the night and Sgt Cressey had found him dead in bed.

The Garrison Padre, Eric Alsopp, was absolutely marvellous; he quickly arranged a very appropriate memorial service in the little garrison church on the following day, and it was filled to capacity with members of the squadron and the Task Force Commander. It was my privilege as Squadron Commander to read the lesson. Since there were no facilities for burial on the island, we were greatly indebted to the Royal Navy for arranging for a committal at sea with full military honours. In spite of the difficulties of the environment, we had provided Sgt Phil Phillips with an impressive and dignified farewell.

The Task Force Commander convened a meeting at Joint Operations Control to inform all Squadron Commanders that due to political pressure the entire programme would be accelerated in order to achieve live drop dates of 2 and 11 September. In outlining the scientific requirement for high explosive drops, the Scientific Director put forward a programme that was going to entail a very heavy work load on the 49 Squadron ground crew.

With the first drop date for 2 September, the initial crew practice bombing and opportunity for crews to become familiar with both visual and radar techniques, was going to be much reduced, for the scientific work-up weapon release programme would be spread over 14 days.

Perhaps it is appropriate at this stage to explain in more detail these two types of bombing techniques.

Visual Method

This method used the T4 bombsight where the graticule must be brought into coincidence with the target indicator on a line of 164°T, the weapon release being subsequently delayed by an appropriate number of seconds to effect the desired burst condition over ground zero. The bomb line of 164°T was marked by a northern marker and the southern marker as shown in the diagram, the Valiant being positioned on this line navigationally by the aid of the Decca system. Once the northern marker became discernible to the bomb aimer, the aircraft commenced its visual run, the bomb aimer then being required to maintain the graticule on the bomb line at the same time as the aircraft's heading was calculated to make good a track of 164°T.

This technique required the aircraft to be moved laterally in space so that the graticule line of sight was maintained on the line markers, with the correct final heading being maintained on the G.IV B compass. To achieve this, correct S turns were essential, with the pilot flying the aircraft to a constant compass heading, to an accuracy of ½°.

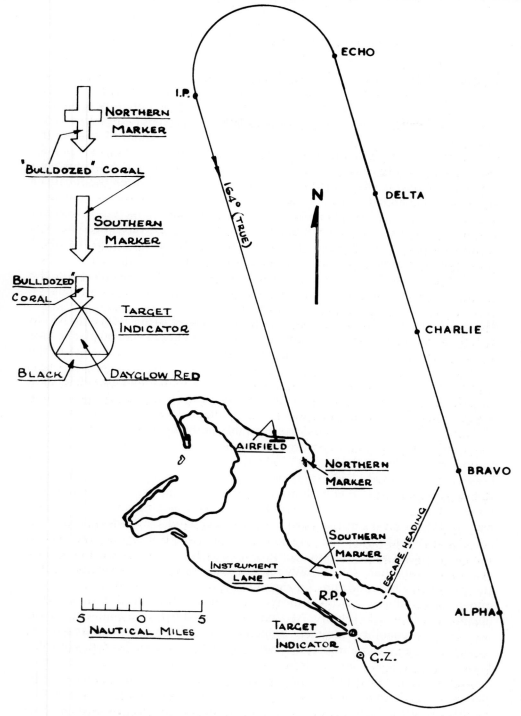

The bombing circuit used on 'Grapple X', 'Y' and 'Z'. A similar circuit was used on the earlier three tests held off Malden Island ('Grapple'). *(Author)*

Blind Method

The Blind Method with the Mk 7 gunlaying radar table required the Valiant to position itself initially on a 164°T bomb line at the intercept point, some 50nm from ground zero. At approximately 4½ minutes from instant of release, the aircraft was picked up by the Mk 7 radar and its position relative to the bomb line fed into the ILS which was set on a map scale. Times from instant of release were called by the Mk 7 ground control, and at 2½ minutes the localiser switched to expanded scale. For the remainder of the run down the bomb line to instant of release, the captain was required to maintain the ILS needles central whilst ensuring that with the elimination of drift, the aircraft's heading was maintained to achieve a track of 164°T. Timing was called from the Mk 7 controller in accordance with the bombing procedure check list being activated by the Valiant crew, followed by a countdown from minus 10sec to enable the bomb aimer to release the weapon at zero.

These were the two methods in which all Valiant crews in this test series had to be fully operationally proficient; although a live drop might well be planned for a visual technique, cloud cover once airborne would dictate a change to the blind method.

Weather during the two weeks prior to 2 September varied between ideal to heavy tropical storms; however, in spite of the difficulties caused by torrential tropical rain, the work up programme was maintained. On one training sortie in Valiant XD818 we were well and truly caught out by the movement of the trop-ical front which competely obscured the island from view, and we were forced to undertake a let-down from 45,000ft through some of the most turbulent heavy cumulus cloud I had experienced for many years. Indeed the turbulence was so great that it needed both myself and the co-pilot to fly the aircraft. The noise of hail beating against the windscreen was deafening and at one time I would not have been surprised had the screen shattered. On reaching 1,500ft the hail changed to torrential rain; we homed on the radio beacon and radar which were able to feed us on to course for final approach to the runway, although we were well aware that in such heavy rain the radar screen would be obscured by clutter. Set on a radar heading for the runway, we continued our let-down with undercarriage down and the windscreen wipers at full speed in an effort to obtain some forward visibility. At 500ft we emerged from the main cloud base, with forward visibility extremely limited. We could see the island and to my relief the runway came into view and in torrential rain we landed. Both Bob Beeson and myself were saturated with perspiration. Having taxied in to dispersal and climbed out of the aircraft, the ferocity of our battle with the elements was there for all to see. The entire front of the aircraft nose area was completely stripped of paint, which meant another task for my overworked ground crew.

With all scientific high explosive drops completed. Valiant XD822 was handed over for loading of the live thermonuclear weapon code named 'Flag Pole 1'. On 2 September, although the weather was suitable for a visual drop, the Task Force Commander ruled that the weapon should be released by the blind radar technique, a disappointing decision for the bomb aimer in Sqn Ldr Bill Bailey's crew.

With all pre-take off drills complete, Valiant XD822 (being flown by Bill Bailey and crew) became airborne at 07.15 local time, closely followed by Flt Lt O'Connor in XD818 to act as grandstand aircraft. Once the aircraft were at 45,000ft Sqn Ldr Bailey reported he was ready to commence the blind initial run, and when this was completed the scientific staff reported that all telemetering recording was satisfactory; therefore the Task Force Commander gave permission for the live run to be carried out.

Since this was our first live weapon drop using the blind radar technique, I listened to the transmission from the Valiant coming through the radio network with intense interest and a degree of apprehension, for I was well aware that this was not the most simple task from the captain's point of view. With Valiant XD822 on its final bombing run, I joined all personnel assembled on the main concrete dispersal, seated on the ground with backs to ground zero.

I noted that all aircraft on the airfield had been parked tail to ground zero, but by this time the instructions came to cover eyes and the radar controller count down to weapon release commenced. At zero we knew that the weapon had left the aircraft and the captain's voice commenced the commentary as he rolled the Valiant into the escape manoeuvre. As the forward controller's voice announced weapon detonation, the flash could be detected through one's fingers shielding the eyes, and there was a warm feeling on the back of the neck. With this past, hands were removed from eyes and we all awaited the bang and over-pressure wave, which followed rapidly and, even at a range of 20nm, was most impressive, particularly as the pressure wave swept across the palm trees. Once it had safely passed, all personnel were allowed to stand up and observe the fire ball and towering cloud development which was, as always, both fascinating and to a degree frightening.

After watching the progressive build-up for a few minutes, I walked over to my squadron office tent to await the return of Valiants XD822 and XD818, for they had both been cleared by the controller to return to base. After landing I congratulated Bill Bailey on a successful sortie, then drove to Joint Operations Control to see if the bombing error had been established, from the high speed camera recordings. This result was not available for about 1 hour, but when it came it certainly was worth waiting for as the error from 45,000ft was 95yd: an absolute record, which proved that there had been really first class team work between the radar plotting team and the aircraft captain's interpretation of the information presented on his ILS needles. With this result, I hastened to inform Bill Bailey and his crew who duly celebrated their success that evening.

The next live drop was scheduled for 11 September and the scientists lost no time in calling for the pre-drop bombing sorties related to the next weapon. For this occasion the Task Force Commander informed me that AOC-in-C Bomber Command, ACM Sir Harry Broadhurst KCB, KBE, DSO, DFC, AFC, would be arriving in a Vulcan. There would also be present the Senior Air Staff Officer, AVM J. G. Davis CB, OBE, and the Air Officer Administration, AVM W. H. Merton CB, OBE.

The C-in-C Bomber Command duly arrived in a Vulcan Mk 2 on the day prior to 'D' Day. Its arrival made a tremendous impact upon all personnel on the island, and as it flew over at low level its massive delta shaped wing gave the impression of something from outer space. After an impressive low level display, it majestically roared into a circuit and made a perfect landing. The Vulcan was captained by Wg Cdr Frank Dodds, without doubt the most experienced Vulcan pilot in the V Force, and the C-in-C was flying as co-pilot. When the Vulcan taxied in, Sir Harry Broadhurst was greeted by the Task Force Commander and myself.

The following day was 11 September; Valiant XD827 would be the aircraft carrying the next live thermonuclear weapon, code named 'Halliard 1' and flown by Flt Lt Tiff O'Connor and crew, with XD824 as grandstand flown by Sqn Ldr Tony Caillard.

In view of the unique success achieved with the previous live weapon release, using the blind radar bombing technique, the Task Force Commander had decided that 'Halliard 1' should also be dropped utilising the same method. This was a decision I accepted with some misgiving, for although admitting that the previous result of 95yd was a considerable improvement on the average of 245yd achieved with the visual bombing technique throughout the training and post operational period on the island, although we had dropped 52 bombs using the blind technique, the average error from 46,000ft had been 235yd. Therefore without decrying the par excellence of our previous blind live drop result of 95yd achieved by Sqn Ldr Bill Bailey, I knew only too well we should be exceptionally lucky to obtain a second result as good as this. I therefore pointed out to the Task Force Commander that it would be wise to assume the dropping crew was more likely to achieve its average of 245yd which was well within the error band stipulated.

Having briefed Flt Lt Tiff O'Connor and his bomb aimer, Flg Off John Muston, to the effect that they were required to make this live thermonuclear weapon a release using the blind technique, I softened the pill for the bomb aimer by saying 'Well, if the radar has any technical problems, remember you will be required to resort to a visual technique.'

From a Valiant crew point of view, the factor that is always disconcerting is that whilst the captain is required to fly by instruments to a high standard of accuracy, particularly as to heading by maintaining the ILS localiser needles precisely on the centre line without any deviation, he is merely following the signals fed in from the ground radar table and has no means of realistically knowing that he is releasing his lethal weapon at a point which has been visually checked by his bomb aimer, or confirmed by a radar display in the aircraft.

Top: A nuclear device explodes off
Christmas Island – the fireball
developing.

Centre: The gas cloud changes
contour and the mushroom form
appears.

Bottom: Finale.

The Commander-in-Chief, Sir Harry Broadhurst, came to see Flt Lt O'Connor and crew before take-off and wished them luck, before departing with the Task Force Commander to forward control in order to observe the entire operation.

At precisely 07.15hrs local time, Valiant XD827 with Tiff O'Connor at the controls roared down the runway and, with weapon 'Halliard 1' aboard, became safely airborne. I waited for the grandstand Valiant XD824, with Sqn Ldr Tony Caillard at the controls, to become airborne, then I drove over to the airfield operations office where it was possible to listen to the transmission from XD827, before I was required to take up my position on the concrete dispersal with all personnel assembled in accordance with the safety plan.

Once the Valiant had reached operational height and completed its navigational run, I heard the controller's voice tell Flt Lt O'Connor that due to a fault in the ground transmitter at the Mk 7 radar site, two-way contact with the Mk 7 plotting installation was impossible. The Task Force Commander had therefore authorised a visual drop. As this came over the air, I allowed myself a slight smile; I could imagine the pleasure this would provide to Tiff O'Connor's crew who now were required to put into practice the results of months of intense training in the visual overshoot technique.

With no further technical problems, the initial run was completed to the satisfaction of the Scientific Team, with all telemetering signals being acceptable, and the controller gave clearance for the Valiant to proceed with a visual live drop.

At this point I moved out of the airfield operations office and positioned myself on the concrete, sitting down, back to ground zero. Looking up, I could see the dropping Valiant at 45,000ft looking like a silver fly with beautifully formed white contrails coming from the four jet engines. It flew effortlessly along the bomb line, followed by the grandstand Valiant behind and at a lower level. As I watched, the order came to 'Cover Eyes' and we could all hear over the tannoy relay system the bomb aimer's steady correction and the AEO's voice calling the switching drills. It all sounded a well controlled and steady bomb run, with every indication that it would be a well co-ordinated release. Then of course came the words everybody was waiting for – 'Weapon Gone' – followed by a steady commentary from the pilot as he rolled the aircraft into the escape manoeuvre, which again sounded from the speed and sensitive 'G' recordings to be progressing well. When the captain called rolling out on heading, I settled back for the weapon explosion and flash which came some 10 seconds later.

Once again all personnel could register the flash through fingers covering the eyes and feel heat on the back of the neck; then of course some 10 seconds later came a fantastic bang, followed by the overpressure wave of displaced air. Thanks to precautions with parked aircraft and buildings, there was no damage, and with the wave past, all personnel were allowed to stand up and look at the incredible development of the fireball and cloud.

Some 4 minutes after weapon detonation, the controller cleared both Valiants for a return to base; at this point I walked over to my squadron office tent to sit outside in the sun and wait for the aircraft to land. From this position, I could still observe the huge mushroom cloud which now towered to well over 60,000ft.

By this time Valiants XD827 and XD824 had landed and taxied in to dispersal. The Commander-in-Chief and Task Force Commander were back from forward control and came over to congratulate Flt Lt Tiff O'Connor on what looked to be a good bombing result. The Task Force Commander commented to the Commander-in-Chief, 'I'm sure Ken willed a jinx on the ground radar to ensure his crew got a visual drop.' I smiled and admitted that my thoughts were on those lines.

That evening I was invited to dine in the Task Force Commander's Mess with the Commander-in-Chief, Sir Harry Broadhurst, AVM John Davies and AVM Willie Merton. After dinner, the Task Force Commander confirmed that the squadron would be returning in a week's time, for a further work-up period for 'Grapple Mike'. But, for political reasons, there was a strong possibility that any further tests would be cancelled. In spite of this, 49 Squadron, once back at RAF Wittering, would be required to prepare for a further test series without delay.

During the course of the evening Sir Harry Broadhurst took me aside and said how impressed he was with all that 49 Squadron had achieved over the past two years. Since it now looked highly unlikely that the weapon testing programme would be continuing at the same intensity, he had decided that the experience gained by 49 Squadron crews should be progressively spread throughout the Command. He then went on to say that by the end of this year I would have completed 2½ years as OC and was therefore on the final stage of my tour of duty. My next appointment was to be on his staff at Bomber Command HQ as his Wing Commander responsible for operational requirements in the V Force. In order to function in this post I would need to have a full working knowledge of the Vulcan and Victor V bombers, and therefore before taking up the appointment I should be given a short conversion course on both types.

I received this news with mixed feelings; on the one hand it was a compliment to be invited to join the C-in-C's staff and a vote of confidence to be given the operational requirements job, which meant that I would be one of a small select band fully qualified on all three V bomber types. On the other hand, 49 Squadron had become my family and one that I had built from scratch: I knew every officer, SNCO and airman by name. We all shared a great pride in '49', had confidence in every man's ability and were a united and disciplined team in every sense of the word. The thought of handing over this great squadron to other hands was something I did not look forward to, for after so long with such a common but highly specialised task only applicable to '49', all enjoying a single aim, an extremely strong band of comradeship and squadron spirit had been established.

Dismissing these thoughts as they raced through my brain, I thanked the C-in-C for his confidence in me and said that although I should be sad to hand over command at the end of my tour, I would be looking foward to putting the experience gained to good use as a member of his staff. Certainly the thought of flying the Vulcan and Victor filled me with pleasure, but the subsequent thought of a desk at Command HQ was somehow lacking in attraction.

Before I left the Task Force Commander's Mess that evening, the visual bombing error was confirmed as 260yd which was extremely good. With this news, I walked slowly back to my own tent, my thoughts already tinged with sadness in the knowledge that by the end of the year I must say farewell to this wonderful squadron. For the time being I decided to keep this information to myself, because after all, if the political masters decided to accelerate another test series, I might be allowed an extension of my present appointment. On that note I retired to bed, knowing only too well that as a regular officer I must be prepared to undertake any appointment given to me, and I had enjoyed a very large slice of good fortune!

With these last tests complete, our attention was turned yet again to preparing all Valiants for return to the UK. I briefed Flt Lt Budden, our Squadron Engineer, that after departure of the Valiants, all ground equipment must be stored carefully as it was doubtful if the next test phase would be carried out. Should this prove to be the case, then no doubt all Valiant specialised ground equipment would be shipped back to the UK ultimately.

All preparations completed, I bade farewell to the Task Force Commander and members of his staff before climbing aboard Valiant XD818, and with my crew took off from Christmas Island on 18 September on the first leg of our homeward journey by way of Honolulu, Travis AFB and Goose Bay, to land back at RAF Wittering on time, on 23 September. By 25 September, all Valiants were back at base, followed by the ground crew two weeks later.

My latest directive indicated that planning was in hand for the next test to be code named 'Grapple Mike' and that 49 Squadron was to resume 'Grapple' training in both visual and blind bombing techniques without delay. Thus, once we had re-established ourselves, flying training was reprogrammed and I settled down to compile a comprehensive report covering not only this recent test series, but to summarise results, problems and outline general experience of the entire 'Grapple X', 'Y' and 'Z' series, concluding with observations and recommendations for future trials.

In order to compile such a wide-ranging and comprehensive report, each Specialist Leader and the Squadron Training Officer was directed to prepare his own report. From these I should be able to present a well balanced and historical summary.

Early in October Alan Boxer, the Station Commander, informed me that RAF Cottesmore was to be honoured by a Royal Visit of HRH Princess Margaret on 21 October. The Commander-in-Chief had decided that the flying display for HRH should include a formation flight of three Valiants from 49 Squadron to be led by XD818. For this we were authorised to undertake a specified number of flying hours for formation practice. I decided that my two wing men would be Sqn Ldr Arthur Steele in XD823 and Sqn Ldr Barney Millett in XD824.

The flypast for HRH Princess Margaret was to be at low level and would include Canberras, Vulcans, Victors and Valiants, each type being allocated a height and a detailed route plan and timing issued by HQ Bomber Command. A full dress rehearsal was flown on 17 October, and with Arthur Steele and Barney Millett with XD823 and XD824 tightly tucked into either side of XD818, I knew the Valiant V formation would look impressive. On 21 October the weather was fine, all aircraft made rendezvous exactly on time and the pattern form-up was good. We flew over the royal dais dead on time and it must have made an impressive picture from the ground. This was a pleasant interlude from bombing training, for formation flying, although hard work, is both exciting and challenging.

November saw us still training for a possible further detachment to Christmas Island. Already a number of experienced crews were being posted to other squadrons and replaced by relatively inexperienced Valiant crews, and by this time the squadron became aware that I should be handing over command some time in December to Ron Payne, who was to be promoted to Wing Commander on taking over. Already he had contacted me and dates had been arranged for him to come over for a comprehensive briefing on the entire 'Grapple' task later in the month.

On 7 November Alan Washbrook and I attended our final conference at HQ 'Grapple', to discuss all aspects of the tests to date, analyse bombing results and decide upon any changes required for the future. My own overall operational report was discussed in some detail, and it was agreed that any recommendations would be considered carefully.

Operation 'Grapple'

The following code names were applied to the seven thermonuclear bombs detonated off Malden and Christmas Islands during the 1957/58 test series. Two smaller devices were also detonated from balloons during the final test, 'Grapple Z'.

Code Name	Location	Test Series
'Short Granite'	Malden Island	'Grapple'
'Orange Herald'	Malden Island	'Grapple'
'Purple Granite'	Malden Island	'Grapple'
'Round C'	Christmas Island	'Grapple X'
'Grapple Y'	Christmas Island	'Grapple Y'
'Flag Pole 1'	Christmas Island	'Grapple Z'
'Halliard 1'	Christmas Island	'Grapple Z'
'Pennant 2' (balloon)	Christmas Island	'Grapple Z'
'Burgee 2' (balloon)	Christmas Island	'Grapple Z'

In concluding the meeting, both the Task Force Commander and the Scientific Director expressed regret that my tour as OC 49 Squadron was now coming to an end, complimented the squadron on the results achieved over the past two years and commented upon the uniquely high standard of morale and squadron spirit displayed at all times. On behalf of the squadron I thanked the Task Force Commander for his kind words and assured him that it had been both a pleasure and privilege to operate under his command and be part of the 'Grapple' team.

By the end of November 1958 the political decision had been made that Britain would not continue its programme of thermonuclear weapon tests on Christmas Island. Simultaneously, a directive was issued by HQ Bomber Command that 49 Squadron, with effect from 1 December 1958, would revert to its standard bomber role, and all aircraft would be demodified from the 'Grapple' standard and refitted with the radar navigational bombing system.

We had arrived at the end of a unique period in the history of the Royal Air Force, in which 49 Squadron had been privileged to play a dominant role. Over this 2½-year period the squadron had become something very personal, having established itself as a strong, well co-ordinated team, and no commanding officer could have enjoyed greater support for no task was beyond its capability. Every man throughout the tests worked exceptionally long hours under at times the most difficult conditions, cheerful in the knowledge that they were involved in an operation of national importance.

It gave me very great pleasure to receive the following signal from the Task Force Commander on the completion of our task on the conclusion of 'Grapple Z'.

It read as follows:

Quote: For Officer Commanding No. 49 Squadron from Task Force Commander. Now that your task in Grapple 'Z' concluded, please convey to all ranks my congratulations on their magnificent contribution to the Nuclear Test Programme. On all counts your high standard has become a tradition. I know full well the hard work and long hours that have been so cheerfully put in, particularly in meeting the accelerated programme. Congratulations and best wishes to you and your squadron. Unquote.

I replied on behalf of the Squadron as follows:

Quote: For Task Force Commander from Officer Commanding 49 Squadron. Your signal of congratulations much appreciated by all ranks. It has been our privilege to be part of the Grapple Organisation for the task has been stimulating. Unquote.

The contents of the above signals were conveyed to all members of the squadron.

Now that the date had been set for me to hand over Command to Wg Cdr R. Payne, I concentrated on tidying up any loose ends of our involvement in Operation Grapple, so that in handing over to my successor he would be clear to concentrate on the transformation of the squadron back to its normal bomber role.

The spirit of 49 Squadron was so strong that a proposal was put to me that because we had all been involved in a task that was unlikely ever to be repeated, we should form a '49' club named 'The Megaton Club' and meet regularly on a reunion basis every year. Membership initially to be restricted only to squadron members serving over the past 2½ years.

I agreed to this proposal but was secretly sceptical as to whether the euphoria

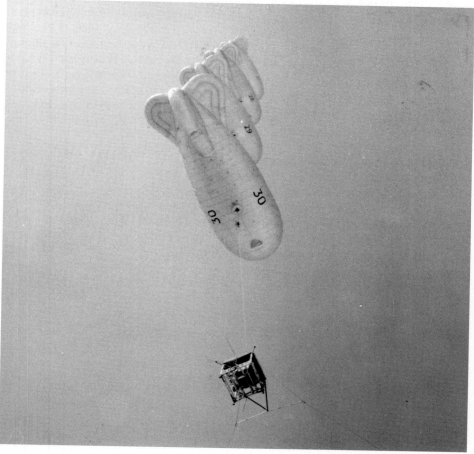

Two balloon detonations were carried out during 'Grapple Z'. Here four barrage balloons lift the cradle that contains the nuclear device.

would be maintained over the coming years. Time, however, has proved me completely wrong, for now some 25 years later we still all assemble once a year at the Royal Air Force Club. Credit for this fine achievement must go to Fred Vening who, as Secretary, has constantly generated enthusiasm and never flinched from the thankless task of correspondence and keeping all members in touch. In this he has been strongly supported by the Treasurer, Arthur Ward.

With farewell parties over and all formal farewells made, I completed the final entries in my Flying Log Book and presented them to the Station Commander, Gp Capt Alan Boxer, for signature on the conclusion of my tour. In the Form 414A he was kind enough to comment as follows: 'A fine leader and outstanding Squadron Commander'. I had flown a total of 559 hours in Valiant XD818.

On 15 December 1958 I formally handed over to Wg Cdr Ron Payne. Then, having already packed, I said farewell to the faithful Mr Stan Dolby, who had taken such great care of both myself and Crusty, the living symbol of 49 'Cave Canem'; then with Crusty in the passenger seat, I drove out of the main gates, heading for a few days' leave before reporting to RAF Gaydon for my conversion to the Victor. As we turned onto the A1, I looked back at RAF Wittering with a feeling of sadness in my heart, for secretly it had been a tremendous wrench to hand over my beloved squadron to other hands. However, a new task lay ahead, one that I must face with renewed determination.

Epilogue

ooking back over the period 1956 to 1958 it is now possible to appreciate fully the uniqueness of Operation 'Grapple', for it was the largest Joint Services Operation ever mounted in peace time. Additionally, it was the only occasion that all three services had worked jointly in an operational role with such a highly specialised Atomic Weapon Scientific Team, under the overall command of a senior officer of Air Rank.

It had been an operation which must have presented formidable problems to the entire 'Grapple' team, firstly in selecting a suitable venue, then planning for converting and building the venue into a relatively full operational area, 9,000nm from the UK.

In this respect every credit must go to the Royal Navy and Fleet Auxiliary ships, for transporting every item of equipment required, and then supporting a garrison which was built up to 3,000 strong; also to the Royal Engineers, who transformed Christmas Island into an operational base, complete with an airfield from which a V bomber could operate. For them no praise is high enough, for under extremely difficult conditions they produced quality results.

Only thanks to the Royal Navy and the Royal Engineers was it possible for the Royal Air Force to operate. Although I have not gone into any detail on the work carried out by 76 Canberra Squadron, which was responsible for taking all the radioactive cloud samples, or 100 Squadron which flew numerous sorties to provide up-to-date high-altitude meteorological information, or the Shackletons of Coastal Command which maintained a constant ocean search to ensure the declared operational area was clear, they all played a vital role.

For the Weapons Scientific Team under the Scientific Director, Bill Cook, their years of research were at last put to the test and the results justified the cost. This entire team fitted into the service element with smoothness and precision, and they were all a pleasure to work with.

Finally, credit for the overall succes of the entire 'Grapple' operation must go to the two Task Force Commanders: firstly AVM Wilf Oulton, who planned 'Grapple' and executed the first two series; then AVM John Grandy, who was in command for 'Grapple Y' and 'Z'. Both men were first-class commanders under whom it was a pleasure to serve.

For the Bomber Command V Force the success of the entire 'Grapple' operation meant that thermonuclear warheads had been operationally tested. Thus Britain's V Force, which with Valiants, Vulcans and Victors had been steadily increasing during 1956/57, was able to receive its first thermonuclear weapons in 1958. This was a year marked by the co-ordination of the RAF/USAF nuclear strike plan and represented the point where Britain's V bomber nuclear deterrent force became an international reality.

From this point in time the operational capability of the V Force steadily improved, as the operational readiness plan came into force and airfields were nominated for dispersal use by the V Force; these airfields were equipped to maintain aircraft and crews at a readiness posture of 3 minutes.

Over a period of some 27 years, Britain's V bomber force has made a constant contribution to the maintenance of world peace – initially backed by Thor missiles, then later by Polaris missiles to be launched by Royal Navy submarines.

Maintaining this effective deterrent force at a constant state of operational readiness, where every V bomber main base was required to hold three aircraft fully armed with crews at a 3 minutes readiness, with the entire force able to be generated to operational readiness and dispersed in a minimum time scale, called for organising efficiency, and a great sense of dedication from all ranks within this force.

Over the years, Bomber Command's V Force had become the envy of Air Forces throughout the world: by participating in international air displays the deterrent had been seen and appreciated; and by participating in bombing competitions held by Strategic Air Command of the USAF, Bomber Command crews have effectively demonstrated their high standards of navigation and bombing accuracy.

The V Force had always been manned by both air and ground crews of quality; every man was dedicated to the task and believed in the deterrent philosophy. Within 3 Group aircrews all were personally interviewed by the Air Officer Commanding before being accepted into the force; all were volunteers, prepared to accept the dedication necessary in maintaining such a force; to a high state of readiness for quick reaction.

The public owes this force a great debt of thanks for ensuring that this country has enjoyed peace and a right to maintain her own democratic way of life over those years, which included such sensitive periods as the Cuban Crisis when World War 3 was almost a reality. However, because both America and Britain possessed a formidable strategic deterrent force, Russia hesitated and eventually recognised that the price was too high.

Now, of course, the V Force has come to the end of its effective life and its responsibilities have been taken over by Polaris and Cruise missiles, the Tornado tactical bomber replacing V Force squadrons in the NATO organisation. Although in different shape, this still represents an effective deterrent, to ensure that Britain's democratic way of life shall not be threatened.

We live today in difficult times, for there are organisations who would achieve their own extreme political ends by breaking the laws passed by Parliament. In the International scene, only an effective deterrent policy can dissuade a major power of abhorrent political views from imposing their will on this country and destroying the freedom of our democratic way of life.

For these reasons, I fail to understand why such organisations as the Campaign for Nuclear Disarmament and the Peace Women cannot comprehend that the only effective way to maintain peace is by being strong and capable of protecting all that we hold dear. They claim to represent a great number of people both in this country and throughout Western Europe. However, if true figures are analysed, their numbers represent a tiny percentage of the population. Even so, by such actions they do a great disservice to their country by indicating to our potential enermies that in the West there is an element weak in resolve, which provides encouragement to the subversive activities of extreme left wing organisations in the UK.

These are the people who would cast aside our nuclear weapons and leave us naked, in the face of dictatorships armed in the most sophisticated manner, thus exposing us to political blackmail resulting in the surrender of our freedom, where the life of every individual is dictated by the State.

The devastation at Hiroshima as seen in 1946. A one megaton H-bomb is 70 times more powerful than the atomic bomb dropped on the city. *(IWM)*

The secure future of this country and the West can only be assured by a strong nuclear deterrent policy, linked with a co-ordinated and well exercised North Atlantic Treaty Organisation. I am proud to have been a part of Britain's V Force and to have played a role in the development of our thermonuclear weapons, and to have dropped the first in the 'Grapple' test series.

In conclusion, I would stress that this book has been produced as a tribute to all those who served under my command in 49 Squadron, throughout the entire 'Grapple' operation. It has not been possible to mention every name, but every man played his part.

Although the V Force is no more, Valiant XD818 which was used for Britain's first live release of a thermonuclear weapon in the megaton range, has been retained; it now resides in the Cold War Museum at RAF Cosford.

Index